for

the precious canaries in our coal mine

I Am My Son's First Sightword

Growing A Child With Autism

Kristin Kucia

Kristin Kucia

ISBN-13: 9780692256879
ISBN-10: 0692256873

Table of Contents

Foreword

WHEN I FIRST met Kristin Kucia, I knew I was in for a ride. I had just dropped off my son, Aidan, at the classroom of his new school 35 miles from our home. After having endured a few disastrous years at another school, he and I were depleted in the ways only an autistic kid and his mom can understand; under-slept, over-anxious, hyper-vigilant, sometimes numb, and sometimes instantly catapulted into biblical realms of grief and anger. We were the new kids on the block that day and on top of everything else, I was in the grip of woozy 7th grade "Will anybody dance with me?" fears. Would Aidan like his school? Would the school have a clue about how to teach him? Would everything ever be OK again? I spied a group of moms in the school courtyard and willed my shaky legs to take me to them.

Oh please, oh please, dance with me.

Kristin stood at the center of the group, radiating an impossible mix of calm and fire, as she extended her hand to mine. She didn't seem to notice my drenched and clammy palm as she instantly enveloped me in a conversation about Aidan and school and Autism, which left me feeling that, yes, everything would be OK and not only that, I was now a member of an Amazon tribe facing a frontier of bright possibilities.

As I drove home that morning, I revisited a belief I'd buried a few years back when things got really hard and the trenches were too deep to see beyond whatever crisis was right in front of me— that raising a child with Autism doesn't have to be a solitary vocation or a fate reserved for the pitied, exhausted, chronically overwhelmed, and on-the-verge-of-tears parent. Sure, these things are all part of the job description but they don't define the job itself, the heart of which is pure backbone and ass-kicking courage. Meeting Kristin that day reawakened in me my own inner Amazonian and banished the scared 7th grader to the past, where she belonged.

In these pages, Kristin describes in kaleidoscopic detail her journey through Autism motherhood. Gut-wrenching, hilarious, indelicate and revelatory, her story covers everything from birth to diagnosis, pizza to poop, classroom disaster to unicycle triumph. It is, indeed, a wild ride, which veers into some pretty dark territory without losing sight of a fierce hope that some day, come hell or high water, her son will come through. And he does.

Buckle up.

Kate Movius
Mother of a child with Autism

CHAPTER 1

Breakfast and A Panic Attack

THE EXPECTATIONS WE have regarding our life, having a family, a career, maintaining friendships, and the general fun of being alive usually unfold in a certain way. A predictable way. We expect it. Same with kids. The experiences of raising children and having a family are familiar to us because we see it in everyone else's lives around us. We see it happen in every one else's world. You get pregnant, you have a kid, endure a couple years of puke on your sleeve, naps, and stinky diapers, skills sets develop and they start to talk, gaining precious shards of developmental independence with each day. And then, those sweet little people begin Kindergarten. We envision Kindergarten as half-days of pure sunshine, and our kids are eager and excited to learn. We practice letters and colors at home. We pack lunches for them in brightly colored sacks, and give them a quarter for popsicles on Fridays. Our kid gets it.

As parents, we envision the commencement of our children reading books, beautiful macaroni artwork, and wonderful moments in the school plays where the every-night practice of the 7-word script of FLOWER 2 is belted out in perfect timing—the fruition of all of our hard work as parents. Our child shits on the toilet with good accuracy and consistency. We deal less with bathroom issues, and more with how much allowance should be given for chores done each day. I imagine my son would say, read the chart, Mom, then he would explain to me, analyzing the chart he had created, to show me how much I owe him. An extra dollar. See? He would point his finger, initiating joint-attention with me with flawless automaticity. His words would be concrete, abstract, and thoughtful. We would marvel at his unique ideas. Beaming. We are so proud. Our dream. Our future. Our plan. Because that's how it is supposed to happen. Add Autism, and things change.

In 2000, as I held my son, Thaddeus, that first day of his life, I was surely the luckiest mama. We had a four-year-old, exquisite, slice-of-sunshine daughter, Ursula. And now, my husband, Rob and I had the perfect boy-and-girl set of precious children to dote love and attention on. I remember that he was born with that great Stauder hair. Long, thick and delicious. His skin looked more olive, more of a Kucia skin tone, with his Eastern European blood. I thought he looked like my dad, his "Grandpa X," and Thaddeus William is named after his other grandpa, Jerry William. I stroke my new son's soft skin, and I call his name. His brown eyes look deeply into mine, imprinting love on my soul.

And he would love being with me because I'm his mama, and we'd be snuggling, kissing, hugging, and tickling each other. As I look deeply into his eyes, he looks back. This Mother sees great things in her Son's future. All the things he will do. The college he will attend. The middle school romances, fun, and secret notes on the school bus. Pizza parties with other families. The children run off together to play video games in the arcade, and the parents casually drink beer at the red and while oilcloth-draped tables. Us relaxed, normal parents just keeping an eye on them, and definitely not concerned about what they are eating or are talking about with their friends. Because, of course, the kids can speak. And, well, obviously, they have friends.

My son would be interested in hobbies and playing games with others, he would play with his toys in so many funny and creative ways and we would marvel at his insights, as we all enjoy life as a family and friends inhabited our social spaces, as he would explore new places independently and successfully, ask such thoughtful questions and learn stuff, just amazing, sometimes seemingly effortless. Because that is what happens. When you have a kid, this is what happens.

He would eat basically whatever he wanted, and maybe he had a little grass allergy or something in the spring, but not bad. At his BFF's birthday party, the blue icing on the Disney character cake, loads of ice cream, and candy at the party would give him a little sugar high but no biggie, he would play the games, and be a good sport if he didn't win. He'd be too busy with the new kids he met at the party to worry about it. If he was sad later about coming in second place, we would have a little talk, a hug, and all would be better, no big deal. And if he were in the other room unsupervised, he would never strip nude (especially in front of other people, strangers even) and never ever, elope out into the darkness in a strange neighborhood merely because he heard an unfamiliar sound that frightened him.

I would daydream and massage my pregnant belly, wondering, if he will be a studious kid, or more of a social guy, hanging with his friends and girls constantly calling? Will he be interested in Little League or Theater Arts at school? All the birthday parties, and boys' sleepovers? Long nights that I would sit at karate class watching him appropriately move his body with precision, excited by his creative drawings in the beginnings of academic book reports, or missing him because he was gone for two days, waiting for him to come home from science camp in the mountain where he went with his fifth-grade class from the local elementary up the street. And I could drop him off, and let him run into the aquatic center alone for swim team practice, while I would run back to my place of employment which is a mile up that way to pick up my bimonthly paycheck associated with expertise in my professional field, grab a quick coffee with a friend, and if I was late, he'd know to wait patiently for my arrival. When we went on vacation, would he bring tons of books along, research all the cool destinations that we would get and deliver insightful updates on our adventures, or would he lament that all of his friends are missing him and be texting, messaging extremely connected with his 12-year old warrior posse of boys, so extremely emotionally connected to others? Who would he choose to be friends with?

Words like "disabled," and "autistic" would be words I would explain to my children regarding the unfortunate life conditions that happen to someone we maybe passed on the street, or a person we vaguely know. I think we saw it on that one-hour long television special on people who live different lives than what we understand as "normal," and now back to our regularly scheduled program. You know, the other people, surely not us. And I would scold my kids if they were to use these words in a derogatory fashion. We would explain to the kids that using words like "mental case," "freak," or "retard" in mean ways is hurtful and damaging. And because we are so socially conscious, we would always speak well of those people in that disabled population. Over there. Way over there. And, certainly, we would never be the receivers of such hateful language ever.

Eighteen years ago, I moved to California with my husband, and our beautiful 6-week old daughter, Ursula. We settled in, I went to massage school and got 1000 hours of training as a Massage Therapist/ Holistic Health Practitioner because I wanted to educate myself about alternative healing methods because I was suspicious of the volatile combination of a bad ear gene in my family, and Ursula's eight sets of PE tubes by second grade. A few years later, I got a graduate degree in English Composition because I enjoy the way words make me feel, and I love to teach.

We prefer mild climates, and the proximity to the ocean and mountains was optimal for what we perceived to be basecamp to our future intense outdoor explorations, and international adventures. We would have two incomes and two offsprings, kids in public school and we lived a 5-mile total triangulation between our jobs, and our children's school. And, most importantly, mangosteen was our favorite fruit from our most recent international adventures in the Philippines, and we found it fresh in Hollywood Farmers Market. Oh yeh, this California adventure was gonna be good.

Our plan was to raise some babies, get some more degrees, have some cool experiences as a family, and for me, to do some groovy dance stuff. I met a delicious mama, Gayle, the first week we arrived in California. That fall, we choreographed a modern dance extravaganza called "Dinner," and performed our cartoon masterpiece at the local community college simulating fruit, and body parts to the tune that asks us to put the lime in the coconut to make us feel better. Ursula called me Mama Coconut Boobies for months to come in honor of our choice in brassieres that evening. Right before we conceived Thad, I had just returned from a 10-day Sufi dance retreat to clear my body, and get ready to create my next child. Every act of being a mother is sacred, and should be cherished.

Before babies, I lived and worked on an organic farm for a while, relished in the plants and the people blooming, and always found a satisfying connection among growing, people, food, music, writing, and movement. In my past, I frequented classes about dying and spinning wool, shimmied a mean bellydance, really enjoyed working in the dirt, and creating food masterpieces in the kitchen.

I worked at a local spa providing hydrotherapy sessions and Swedish massage until I was nine months pregnant with Thad. I would slather bodies in dead sea salt and mango lush, and press stress and illness out of muscles, and end my day deliciously dewy and hydrated. I am the mama to two beautiful children, and I find the primalness of life a real rush.

This story is a lovesong for my son, my heartache, my *raison d'etre*, my challenge, my champion. It is about intensive therapy to help remediate the devastation of Autism in our boy, endless possibilities, lifechoices, and fruit. It is a memoir of my passion for the health, safety and a quality of life my child deserves. It is a story about slowing down to smell the orange blossoms, learning to surf, learning to read, falling down, getting up, falling down again, getting up again, climbing rocks and moving mountains, organic food and great beer, amazing friends and bad guys, sadness and joy, weapons and perception, love and remorse, primal anger and release, poop and puke, water and wine, disability and ability, laughter and tears, words and vision, all the while mentally foraging for the answer to unlock a small boy with a big mind, and finding peace in our family, in our world touched by Autism.

Our grand plan was to travel the world—everywhere, and often. We live near LAX, so all international flights would be uber-cheap. We would go on great family vacations, and never really worry too much about money because our plan was to have enough money to comfortably do whatever we pleased, and the children's college savings funds would be huge. Absolutely. Perfection. So much cash to do whatever the fuck we wanted, yes, the dream had been realized. Order those sweet French doors, and check out the blueprints for the fancy in-ground pool and spa construction, honey. We have it all.

We adore and feel proud of the lush palm and fruit trees that dot our beautifully landscaped corner lot, bursting with coconuts and plums and bounty from high above, as the gardener toils outside in the broiling heat, and us in our air-conditioned kitchen with shiny new appliances, stressing out over our most recent large anxiety of what color to paint the patio we had just added in our backyard, blue trim or green, purple or green Pebbletec in the pool, how the construction might impede the timelines of the cool vacations we were planning, and fuck if we couldn't agree on the hue of the decking trim in this about-to-happen backyard masterpiece, sitting, sipping coffee calmly, poring over our elaborate plans in our brand-new house, full of possibility, as we relish our comfortable citrus living.

Then, Life plays a wild card, and the coconuts start falling off the tree at alarming speeds. Thaddeus was a normally-developing baby, and started preschool at 18 months old. He met all the important developmental milestones at the appropriate times. At nine months old, he said Ursula's best friend's name, Emily, with clarity, and at ten months of age, we marveled at the multiple-consonant-blending involved with his loud, clear voicing of "stroller" as his way of letting us know it was time to go out and cruise the neighborhood. He swam in the pool, and the ocean. He was a great eater. We lovingly called him Fruitbat because he could polish off a half of a cantaloupe at a time. So sweet and fruity himself. An armful of baby-boy-love. He nursed often, and we stared at each other for hours. I taught yoga at his Montessori school, and we were all so happy.

It's difficult to say exactly where this tale begins. On that dreaded day, when he got seven live vaccines in one "well-baby" appointment whilst sick and jacked-up on antibiotics and Tylenol? Or the next day, when he was bitten by a black widow spider, and my 18-month-old child emotionally disappeared? Those dark days when our son slipped slowly away from us and into a dark, lonely world of his own? Or when the 299.0 (Autism Spectrum Disorder) DSM Diagnosis was placed on my child's future?

So, Gentle Reader, I invite you to stay with me emotionally in my endless moments with Autism, to be with me in this uncensored rawness of the true feelings I display as a life and a family affected by Autism, and to set aside any preconceived notions of an Autism story. Truth is, Autism is not all rah-rah peaced-out puzzle piece heaven. Honestly, Autism is a very difficult road, a complicated dance with a partner who no-shows and constantly steps on your toes. I invite you to listen with me to the pulse of Thad and his Autism, to feel my sadness and pain, to rejoice in his journey, and to celebrate my hope and deep fierce love for this delicious specimen of a boy, my son, my Thaddeus. I invite you to laugh, cry, and feel with me as I tell you these very real feelings that might be sometimes not exactly what polite company might wish for or expect. Autism has changed my life dramatically, significantly, profoundly, and permanently, and I would like to share with you exactly how.

All of a sudden, we fell face-first onto the Autism path. Smack. Just like that. We went to the doctor to get vaccines per the prescribed schedule. Thad was on constant rounds of antibiotics for ear infections throughout his first two years of life. Two sets of ear tubes, hearing concerns and a bunch of doctors later, we gave him his antibiotics, and Tylenol, and took a sick boy in for his routine immunizations. All according to schedule, just what the doctor ordered. He got injections of live vaccines, some grown in eggs, some with aluminum boosters, and all launching a relentless, unabated assault on his immune system. Then, there was a horrible darkness that set over our life.

The next afternoon, I was teaching "Mommy and Me" yoga at the local studio. Ursula sat, pretending her knees were butterflies, gently flapping them up and down. Thaddeus had been a bit distant and lethargic that morning. He had a low-grade fever, and I was on the phone with nurse triage various times the night before. As the class stretched, pulled, and visualized, Thaddeus crawled around the bolster pillows that bathed in the sunshine of the studio's front window.

I hear him yell in pain. A different cry I had not heard before. "A bug bit me," he wails. My eyes focused with deafening accuracy on the little red violin on the back of the black widow spider, scurrying behind the bamboo screens propped in the corner. Class is finished, I have to take him to the emergency room, I tell the room of people. These are the last words I hear from my son's sweet lips for years to follow.

Vaccines related to Autism? What do I think, you inquire. Just like there is no correlation between the fact that my husband and I engaged in lusty intercourse whilst I was ovulating, and hence, I became pregnant with Thaddeus. Maybe the conception was a genetic response to the introduction of Rob's DNA matter in my body? Perhaps it was an environmental response to flirty sperm swimming around in my fluffy uterus looking for love, and a place to settle down? Dr. Andrew Wakefield, rock on.

In the dark days and months that followed, Thaddeus changed, twisted and slipped down this dangerous slope into the lonely scary world of Autism. And we had no fucking idea it was even happening.

Slowly, the light faded from his eyes. He limited his diet to four things and stopped eating fruits and vegetables entirely, he puked constantly, he stopped talking, he got permanently sweaty with an acrid, yeasty twinge that lingered no matter how high we cranked the AC, his raw diaper zone increased to include all areas between his shoulders and ankles, with unending, exploding diapers full of yellow toxic waste, and he looked right through me. What I saw was visible pain, as he unsuccessfully attempted to return his mother's loving gaze. Physical touch, and loud noise were received with massive tantrums that lasted long enough for all of us to comply with his new wishes of complete physical and emotional solitude.

He also became rigid physically and emotionally. He only wanted to remain unbothered in front of the television, with an undying loop of the movie Toy Story filling in his new mental blanks, and satisfying any type of interaction that he could even tolerate. Looking back, I am crushed every time I think about the environmental overload I accidentally exposed him to. Too much shit had blasted his immune system and had destroyed it.

Once again, I had no fucking idea what was happening. He became the dictator of the house, his tantrums and strange perseverations ruling every aspect of a once-calm, now out-of-control home. He would throw tantrums for too much noise, too many people, if we did not adhere to his ritualistic behaviors and expectations of everyday events, and on and on and on.

One such ritualistic behavior is a phenomenon here in *mi casa* is called "Shirts On." This is Thad's determination that when in the house, Rob and Thad will be dressed identically. If we are doing "shirts off," then the gentlemen of the house will strip to skins, and if Thad deems it a "shirts on" moment, Rob is required to replace or acquire a shirt. Many other odd demands by Thad of particular behaviors, scripts and body movements by Rob, Ursula and me became part of our very strange, sad existence.

Thad would get so very angry at me, almost like my words were fingernails on the chalkboard to his ears. He would tense up, fume, yell, and get verbally aggressive with anyone within listening distance. Wild stuff started to happen every day. All day.

He would threaten to vomit if we asked him to eat vegetables. He would threaten tantrums, and would use all of his "weapons," which were anything that he determined as such from invisible swords to tall lightsabers to yardsticks to lamps to anything he envisioned as dangerous, to shoot, decapitate, dismember, and disengage from us. In every way possible, he controlled the roost. No doubt about it. Every time we would go out, Rob or I would end up outside in the parking lot with Thad, or spend extended time in the basement with him alone because T could not tolerate the noise, or the physical proximity of the other people at the party. I quit my spot in a local modern dance company, something fun I used to do, because I could no longer go to the evening rehearsals. Someone had to have two eyes on him at all times. And the other person would do whatever needed to be done, like make dinner, take out the trash, or clean up the food he just barfed up on the table.

Or if Rob or I were alone with him, we would just handle him, and nothing else. No multi-tasking was possible. Very often, he was more than we could handle. He could sustain enormous tantrums for way longer than any of our emotions or nerves could tolerate. Our family's life got a lot less fun.

When we would try to hang out at our friends' houses, he would disappear, and go into their closets and smell their stuff, get under the covers in random people's beds, and search for "weapons" in their house. To Thad, a "weapon" could be a kitchen knife, a mousetrap, a light saber, a plastic sword, or a very real burning candle lit and left unattended in the bathroom. Maybe really dangerous, or maybe "pretend dangerous." If Thaddeus perceived it to be "dangerous," or a "weapon," he wanted it. Decorative swords particularly enamored him, but anything long and pointy could suffice his need to have a "weapon" to "fight" the following scripted scene per Thad's relentless instruction. A real or pretend sword, umbrellas, tall lamps, rolling pins, and toilet plungers were all game-on. We usually left the party abruptly, or early. And we eventually stopped going all together.

It became necessary to sequester my child at home due to his crazy antics out in the world, and then, if we had guests for a meal or a visit, a *tantrum grande* would ensue. We had less and less parties, less and less visitors, and offered and received less and less invitations to participate in social events with other families. Our house was quiet, solitary, and cold. Just as Thad wanted it.

In 2002, Thad was identified by his Montessori preschool teacher as having a possible speech delay. He was assessed, and was found to have challenges with severe challenges and delays in Expressive and Receptive Language, which means that he had severe difficulty understanding communications that was directed at him, and he had severe difficulty producing communication. All the information going in language-wise was jumbled, and everything trying to come out with words just wasn't.

He became a Regional Center (RC) client, California's public entity dedicated to the health and safety of disabled pre-3 kids and post-22 adults, at 2 1/2, he began to receive speech services weekly for his language delay. We had therapists, nurses, and staff at our house multiple times each week for multiple hours at a time, doing speech-related early intervention with him. He became a RC client at age two-and-a-half, and at three years old, he was reassessed to see if he continued to qualify for services through Regional Center, as he transitioned into preschool age special education programming in the school district.

Speech Delay was not a qualifier for continued RC services, but Autism was. We still suspected problems, and yet, we breathed a sigh of relief when we received a form letter from the Regional Center. The two boxes read: Your child does have Autism/ Your child does not have Autism. "Does not" was checked. We were elated. He did not have Autism. Hooray. What we did not realize then was that with this proclamation, Thad became ineligible for Regional Center services, and he was dropped from the state program. We continued to be as confused as ever about his peculiar interests, emotional vacuity, and strange behavior. The earlier the intervention for Autism, the better the prognosis and long-term outcome, they say. Early intervention loosely interprets as pre-6, before elementary school.

As I look back through the endless assessments, protocols, forms and questionnaires that I filled out in 2003, I feel so mad at myself that I did not see what was happening. He was three years old by this point, and probably had ten coherent words, all related to concrete needs and wants, eggs, and Toy Story. In my own handwriting, I unknowingly had detailed copious, endless observations of an autistic child. Mine.

One questionnaire asked me to check off which one of these words does he say, and have I heard him say ever. I highlighted the few words he was saying currently, and then put loads of checkmarks next to other words with the qualifier that I had not heard these words since he was eighteen months old. A symptom of Regressive Autism is an abrupt language loss with the majority of all normal prior developmental milestones met. All words he had, and had used correctly in the past, he no longer had and didn't use at all. Why didn't I see it?

I would fill out mountains of assessments, and forms about him, detailing his rigid behaviors, uncontrollable unceasing tantrums, him walking around the house in the middle of the night with the goal of shining his collection of flashlights into our sleeping eyes, the episodes, the incidents, the social challenges, the tummy issues, the level of physical pain he seemed to be in when sand got between his toes on the playground, and the excruciating academic difficulties in school. All of it. Geneticists, Neurologists, Doctors, and Teachers all told me not to worry.

Years later, in my quest to get my child an appropriate education, I would request a copy of his cumulative school records. At the very bottom of the stack of District records was the Psychologist report from the 2003 Regional Center Assessment that I never received somehow, and I did not know that assessments have accompanying reports detailing the findings, as I do now. At age three, he was not diagnosed with Autism. According to this report, he was diagnosed with Pervasive Development Disorder (PDD), also know as Autism. But PDD was not a condition that warranted RC services like Autism, so he just got a different diagnosis. Get it? Jokes on me. Not only did he get a diagnosis, that diagnosis was never officially revealed to us. Years later, I found out accidentally that he was diagnosed with Autism, a-hem PDD, at age three. No intensive early intervention for him. Oops.

We celebrated our big entrance into the Autism Nation in 2003, on Thad's third birthday with our first meeting with the School District, in the form of an annual meeting called the Individual Education Plan, or the IEP, where at a minimum-of-annual-but-can-be-more-frequent-meeting, disabled children and their parents participate in the right to an appropriate education by the local school district.

In 2003, our boy, who hardly talked, and was definitely having something loopy going on upstairs, was offered a county Speech class twice per week for forty-five minutes by the school district. We signed on the dotted line. The rest of the time, he would watch Toy Story, eat macaroni and cheese, and fly miniature cars in front of his eyes at close range as a calming mechanism. We later learned that this is called visual stimming, as in stimulation. He was trying to regulate something that is disordered in his body's sensory system with this repetitive movement. He would also flick his fingers in front of his eyes for the same effect. We still had no idea this action was a symptom of anything, and we called the behavior, "Thad's screensaver." Endlessly fascinated with his wiggling fingers centimeters from his pupils. Autism, yep. Still, we had no idea.

In 2004, he started in a preschool Language Impairment program in the school district. Yet, something was odd about the class. I speak Spanish, and would stand outside with the ladies chatting *en espanol,* waiting for our kids to leave the class for speech-delayed kids. When the children would exit, they would run to their mommies chattering in Spanish, mute in English, but chattering in Spanish. These kids just need some exposure to English, I thought. These kids are not speech-delayed, like Thad.

I asked the teacher if there was delineation between the goals of the Spanish native speakers, and English native speakers in the Speech class. I was basically trying to understand if this was a preschool English as a Second Language class. Kinda seemed like it to me.

We switched to individual Speech Therapy for 45 minutes per week. He worked for the Therapist for rewards of pretend food, except for corn because he had a huge fear of corn for years. Reason unknown. He spent a lot of the therapy time crying under the table, would incessantly ask for his mom, or to flat out leave during most of the sessions. At home, Thad would sit at the kitchen table for hours, mesmerized by and only interested in interacting with a carton of raw eggs. Alone, at the kitchen table with a dozen eggs, endlessly, hours and hours, gazing lovingly into their blank shells.

I knew there was something very wrong with him, as each day continued. But I could not figure out what it was. He's a late bloomer, he's a boy, his big sister talks a lot and is speaking for him, he will catch up don't worry, they would tell me. Also, I was advised to not worry that he had abruptly lost the words he had one year ago, that he is speaking in some sort of made-up language that only he understands, that he is screaming under the table during attempted standardized testing, that he was not complying with adult directives, that he was avoiding eye contact with everyone, and that he was freakishly perseverating on chicken eggs. Something was not right.

I requested everyone's opinion about Thad, and I asked anyone and everyone what could possibly be wrong with him. I asked school therapists, teachers, doctors, neurologists, all flavors of specialists, and nothing. A little speech delay, that's all. Look, his bad behavior is controlling the room, the room full of specialists would say to us. Of course he doesn't have Autism because he is emotionally engaging his father by shrieking at him and hitting him in the face with a plastic Buzz Lightyear. Kids with Autism rock in the corner, they don't engage like he is, as their expertise flooded the room and drowned me.

I stopped teaching yoga, and exited T from the Montessori preschool because he was beginning to have issues there also. We decided that the Montessori structure was too "academic," and we placed him in a "play-based" preschool run by a fabulous pack of older ladies with about 200 years of combined experience with children. Surely, they could help me figure him out. I asked them what they thought. Autism? I asked. They had never seen it. Prevalence of Autism before 1985 used to be about 4 or 5 kids per 10,000. Now, in 2004, it's 1 in 91. Thad was their first knock on the Autism door.

The Special Education Department at the School District stopped Thad's speech services when he turned five in 2005 because we chose to let him go to another year of preschool to let him "mature more," because his behavior might perhaps be an issue with maturity, not Autism. They informed us that he is, therefore, not eligible for Special Education Services until he started Kindergarten in a District classroom. Mid-year of his third year of preschool, he was still not emotionally progressing, still not catching up, or catching on to what was going on in the world around him. He had sealed himself up in a very tight shell, and it was getting more obvious every day, every moment that our child was very sick.

I would pick him up at preschool, and most of the time, my 5-year old would be laying facedown on a bench alone, or crumpled-up asleep in a doorway. He would only paint with the color blue, he incessantly recreated fight scenes on the playground solo, and obsessively collected small sticks to flick in front of his eyes. He refused to do everything, even things we knew he wanted to do.

The term "quiet defiance" is created to describe his aloof behavior. Something was so wrong, and our family was falling apart. We decided to search for more answers, more expertise, and for doctors, and experts who saw what we saw in our son as a problem.

We met Kelli, a Speech and Language Pathologist, who assessed him and delivered a diagnosis of severe mixed Expressive/Receptive Language Disorder "with a history of language regression, significant social communication difficulties, and particular challenges in comprehension." This description of his condition means that there is a problem with his speech output, expressive, and there is a problem with how he understands language, receptive. Everything going in, and coming out had huge comprehension and meaning problems. His impaired language, social, and communication skills were delayed by years.

We ask Dr. Gwen, Clinical Psychologist, to perform the ADOS, Autism Diagnostic Observation Scale, a gold-standard autism diagnostic tool, on our son. During testing, we watched as Thad would not comply with Gwen's request that he blow out the candle on the birthday cake for her, he would not engage in joint attention with her, and he would not answer questions about his feelings. He only had two emotions that he displayed at all, at the point—mad, and not mad. The assessment went on for multiple days, as Gwen visited Thad at preschool, observed his interaction and family dynamic at home, and conducted a series of lengthy verbal and written interviews with Rob and me.

On June 2, 2006, seventeen days before his sixth birthday, I sit in a cushy, white chair, crying. Rob sits on the floor. Dr. Gwen delivers the findings of her observations, assessments and testing to us, and Thad receives this diagnosis:

The DSM Diagnostic Criteria for Autistic Disorder (299.0 AUTISM SPECTRUM DISORDER) describes impairments in:
Communication
Delay in or lack of spoken language development
Marked impairment in conversational skills
Stereotyped and repetitive use of language
Lack of spontaneous age-appropriate make-believe or social-imitative play
Social interaction
Marked impairment in the use of multiple nonverbal behaviors

Failure to develop age-appropriate peer relationships

Lack of spontaneous seeking to share interests and achievements with others

Behavior

Preoccupation with at least one stereotyped and restricted pattern of interest to an abnormal degree

Inflexible adherence to nonfunctional routines or rituals

Repetitive motor mannerisms and preoccupations with parts of objects

Persistent preoccupation with parts of objects

The DSM IV (Diagnostic and Statistical Manual, 2000) is a reference published by the American Psychiatric Association. A child is thought to have some form of Autism with a minimum of six positive associations to the criteria listed above. Thad had all of the characteristics. Wow, we certainly did have it all.

Having my child diagnosed with Autism that day felt like heading out to go surfing. You arrive at the beach, board under your arm. Not only are there no waves, someone has sucked the ocean dry.

Yes, it's true. A diagnosis of Autism trips up this perfect picture of domestic bliss with our family, kids, and life expectations, slightly. Just kidding. Actually, imagine your whole, perfectly calculated world knocked on its ass. Autism affects the pulp of our family, and controls most aspects—lifechoices, finances, time, resources, and a whole fuck lot of emotion.

When Thad was born, I wondered *what* in the world he would be interested in, not *if* he would be interested in the world, at all. I also did not consider how I would feel if my child's eyes looked through me as I attempted to engage his lifeless soul. I did not think about the heartache I would endure as I got the moment-by-moment audio and the visual to the behavioral therapists in my dining-room-turned-behavior-therapy-clinic-and-homeschool reinforcing my tantrumming child into compliance through various protocols in critical behavioral therapies for Thad's Autism.

I did not prepare emotionally for my morning coffee to include my child's lack of adherence to the therapists in my living room to the simple request to clap twice and tap your nose once, the torrential non-compliance and ceaseless tantrums, and the consequences that followed. As he sat in protest, his anger was timed, the way he manifested each particular outrage was charted, and it was reviewed by team members and supervisors at our weekly team meetings. His behavioral response was noted at each meltdown--the Antecedent, the Behavior and the Consequence of each autistic behavior. Weekly. Daily. Hourly. By the minute. By the second.

And then another therapist would arrive and repeat the same scenario, and again recording every aspect of him, his behavior, his responses, his interactions and lack of interactions, his compliance to adult directives, his refusal toward relaxation techniques, teaching food tolerance, learning playground sports, and the slow inching progress of the various skill sets he lacked documented in a large white binder. It took hours and hours of individual therapy for Thad to learn to tie his shoes, to learn how to ride a two-wheeler bike, and to learn how to sit up straight in class.

I did not realized that I would be teaching a child overtly how to interact with others, how to successfully chew a celery stick, or suck on a coughdrop appropriately. Everything must be taught to my child. Down to the minutia. In second grade, T would have a series of teaching interactions with an instructional aide at school, about how to, and when it is appropriate to throw water in someone's face. Everything must be taught.

I continued to realize more and more how huge this problem was, and we immediately started intensive therapy for Thaddeus, and parent training with Kelli and Gwen to help us try to unlock our boy. I am forever grateful to them as the first experts who listened to my concerns, and began to show me how to access my son, and bring him back into our world.

Kelli was the very first therapist that acknowledged that there was a serious problem with Thaddeus, his behavior, his social skills and his communication skills. She assessed him, and immediately started treating him after. We snatched up any and every extra session with Kelli that we could. We were like people scrounging for morsels in the desert that haven't eaten in weeks, and had finally found an oasis of resources and information. A cornucopia of expertise on how to help our child. We felt so hopeful that we had found someone to help us find our boy. She cracked the first layer of the Thaddeus mystery, and Kelli is Thad's first true friend. The big mystery question, how to emotionally engage the boy? How to get in, and how to stay in? Rob and I found it so difficult to emotionally engage with him because he literally did not like anything but "Pretend Peril," eggs, and Toy Story. Nothing.

"Pretend Peril" is our family-created definition of T pretending to beat up someone with Incredible Hulk hands, feeling the cartoon character strength and power of being able to pretend cut off your mom's arm, and then pretend sew it back on, or throwing a pretend bomb in the kitchen that blows up, or pretending the excitement of being attacked by a million mad bees. In the shower, he will yell, take my hand, outstretched arm, crawling on all 4s on the shower floor with water pouring on his head, as if he needs to be saved from the tsunami he is in. It is the gentlest dangerous moment or dismemberment possible, it is never a violent act, and as long as it is monitored, our little actor is usually quite amusing. I request that Thad feed the dogs, and his response might include a pretend punch in my nose, a big bad-guy face on him, and my little darling telling me it's not his job. Although it is.

And Rob, Ursula and I have this problem with the movie, Toy Story, because it is extremely associated with his Autism to us, as it was the unceasing, perseverative focus of Thad's little, tiny universe. If it was not playing on the television, he was requesting it or crying because his sister wanted a turn. Rob lost a chunk of his nose due to a large Buzz being lobbed at his face at close range, and Thad clung to his large stash of Buzzes in all social situations, and slept cuddling his plastic swords. He did not touch us, he would not allow physical contact with him of any kind, he was a complete mystery to us, and we were scared shitless on so many different levels. So many that we did not even realize it until after hours and hours of parent training on how to successfully engage with our son, and help him access the world.

Rob and I would literally peer around the corner at the clinic, so nervous that he was going to melt down during his therapy, be kicked out, or be worried that the therapists couldn't handle him either. Thaddeus was so emotionally sealed up, and we were so well trained through the years by our kid to be scared to death of his wrath, his rage, his Autism.

But Kelli got in. She unlocked Level One. She got in with the two things that freaked us out most—Toy Story, and Pretend Peril. For years, the way Thaddeus would start his speech therapy session—*Kelli, I am going to kick your butt.*

Trash-talk between the two would commence, almost like their own private salutation, as the therapy door closed. Thad likes cuts and injuries. He would draw fake injuries on himself with red markers, he and Kelli would have intense light saber fights, and loud, raucous sword battles, and then he would continue to draw elaborate wounds all over Kelli's face, arms and legs. Thad would have to pretend to be the doctor, and make her better. Thad would leave the clinic session stabilized, refreshed and so happy that someone would go head-to-head with him in dangerous battle. Through the years, Kelli would dress as General Grievous, a six-armed, six-light saber-sworded bad guy at Thad's request, or play "To infinity and beyond" with blow-up spacewings with him to entice him emotionally to engage with her. Right up Thad's alley, and a valuable piece of our puzzle.

Kelli follows a model for teaching children with Autism called DIR (Developmental, Individual-differences, Relationship-based) or Floortime, developed by Stanley Greenspan. This form of therapy asks therapists to start working with the children where they are not where they should be developmentally or where therapist wants them to be, to use their unique interests as a hook to enter into the child's world, their space and their interests, and to start there, wherever "there" is.

What she was doing was working, slowly getting into his psyche using his perseverative stuff as a hook. Kelli started off playing with Thad and the Buzz Lightyear crew of characters for the entire session, then slowly, in a few sessions, a task would be required of Thad first, then Buzz, then, a week or so later, two tasks then Buzz. And Kelli has great toys in her clinic. She explained her strategy with Thad to me. I gotta show him I am worth playing with, she said. And that it is more fun to play cool games with awesome toys with her, than sit and tantrum in the corner. She was getting inside him, and he was starting to slowly respond to life again.

Thaddeus also began to understand that words could elicit an emotional response from others, and he was particularly keen and acute on the movie phrases that made others mad, scared, or shocked. The Autism characteristic, scripting, is the incessant repetition of a particular word, phrase, or sound, and Thad is stellar at repeating phrases from television or movies over and over.

A particular favorite phrase during Kindergarten was a script of Woody, from you guessed it, Toy Story. A teacher or therapist would spend her precious 50-minute hour with him, trying to get a morsel of knowledge to stick in his noggin. He would be cute and mischievous and spacey during class, and then abruptly end the session with a mean scowl and mad eyes and say, "You're wasting your time," just like Woody said to Buzz under the car in front of Pizza Planet.

The School Therapist would then tell me how rude and naughty Thad was for saying that, and I would explain that he was scripting a scene from a movie. And how I was certain that a child with such limited speech, and such severe challenges in language comprehension did not understand the literal meaning of that statement, but that he certainly delighted in the mad emotional response you gave him. No one believed me, and I was directed to parenting class to get his behavior under control. His behavior challenges were a parenting issue, the School Psych told me.

He would play, replay, and rewatch specific scenes in specific movies over and over, watching each person's inflection, pulse or movement closely, like a surfer examining a wave set to get the intimate details of the swell. As if he was learning life, and human interaction from the screen because he couldn't quite see it in, or on other people. Thad also became enamored with the vast variety of emotionally charged responses that cuss words could elicit; it was getting him into certain unfavorable predicaments.

To his defense, and as his parent, I do believe that it is intrinsic to young boys, autistic or not, to want to cuss, so I could sympathize with his unfortunate dilemma. A compromise emerged between us. We agreed that he could only say the naughty words underwater. He would lay in the bath, underwater for hours, with a straw in his mouth, shit, dammit, stupid all flooding out of the straw.

In the 1960s, what was more enraging to those police officers than those damn hippies putting daisies in the barrels of their big, scary cocked rifles? During the early years of Autism, Thad would engage in behavior tantrums that resembled a non-violent protest that we termed a "Man-Down." as in the police walkie-talkie conversations—*"We have a man down in the living room."* A family definition, the "man-down" is a silent boy laying face directly down on the ground, stick-straight arms and legs, non-responsive, and refusing to move.

A "man-down" in the living room or the kitchen is at most irritating, but not so problematic. But, a man-down in the international airport or the grocery store or God forbid, a public bathroom (yes, it happened) is downright disgusting, and takes hygiene to a new low. As T gained language, he would threaten to do a man-down if he did not get his way, and down he would go if there was any rebuttal to his commands.

The Autism party usually starts in the morning, and continues all day long. Usually long into the night, and usually right into tomorrow. One memorable morning, I felt mad, sad, and mostly scared. As I waited for Thaddeus to come downstairs to breakfast, I chatted on the phone to my friend, Jessica. It was later in the morning than usual for his breakfast. But, he had just yelled to tell me that he was cutting paper, and that he would be down for granola, pears, toast and nutritional supplements shortly. I recounted my previous day's events in no particular order to Jessica as I buttered his rice toast and cut the crusts off for him to eat separately.

Out of the corner of my eye, I noticed something flutter to the ground outside the kitchen window. I thought that the gardeners were getting aggressive with their leafblowers, and had blustered a palm frond over my fence. The hot sun beat down hard on the sassy magenta bougainvillea blossoms, outside, beckoning my attention, as I balanced his full plate of food.

Mother's intuition kicked in full-force as my son walked quickly past me, out the back door and toward the kitchen window, full of flowers and mid-morning action. He did not address me as he walked past nor did he stop at the kitchen table, as he typically does for a delicious rice bread crust treat. Something was up. I followed him out the door, and as I turned the corner, I watched him pick something up. He is throwing things out the window, I thought, disgruntled. I calculated the amount of minutes we would spend discussing how it is inappropriate to throw one's belongings out of the second story window, and then we would revisit all of the better choices we could be making with our toys and with our time.

A vision of my child picking up something black and net-like from the hot concrete walkway smacked me in the face like a metal bat, aluminum perhaps. Plastic, shiny, and missing from the appropriate place, I watched him gather the remnant pieces of the screen from his bedroom window. He had cut the fucking screen out of his window. I had let this happen. My kid could have fallen. He could have been hurt. And I did not know. This was the first time Autism had stopped me cold in my tracks. I was so scared, completely numb. I did not know what to do next. I was shaking in fear, anger, and confusion. I looked up at his bedroom window to see the screen not-so-neatly but ever-so-accurately cut out of his window.

"Sweetheart, why did you do that?" I asked him, shaking.

"I needed some fresh air," he replied, in a small, too-soft, sing-songy voice, flicking the net very near his eyes.

I ran upstairs to assess the scene of the crime. We live in an orange grove in southern California, with loads of flying insects that are equipped with stingers. Coincidentally, a colony of wasps had moved in to the eves of his second-story bedroom window the night before. I wondered if the loud buzzing and the hive activities of the hefty wasp tribe were comforting, loud, or annoying as he cut. Or did he even notice? Did he sense the danger of cutting out a second-story screen window, and gaining direct access to a pack of wasps hanging in their domicile, and the possibility of him falling on the hot, hard concrete below? My child had chosen to stand on a desk in front of a large window in his bedroom, and with my sharp sewing scissors that he had extracted from what I had perceived to be a good hiding place, he had cut the screen out of his window. Thaddeus has an impaired sense of danger, and a lack of safety awareness. Additionally, he is interested in all things he perceives to be "dangerous," which is very often problematic and a big safety concern.

Danger Dog, we call him in jest. But, he was really a shy gentle boy, and the idea of a wasp attack for the morning happenings was not on my preferred list. Nothing really happened. But the "what-if" factor of the situation knocked me sideways. What if this happened again? Or something like it, or something different? I called his therapists, gasping, sobbing. Should I yell at him? Should I give him a time-out? Should I give myself a time-out? He just...he just... I am numb. I am scared, and blood is racing through my crevices.

We had recently sold the large, wooden playset in our backyard on craigslist because Thad was being dangerous with it by sitting on the roof of the fort in his underwear, dangling by one arm from tall, horizontal bars, flailing and scream-ing for fake help from unknowing passerbys. We had alarms, locks, dogs, gates, therapists, and keys at home. Wasn't this enough to keep him safe?

Due to the intense nature of emotional heartbreak, and this scary stuff of life happening, my morning meal consists quite regularly of breakfast and a panic attack. Panic attacks are similar to Autism. Never know when it's going to strike. I am relaxed, and hanging out one moment. And then, all of a sudden, I am having a panic attack. Why are you stressed right now? I have no idea. I say, not lying. It is a physiological response to this palpable level of stress rushing at me constantly and incessantly, comparable to gripping terror, or the oxygen being turned off in your scuba tank, as I continue to viscerally experience the magnitude of the situation.

Unexpected, cold blasts of water in my face that feel like sharp icicles, slough-ing away my sanity pore by pore. Beating butterfly wings grip my stomach into pangs of nausea. I often manifest my fear of the unknown in Thad's future, my depression, and the gravity of my child's illness in my body with heart-stopping, violent panic attacks that have hospitalized me.

These vicious panic attacks seem to sneak out of nowhere. My body had trained itself to crank up the adrenaline, and engage in a blood-coursing, internal-turmoil freak-out. Swirling my hand around in a pot of boiling water, attempting to grab hold of my baby's lost soul. Debilitating feelings of doom. Panic attacks are invisible. So is Autism. Only the person experiencing it truly knows what it feels like.

CHAPTER 2

I Am My Son's First Sightword

IN 2006, THAD starts public school Kindergarten. The Individual Education Plan (IEP) team decides that based on his unique needs, he requires an individual adult aide (commonly known as a one-to-one, or a 1:1) with him 100% of his academic day, Speech Therapy, Resource Specialist support (commonly known as RSP at this time), and eventually Occupational Therapy (OT) in order to help him access the curriculum and learn. Then, the IEP team changes his special education eligibility under the Individuals with Disabilities Act (IDEA), the law that guides and informs the IEP process, to Autism. We had also realized by this point that he had sensory integration challenges, and has struggled significantly with basic academic tasks. In addition, he is also eventually diagnosed with Central Auditory Processing Disorder (CAPD), Speech-Language Impairment (SLI), Sensory Integration Disorder (SID), Dyslexia, Dysgraphia, and Dyscalculia.

So, Thad went to public Elementary School for Kindergarten, and First Grade. And I went to teach English Composition at the local university for exactly two academic years.

Thaddeus had quite a big temper by the time he started Kindergarten, and held grudges a mile wide, and just as deep. He would stomp down the stairs angrily each morning. Dad, I am mad at your wife for making me go to school, he would declare over fried bacon, and potatoes. We would put fruit on his plate at each meal, too. He regularly threw the fruit across the room or in the trash, along with every fucking fork in our house because he had numerous, odd biases against forks for years.

I would tell him that I was putting the fruit on his plate just for a joke, and hoped secretly, that I could slowly, incrementally, over time, desensitize whatever was messing with him inside by him tolerating the fruit actually on his plate, and then eventually get the juicy orange smile to touch his lips, and someday, actually get him to chew it, and ultimately, down the road, swallow the damn thing. Every new thing we tried to teach him or introduce to him, especially things he perceived that he already did not like, would be met with hours and hours of resistance, before any new learning could even occur. And it usually didn't.

Rob and I do extensive nutritional research, and that fall, Thaddeus begins a biomedical protocol sometimes referred to as the Defeat Autism Now (DAN) protocol, which addresses, acknowledges, and remediates the physical imbalances and environmental symptoms that might contribute to the Autism symptoms he experienced. We visit our naturopathic doctor once per month, work on developing a concise nutritional supplement schedule, make extreme diet changes, do intensive gut remediation based on the precise testing of his sensitive systems, and we are so relieved to have finally found a doctor following T who knew what was up. She does extensive bloodwork on Thad, and finds that he is severely allergic to gluten (wheat protein), casein (milk protein), and eggs. We immediately begin the Gluten-Free, Casein-Free Diet (GFCF), and we eliminate eggs from our cupboards. In addition, he stops eating soy because it mimics milk's molecular structure, and we exit all artificial dyes, chemicals and colors from his diet because he becomes a lunatic fringe each time he ingested anything gummy or chewy because of his behavioral reactions to the chemical neurotoxins. We green our soaps and cleaning chemicals, and we actively block any and all vaccine protocols that he might fall victim to. I have always found what a person eats to be important, I have always found food to be significant in my life in so many active ways, and that what you eat determines how you feel, and I add to my list, what you eat determines how you behave.

We learn quickly that a fast food cheeseburger with a DumDum sucker chaser was a sure fire way to amplify T's Autism, and scrupulously make all of the food he eats for the next four years from scratch in our kitchen. Rob and I move forward each day rhythmically, a tedious medicinal tango. A large amount of our collective time was spent in a complicated series of meticulous culinary movements, and measurements to the microgram of oral, topical, and intravenous supplementation to nourish our child's body and mind, and to unfog his brain.

When we started the GFCF diet, I asked my friend, Hannah, if I could come over and look in her gluten-free, casein-free cabinets, and fridge. I was willing to try anything, and I seriously needed a crash course from a savvy mama. I could not imagine what we would eat. What would I throw in the cart at the grocery, and what could replace the gluey goodness of soft, freshly baked French bread with garlic and fresh Parmesan, or warm, stretchy cheese on mounds of heavenly pasta? Both professors at the university, we would meet at the university swimming pool to hang, and the rigidity and impaired social skills of our boys' Autism would emerge. Thad firmly only wanted to swim in the deep end, and her boy firmly only wanted to swim in the shallow end. A few hours later, we would wave at each other, and consider the playdate a moderate success.

We then realize through testing and observation that T had a "leaky gut," and something must be done. All the undigested proteins in his tummy were leaking through his intestinal lining into his bloodstream, and mimicking opiate receptors in his brain. Basically, the gluten and casein made it hard for him to focus and engage with the world because he was tripping out on his body's morphine-like response these proteins had tricked his brain into craving. And he would respond to the allergen in eggs with crazy odd behaviors, lack of memory, decreased focus and attention to reality, and overt spaciness. Basically, eggs made him act more autistic. No wonder, they say you crave your allergy. He had been eating up to six eggs per day, and touching or talking about them the rest of the day. Like a cat and catnip.

I explain all this to the teacher, and she responds that she's been meaning to tell me that she and the kids in the class think Thad eating salmon patties for lunch is weird, and then shakes a cup of Skittles in his face, asking me if T can have them, immediately after I specifically said I would provide all of his food from home. No, he cannot, I reply. And then I thank her for the extended tantrum about to commence from Thad, and his lack of possibly-promised-but-only-if-your-mom-says-yes Skittles rage machine.

Thad had a quick honeymoon period in the afternoon Kindergarten, and soon he began shuffling through an endless supply of untrained, unsupervised permanent aides, and boatloads of substitute aides. A skin-brushing protocol called Wilbarger was started on him that was supposed to help him overcome tactile defensiveness, and instead makes him overstimulated and completely emotionally shut-down. I asked them to please stop because he was getting a sensory overload, and the school staff refused to stop stimulating my child's skin with a plastic-bristled, white sensory brush while on campus until we had a meeting to decide to stop. My words were not enough. I kept him home, unbrushed, for a few days until we could meet, and I watched his wackiness decrease without this particular therapy. No one knew how to handle T at school. Thad would just say, "I don't know" to every question anyone asked him. Even stuff he knew. And everyone was okay with that, except me.

I started to get more concerned because I had to remind the Teacher and his 1:1 Aide regularly that Thad could not use free time to lay on the little blue couch in the reading area and pass out, or hide in the playhouse alone, which was what I kept seeing. And as I said, each new thing needs to be taught. I would volunteer in class, and work with him writing on the whiteboards as a class, and then everyone erasing everything on their boards in unison. One day, the teacher changed the expectation, and asked the children to erase only one thing at a time on the board. We had not yet practiced only erasing one thing at a time at home, so Thad erased everything on the board, and got in trouble for not listening to the directions. He got mad, and I took him home early to overtly practice wiping things off of a whiteboard one-by-one for the next few hours.

I repeatedly ask the Special Services in the School District for more help, as we continue to be challenged by Thad's behavior at home and at school, we are very concerned about his lack of interest, ability, and progress in academics, and we are the most worried about his lack of interest in human interaction and life. I could not understand why they just wanted to label him "disabled" and "autistic," and sort of forget about it after that. He'll be our "special child" in the class, they would tell me. We won't expect much, he'll skate through and not learn too much, but at least there is no boat-rocking, they tell me. And, what are we going to do about the fact that he's not paying attention in class, was my continuous query in daily communication book. "Oh, autistic kids are like that" would be the common response.

Part of his biomedical protocol involved an aggressive attack on the yeasty beasts that were partying down in his intestinal track. And when yeast die, they explode. So, Thad developed the term, "spicy poop," to let us know that he needed to hit the bathroom double-time for an imminent diarrhea explosion. Bathrooms are also an avoidance location for Thad, and he spent a significant amount of his Kindergarten year in the gentlemen's lounge. Significant amounts of time chilling in the restroom, sometimes for avoidance and sensory overload reasons, and sometimes for spicy poop. I don't think anyone really believed me about the spicy poop or the yeast challenges. I got the feeling that the staff thought I was making excuses for his bad behavior, and poor attending skills in class. In addition, it was difficult to figure out if the dash to the restroom was for spicy poop, or because he needed a moment alone. Eventually, I ask the teacher to kindly stop writing, "He went to the bathroom" all over Thad's unfinished worksheets.

I found myself calling more and more meetings at school. I had noticed that the current Aide was physically writing in his journal for him, instead of helping him to write in his journal himself. I requested he have "paper-and-pencil-independence" in journal writing because the Aide appeared to be more concerned about Thad getting his work done in the same amount of time as the other children. Very often, I watched her give him the answers to speed him up, or she would actually do his work herself. And, by the way, who the fuck was in charge of the rotating, perpetual cast of untrained aides for Thad anyway? No one knew. I audiotaped many of the meetings, so Rob could follow the unending conversation of how to successfully teach Thad.

TRANSCRIPT OF A RECORDED CONVERSATION BETWEEN PUBLIC SCHOOL PERSONNEL, AND ME
NAMES HAVE BEEN CHANGED TO PROTECT THE INNOCENT

PLAYERS
PRINCIPAL OF THE LOCAL ELEMENTARY SCHOOL
GENERAL EDUCATION TEACHER AT THE LOCAL ELEMENTARY SCHOOL

SPECIAL EDUCATION TEACHER AT THE LOCAL ELEMENTARY SCHOOL
MOTHER OF BOY WITH AUTISM

033
GENERAL EDUCATION KINDER-YEAR TEACHER—His phoneme sounds are weak. He hasn't shown me that he knows any letter sounds yet. He doesn't have any sight words except the word "a," which is also a letter, so let's count that as two skills.

071
PARENT—Sometimes at the beginning of asking LITTLE MR. WONDERFUL to do something, he is resistant for his own personal reasons. I asked him to think of a sentence, I wrote it on the white board, and then he was resistant to doing the writing. Then, he started copying the sentence, and NEW AIDE, AS OF 2 WEEKS said "Oh, it's too hard for him, let's make it easier." And I was like no, no, let's not make it easier. Let's, you know, keep him at the level. So, I just wonder if when she does the journaling that er, when he does the journaling, if the sentence could be written on the white board by her and he could have complete control over writing with the pencil on the page. Because it looks like she's writing on the page, and he's…

EXTREMELY CREDENTIALED TEACHER WHO KNOWS EVERYTHING THERE IS TO KNOW ABOUT EVERYTHING—I think that's what AUTISM PROGRAM SPECIALIST TO THE UNIVERSE instructed her to do. That was part of the back-chaining idea. Was that writing the whole thing did seem too daunting for him. So, that's why they are just picking the one word at the end for him to copy, and eventually, it was going to be two words, and eventually 3. It was my understanding.

MOTHER (BITCH)—But I can say, from experience at home and from experience on Friday, that he can copy a whole sentence. And so, um, I'm going to come in tomorrow too, and I can, you know, model that for STUPID, UNTRAINED CLASSROOM AIDE or anybody. But, in relation to his writing, he has the ability to write. For whatever reason, our little tendencies… In the beginning, it seems hard, it seems daunting, it seems, whatever…we just can't lower the bar for him when I have seen him copy a whole sentence. And he just did it on Friday, too. If you look on the word wall…

RED-FACED KINDERGARTEN EXECUTIVE DIRECTOR (interrupting)—Right. I know he didn't do it at all earlier in the week, which is why it was incomplete. I mean, he refused to write anything that day. Except maybe the one word that was there.

MOTHER PRACTICING PRANAYAMA—But what I'm just concerned about is that on Friday, what I saw him…All I'm doing is making an observation because I know what he does at home. And I'm just saying that if he has control over what he's writing then he will be more motivated to write it himself. When you look in his journal, there is very little written by POOR LITTLE DEVELOPMENTALLY-BEHIND BOY. And I'm saying that yes, he can do this because he does it at home. So, it's not that big of a deal. Well, yes, it is that big of a deal. What I'm saying is that he can do it, and if he could have the pencil in his hand, and the control over that journal…

SPECIAL ED TEACHER WHO SMELLS LIKE YESTERDAY—We could try. But, you know, it will take a ton of redirecting.

MOM—That's why it's great that he has an individual behavioral aide at school for the entire day. To keep him safe, to keep him on task, to reinforce, you know…follow-thru, continuity….

122

TEACHER (TEACHES WITH HER EGO, NOT WITH HER HEART)—So, I think that from IDIOT WHO DOESN'T KNOW HER ASS FROM HER EYEBALL's professional observation that the back-chaining idea was to not overwhelm him.

ADVOCATE FOR HER LITTLE ONE—Well, I understand that. But I would like to request, due to the fact that SMART SHINING YOUNG EXAMPLE OF GOODNESS AND UNIQUE IDEAS has someone working with him 100% of the time, that we try it the way I am asking. Paper and pencil independence in his journal writing. Because to me, that seems like more of a challenge to him, as opposed to less of a challenge for him. And more of an independent way of doing the journaling.

PRINCIPAL OF SCHOOL WHO HAS NO IDEA THAT THE PESKY '1 IN 91 AUTISM SPECTRUM DISORDER DIAGNOSIS' IS HERE, AND IT CONTINUES A-KNOCKIN' AT HER KINDERGARTEN

ENROLLMENT DOOR—And I think that that would be a good discussion to have with TALKS BUT SEZ NUTHIN. And she's here on...

CRABBY, INDEBTED MOM OF A BOY WHO DRAWS MUSTACHES ON HIS FACE WITH PERMANENT MARKER —Tomorrow. At 2.

130

EVIL WITCH SCHOOL PRINCIPAL—So that would be a good conversation to have with her because AIDE takes her direction from LA SPECIALISTA.

MOM OF BOY WHO CLIMBS INAPPROPRIATE POLES AT SCHOOL—Exactly.

SOUR APPLE IN CHARGE—So, rather than giving NO, SHE'S NOT A DUMBSHIT, SHE'S JUST UNTRAINED mixed messages...

SLEEPY MADRE (SOMETIMES IN CHARGE)—and AIDE, DON'T WORRY SHE'LL BE GONE IN 2 MONTHS ANYWAY and I talked about that on Friday, that she is receiving mixed messages from all of you about how to appropriately support my child at school...

Eloquent whispers of *fuckyoulady* glistened in their eyes, as they talked about his shortcomings, his academic deficits, his wrongdoings in class, and the ways that will not inconvenience them to deal with his poor classroom behavior. No one talked about how to help him overcome or control his bad behavior, poor attention, and enormous classroom challenges. No one talked about how to help him, only how to tolerate him. Kristin, we are out of ideas, they would tell me. Okay, I would respond, but it's not okay to BE OKAY with being out of ideas.

More District specialists are brought in to train teachers, aides, and staff. I participated in parent training on the school campus, and host a separate training at my house. Thad gets another new permanent aide, and a sensory diet is put in place for him. In his sensory diet, he would leave the classroom every hour and do some sort of physical exercise to keep him physically alert, regulated, and help him pay attention in class. Paying attention is a huge challenge for him.

Thad is the master of memorizing other people's words, a funny actor, and he was excited to participate in the Kindergarten spring play. On the big day, Thad was playing with the microphone inappropriately during rehearsal, and the teacher clapped her hands loudly in his face, and yelled at him to stop. I had alerted her previously to his extreme sensitivity to sounds, and now he told me he was too scared to participate in play because he was extremely worried the teacher would clap loudly in his face again if he made a mistake. He did not participate in the class play that night; instead he stayed home, ate organic, gluten-free ricechips, and watched Toy Story.

I would pick Thaddeus up at school each day. Usually, in my first twenty or so steps on campus on my path to collect him at his classroom, every adult that worked with him throughout the day would accost me with a hefty list of his daily behavioral, social and academic infractions for the day. He mustached himself with the permanent marker again, he broke more of the antique Curious George stuff in the Principal's office, he climbed up poles at school on two occasions, one before lunch and one after, and then refused to get down. He hit his reading partner, and as a punishment, he missed recess. He spent math time on a sensory break because he broke the manipulatives. The entire class counted cookies today, and he did not get one because we know how you like to follow that Jenny McCarthy diet. He was mad for the first hour of the day because of his lack of cookies to count, and did not do the painting project. Oh, and that's why the George Washington art project in his backpack has no head.

On a sunny Wednesday, I arrived at school to pick Thaddeus up. I noticed that he was seated on top of the tall metal swing set, the cool old kind that unfortunately is leaving public school campuses daily. He got up there and he won't get down, they say. I looked around at The Principal, The Teacher, The Resource Teacher, The Speech Therapist, the Occupational Therapist, The Aide, and The Autism Program Specialist. Let's see, according to the IEP, he has 100% of your time, as I pointed to one person, and 20% of your time daily, and 1/528% of your time, and 1/5% of yours. And on and on. So, I asked, who was not doing their job? Initiate eye contact aversion.

Who is not keeping my child safe? Everyone looks around, fingers unpointed and faces crunched up in confusion at the perplexing question, peering suspiciously up at Thaddeus on the top of the swing set. How did he get up there? It must have taken him a while, I question. I looked at the long fire-engine-red supporting crossbars that he would have had to shinny up to reach the ocean-blue horizontal bar, where Thad sat with a smug, yet confused look in his eyes.

They were about to call the Fire Department to get him down, and the situation was definitely looking grim. Did anyone ask why he was up there? I questioned. No, no, but he might fall, they cried in unison. I knew from experience with his dangerous interactions with our backyard playset, and his rock-climbing proficiency out on the desert rocks we frequented that he would not fall. But, he did need to come down. Hey Thad, why are you up there? I ask. I am playing "hot lava," he tells me. Red lava, and blue water. I understood. He was at top of swing set at school because, in his mind, he was climbing away from the dangerous, hot lava bars. Will you come down Thad, and we can play "hot lava" at home? I asked him. Sure, he said, and he climbed down. No one had asked him why he was up there. Yes, the reason was inappropriate, but he did have a reason, and a remedy soon followed. Another teachable moment, lost in the sauce.

The Kindergarten teacher was also the Reading Recovery Teacher. She looked into my eyes the last day of school, and said, "If I cannot teach him to read, then no one can." She did not teach him to read, and when he left Kindergarten, he still did not know the letters of the alphabet. He could not cut successfully or safely with scissors, and he had problems listening and looking at the teacher at the same time. Very often, he was listening, just not looking. Or looking, but not listening. These were all characteristics of his sensory challenges, and no one seemed to understand how to appropriately or effectively teach him.

In the summer between Kindergarten and First Grade, I thought a lot about the abstract quality of Sightword List One. Sightwords are the backbone of elementary school learning, I realize. Recognizable by sight, immediately, and an important batch of words to know that strengthen your reading fluency, islands of certainty in a sea of words, some shit like that. I mean, really, why should Thaddeus seriously care about learning how to spell "it," "is," "my," and "so?" Yes, these words are only two letters long. Yes, they are in the top one hundred most used words in the English language. And, yes, for many children, these words are desperately easy to remember.

But for certain children, such as mine, these sight words also cover some seriously abstract concepts for a child who already suffers from receptive and expressive language disorders, and has severe comprehension challenges. How does one truly overtly, explicitly, clearly, and correctly explain the concepts of "so" or "the" or "me?" Or even more basically, why he should even care in the first place? Try to explain the importance, and abstract significance of the concept "the" to child who has very limited, mostly needs-based vocabulary. It's quite a challenge.

I wrote my name, MOM, on a white index card one morning, and pointed at myself. Then, I wrote THAD on a card, and pointed to him. We went back and forth, and he was able to identify me, MOM, and point to the correct corresponding card. Two years of blindness to the Sightword List One, and it took him 20 minutes that morning to recognize me, his mom written symbolically. Overjoyed, I realize that I am my son's first sightword. MOM. I had taught Thaddeus his first sightword, and I was beyond ecstatic. Make the words meaningful and salient, I thought. So we moved forward with other concrete words that are important to him, other words that have emotional meaning to him, DAD, URSULA, and his beloved mutt-siblings, NIC, GLOB and JOSIE. By the end of the summer, he could pick the words out of a random group, and write them from a visual cue. The names of the members of his family are the sightwords he went to First Grade with, and these are the sightwords he left First Grade with.

I also noticed that when he sat still, erect, for more than say, fifteen seconds, to do his tabletop work with me, he would slowly deflate like an old circus balloon, and ooze gently in a deep sleep on top of his incomplete math worksheets. So, Thad and I created the Smart Boy Body, as the protocol for how he would sit when he did his work. Every part of his body had a job to engage in, and focus on. We gave each part of his body a job. The body was firm, with a straight back, and both hands on the table. The brain's job was to think about the work. Feet on floor with shoes on so we don't get unfocused by worrying about temperature of our feet, eyes on the book and mouth quiet, pointer-underliner finger, and strong wrists and fingers to hold the book. Also, we decided that the opposite of 'smart' was 'cheesy,' because 'stupid' is a mean word.

Thad also started on the swim team that summer, and I am sure I looked like the bitchiest mom there. I would walk up and down the pool with him when he was doing laps because literally mid-lap, he would forget what he was doing, stop, bob up and down, and look around. I was the constant reminding him to keep moving, don't stop, get going, go that way. The coaches were extremely understanding, and allowed my march to continue every Monday and Wednesday evening for months. He would take off his goggles and lose them, or leave them somewhere almost weekly, and he was usually underwater when the directions for the next swim sets occurred. But, he felt great in the water, and with a little behavioral support from me at practice, it worked. Thad and I got our visual language down well enough into the season that I could bust him for any of the previous infractions with hand commands from the other side of the pool because I eventually faded back to just standing at the end of his lane, noodling at him to hurry up with my fingers. I had taught him these signs specifically for that purpose, and usually they went something like, if you don't put your goggles back on, I will chop you in half.

When I was cool and twenty years old, I went backpacking through Old Yugoslavia. All the signs were in Cyrillic, and I cannot read Cyrillic, therefore I am illiterate in the country. I experienced not being able to read signs, or menus one morning. I couldn't find a single person in Belgrade who I could communicate successfully with, so I held out my hands with a fanned stack of bills to pay for my meals, and busfare. I could not even understand the money because about four different editions were in circulation, and I did not understand its logic. The 0s mean this and the 2 0s mean this, and subtract two. I am sure that morning, I probably paid like one hundred bucks for my Turkish coffee, and olive-infused scrambled eggs.

I felt disoriented, and really fucking stupid in this small enclave where I could only point, and my multiple attempts at communication regarding the train schedule to Istanbul meant nothing to anyone. I hoped that someone understood me, and could tell me which sign said my designation. Not being able to read the words that tell us what's going on in our surroundings is really scary. And frustrating. Finally, someone understood my words, and was able to help me. It is important to help people in need.

In the fall of 2007, he started First Grade, and I was so hopeful for his success. I had taught him how to successfully copy the alphabet, capital letters and small letters all over the summer. He could imitate the letter formations with a visual model, but not by memory. Not yet. He was still significantly behind the classmates academically, but he had made huge progress over the summer, and he felt confident. He had some sight words he knew, just like the other kids. He was still on Sightword List One from the California state standards list, where he started on the first day of Kindergarten. But, we had made progress in the summer, and I was sure this was going to be the year it all came together for him.

The year began well with Thad's first sensory break of the day including the entire class on the playground for twenty minutes of stretches and warm-ups. The one positive quality I did admire in his first grade teacher was that she could run quite fast across playground in her four-inch heels. I spent those days expecting that those commissioned to teach my child would actually teach him something. I spent those days hoping that the hours he spent away from me were, at least, microscopically productive. He got lots of praise for trying hard in the first few moments of his new classroom. The big highlight was at the weekly school assembly when he played the part of famous music conductor in an educational play. He said his words loudly in the microphone, knee-socks pulled up far, gymshoes tied extra-tight, and he gave me constant thumbs-up during his little speech. I was so proud of him. It's finally working, I thought. I felt peaceful inside for about two weeks.

Schoolwork got harder, and more attention and language demands were made on the students. Other children learned, and Thad did not move forward. Boys in his class started to bully him. They would imitate him, jumping up and down, taunting, I'm autistic, I'm autistic. They knew he was sensitive to touch, and they would grab him and not let go. They thought it was funny to see him freak out, I guess. I alerted the Program Specialists, the Director of Special Education, the Principal, and the Teacher. Nothing happened. Every day, on his personal check-in list, he circled "mad' and "sad.' Every day.

His behavioral, and sensory challenges were quickly turning his school day into one big sensory break. He would gain access to the swings, and climbing stuff for tantrumming in class, refusing whatever, generally passing out on his desk in boredom, or some other demonstrations of lack of compliance to adult directives. And he usually was on some sort of catch-all, "sensory break," because I would show up for my frequent meetings with the Principal, and see Thad and his Aide off in the field at farthest monkey bars, T, dangling motionless by one arm, and the Aide, chatting on her cellphone. Meetings became weekly, and were named Team Thad. We sat in the Principal's Office, and talked about all the things he could not do.

He would regularly pretend he was asleep, or "dead" in order to get out of academic tasks. A common conversation:

Me—How was the spelling test?

Teacher—Well, he pretended he was dead during the entire spelling period, so he did not take the test.

In First Grade, he had a speaking part in the class play, and he appeared excited. Yet, when we arrived, he flat-out would not wake up from a deep sleep he had fallen into in the ten minutes it took to arrive at school. Finally, he awoke in a fit. School staff and I collectively did not know what to do that night either to handle his explosive, unexpected behavior. He did not participate in the school play that night, and his proud voice saying the lines we rehearsed endlessly were never heard. My participation in solving this problem was not welcomed by the staff, as a thick, painful wall of hatred and resentment slowly built between me and Thad's IEP team members.

Every morning, he would be mad that I woke him up for school, I would drop him off at school mad, and I would pick him up six hours later, and he would still be mad at me for dropping him off at school that morning. Needless to say, progress was slight. Actually, he regressed significantly academically and emotionally.

I began writing letters to the Special Services Administration directly. I thought that if I outlined in writing exactly how serious the situation was to them, that they would understand. They would help me. They would help Thaddeus. They would help me help Thaddeus. Egos started getting involved, and his Teacher told me I was "mean" and "could not be trusted" for bringing up the problems Thad had in her classroom at the weekly meetings held to discuss his problems.

I bought books about Autism, how to educate, respect, support, understand, remediate and teach children on the spectrum for the staff, I read endless picture-book stories about being a friend to someone with Autism to his class-rooms both years, as I continued to learn more about Autism protocols, methods and therapies myself. I asked the children in his class directly to be a "friend" to Thad, and I tried to explore and explain to them how to interact with him. Although, honestly at that point, I was unsure that anything I was doing to help the staff access him was doing anything. Through parent training with Kelli and Gwen, I was only just starting to learn and understand myself how to engage with him, by starting with where he was on the developmental ladder. Not where he should be, where he is.

Inclusion, the practice of mixing kids with special needs into general education environments, is a great concept, if done properly, and appropriately managed. Unfortunately, the only inclusion that was happening for Thad in his classroom was that he was breathing same air as his classmates. He spent his days on extended sensory breaks, doing who-knows-what in RSP, or connected for hours to the black, shiny earphones on the classroom computer, completely disconnected from the world. He was bringing no work home in his backpack, and so far away emotionally. I had no idea what he was doing during the day, and the more I asked, the less I was told. Just let us do our jobs, they would implore. I would love for you to do your jobs. But my son is sad and failing school, so obviously we need to be doing something more, I would respond.

I called yet another IEP meeting in March 2008 because of my concerns about his worsening behavior, his lack of progress in reading, and the slurry of unsupervised aides. I had written an agenda outlining my specific concerns, and expounded on my observations, my fears, and my utter confusion as to why he could not seem to learn. I wanted to know who was in charge of the Aide, what did all this documentation meant, who was supervising his case, and why he was still on Sightword List One? They replied that because the last Aide was going on maternity leave, he was going to get a super-duper new Aide, who was super-duper trained, and knew sign language. Super-duper, that's nice, but Thad did not use sign language at this point. He just hardly talked.

Don't worry about reading. He will catch up someday, the IEP Team assured me. I was starting to feel immediate nausea waves every time I heard the words, trust me. If he can't read by Fifth Grade, they told me, the mom of a first grader, then we should worry. What should he do til then, I asked. Silence. The IEP team then decided that I would teach him to read because the school could not. They told me in voices laced with shit, that since I was "the College English Professor," and clearly the most *passionate* about him learning to read, I should just teach him. I got a lawyer, and I set out to learn how to teach him to read myself. We started to work on reading every day, seven days per week, no holidays, and no breaks.

A positive aspect of this Autism journey is that I have met some of the most amazing, kind, caring people I probably would not have had the true pleasure to know otherwise. I also have intense discussions with these important people that stay in my mind forever, and consistently guide my decisions regarding Thaddeus. I had a conversation with my friend, Mark, about how our autistic boys climb up, over, on, and under everything with no fear, and very often with a twinge of danger present, real or pretend. We chatted about too-tall, twisty, pink pepper trees, dangerous forays in kitchen pantries, on pointy Joshua Tree rocks, and all the other cool places boys like to climb up to and into, and refuse to descend from. Mark explained to me that our boys were just born in the wrong time period.

They are Hunter and Gatherer boys, he would tell me. They would be the boys that could climb to the tops of the tallest trees quickly and effortlessly, and pick the finest fruit. They would then scale the sides of the cliffs, unwinded, to carry the bountiful harvest home. We mused that our boys were the strong, silent, handsome type, and they would be revered in their tribe as those specially charged to feed the people with the best of nature's bounty, the most luscious fruit. Mark is also my special education lawyer.

Me teaching Thad to read officially began the next Monday. I picked five random words that I perceived to be important each week, and emailed them to the multitude of Team Thad members. I started with concrete words, such as colors, and things in our house. I filled a binder with empty page protectors, and started a journal of his reading, drawing the words, rainbow writing it, spelling it over and over, every way I could think of. We also added foundations of reading, and academics into our therapy plan and continued to pay for it all ourselves. Meanwhile, at school, he continued to work on articulation in his group speech class. Thad has never had any issues with his articulation.

Springtime came, the air was sodden with orange blossoms, and my 8-year-old Thaddeus was very sure that he "did not go to school," and definitely "did not like learning to read." In addition, he continued to be a victim of repeated bullying by some of the boys in his class, a guinea pig to ineffective classroom inclusion models, and a recipient of the damaging ignorance of inappropriately trained staff. Thad had spent two years on Sightword List One, and by the end of First Grade, he still did not have a full grasp of the alphabet. He would come home upset each day, telling me he was "stupid" or a "fool." His autistic tendencies amplified, he lost academic skill sets, sunk further into maladaptive behaviors, and had decreased social communication.

In May 2008, the School District held Thad's annual IEP. The teacher promoted him to Second Grade, although he had failed all of the expectations of First Grade curriculum, and he was clearly in distress. Under Individuals with Disabilities Education Act (IDEA), the governing body of special education law, disabled children are entitled to the following fundamental educational rights (20 U.S.C. 1401 (9)):

FREE AND APPROPRIATE PUBLIC EDUCATION (FAPE). The term "free appropriate public education" means special education and related services that:

have been provided at public expense, under public supervision and direction, and without charge; meet the standards of the State educational agency; and include an appropriate preschool, elementary, or secondary school in the State involved.

Basically, children with certain disabilities, such as Autism, were entitled to an education that considers the child's unique needs, provides appropriate placement and adequate support that offers meaningful access to the school curriculum at "public expense," also know as "free."

The meeting included the results of the District Triennial Assessments, endless laundry lists of his shortcomings and deficits in all academic, social, behavioral, and emotional domains. But there still was no plan to do anything to help him, or to figure out how to teach him. I could not believe what I was hearing. I begged them, I told them that he was out of control again, and regressing back into himself at a scary pace. I told the team that he had been moved out of the social groups at the clinic back into individual therapy because of his waning inability to tolerate the other children.

At the end of an IEP, a school district will make an offer of FAPE to the parents with the legal interpretation of the offer as, here's what we will offer your child for an appropriate placement that supports his or her unique needs, as the parents can accept and sign on the dotted line, or refuse to sign which starts a series of timelines in motion and usually moves both parties into a heightened, possibly contentious, environment. The District's offer for FAPE that year for Thaddeus was to warehouse my son, the current emotional trainwreck, in a Special Day Class (SDC), a non-specific classroom which was a catch-all educational receptacle for children suffering from varying conditions in a classroom without a definitive model for remediation that meets my boy's unique needs. In the presence of my attorney, and in a voice loud enough for my whirring audiotape to remember, the Special Services Coordinator continued to reassure me to not to worry about my son not reading, and told me that I should probably start getting used to his primary deficit being listed on the IEP as MR (Mental Retardation). They couldn't figure out how to teach him, so obviously he was mentally retarded?

I did not sign off on their offer, left the IEP feeling more than a little flustered, and arrived at my son's school on May 28, 2008. His Aide told me that she had been feeding him rocks at recess.

Aide—"Thad is so stressed out and scared of the kids, so we walked around the perimeter of the playgrounds, and looked at the flowers. We played a dinosaur game too, and I was feeding him rocks.

Me—(sure that I had misunderstood her comment) "Feeding him rocks?"

Aide—"Yeh. But, don't worry. I washed the rock off each time I put it in his mouth, so he wouldn't get germs. Boy, he sure liked that game. I put that rock in his mouth eight or ten times."

She handed me the grey, mottled rock. It was three-inches long, one-inch wide, and smooth. As the blood drained from my appendages, and I quickly calculated the "what-if" factor of the rock in my son's mouth. I will never bring him back here, I realized, as we walked the expanse of green grass at his elementary school. We would not set foot on that campus ever again. I still have the rock. When I doubt my personal mission, my life choices, and myself, I look at it to remind, to remember, the who, and the why.

I realized we were in the "family emergency" mode, and resigned from my job that evening. My child was failing, sinking further into himself, and I was losing him again. I kinda wanted to peel off the first layer of skin on my entire body, and dive in the ocean. Just to calm down.

The Principal called me to ask why I had taken him out of school, and why I didn't come and talk with her about it before informing them in writing that he would not be returning. I responded that I did not see what there was to discuss. She persisted in this phone conversation and others, trying to coax my boy back into the danger pit, his school, and I finally asked if she condoned rock-eating on her campus. That subject was one that I was willing to discuss. I did not hear from her all summer.

My eyes are white disks in a blackened bed. I try to go to that happy place, the calm place. The door is too small. Tonight, as many other nights, there is no door. My chest pounds gallons of anxiety behind my heart, pushing my pulse into my temples and my eyelashes. My whole being beats in fear. Fear for my son, his future, his now.

That summer of 2008, Thad and I went to the Diagnostic Center (DC) on the campus of Cal State LA. The School District, and the parents make a co-referral to this particular type of intensive assessment, which is extensive testing executed by a large team of doctors and experts who specialize in difficult, complex cases, and is done when a school district has exhausted its own ideas, programs, and resources. Thousands of referral requests come in each year to the Diagnostic Centers from across California. The teams decide the severity of the problem based on information provided by the school district, and the parents, and then decide the level of assessment necessary. Four full days of assessment was the maximum amount of time that children stayed at the facility to be assessed.

We stayed in a hotel for four days with a pool, across from a supermarket that had live carp swimming in the window. We spent lots of time looking at the fish, and not a lot of time swimming because Thad was recovering from an ear infection, and needed his ears to be dry during testing. A van picked up about six guardians, and our lot of highly complex kids at the hotel, and transported us to the DC each morning. The children would be assessed by various types of professionals and doctors who specialize in different, atypical presentation, and complex cases all day long, and at dinnertime, the van would return, and take us all to dinner. I was so happy to talk to, and learn from the specialized knowledge at the Diagnostic Center about so many new avenues, unique activities, and thoughtful ways to help us understand how to best teach Thad.

We met with the DC Team Leader three months later to receive a thick report full of results, impressions, and recommendations. A big pack of district representatives sat across from Rob and me. She delivers results of Speech and Psych tests, and then turns her entire body towards the district folk. And as for your other question, and they all lean forward in anticipation. Please do not continue to try to test this child for mental retardation. Apparently, as I read the paperwork later, they asked to have him assessed for mental retardation covertly. All the District folks slumped in their seats. Bummer, we got nothing now to get us off the hook, I am sure they were thinking. It is unfortunately a common practice to attempt to diagnose an autistic child with mental retardation, so not as much growth and progress is expected from him, so I hear.

Summer passes like a kidney stone, and on the first day of the 2008 school year, I receive a call from the Principal, all bright, cheery, and all-sins-forgotten-esque. "First day of school," she chirped. "Where's Thad? We have a new trained aide, and everything set up for him in the classroom." I ask her if she remembers our previous conversations, and I explain that Thad is so stressed out, disregulated, and very sad. In addition, I tell her that we fear for his safety in their care.

We just had spent two academic school years of my boy as the "project-child" that loses his luster somewhere around Thanksgiving break, and then spends the rest of the year sinking deeper into sadness, losing self-confidence and skill sets faster than the hours that click by all night. As I lay awake each night, I know that something different must happen.

In this Autism-fueled lifestyle, I continually strive to find the funny stuff, and constantly undertake odd, weird attempts at finding the good, the humorous or the unique in order to amuse myself, and others in what is very often an un-funny situation. If I took everything 100% seriously, I might really get my feelings hurt. Laughter makes everyone feel good, and feel better. Sometimes, it's a challenge. But, the positive can be found in many unexpected places. Yes, including in a pile of shit. For example, Thaddeus greeted me in early dawn hours one morning with a headbutt, and the words "Good morning Mom. There are three kinds of poop downstairs."

Now, as a glass-half-full-kind-o-gal, I hastily spun a web of good out of a potentially negative moment. I felt gratitude about how lucky I was that my son was able to:

1. Tell me with his words that the dogs had shit in the front of the TV again

2. Remain calm with the *eau de poo* aroma, and his acute nostrils

3. Notice the details of each pool or puddle of excrement, and able to qualify their differences.

I was thrilled that we had worked on categories. eye contact, and appropriate salutation, all by 6am. What a great way to begin the day.

Thick, spiky, creamy Yucca Whipleys bloom on our back hill like enormous vanilla ice cream cones that summer. Sunsets bathes our dusty orange groves in pink and purple, and we file Due Process, a formal legal complaint with the state, against the School District because we believed that their offer of FAPE did not address Thad's unique learning needs. In late September, Mark and I participated in Mediation with representatives of the School District for six hours. An Administrative Law Judge (ALJ) from the Office of Administrative Hearings (OAH), a representative from the type of state court that settles disputes between families and school districts, and provides informed interpretations of the laws that support and protect individuals with disabilities, and their legal rights to appropriately delivered education, facilitated the proceeding, and the School District offered funding for 30 hours toward an ABA in-home program, and they paid for a portion of his private Speech, Occupational Therapy, and Cognitive Therapy for that academic year. They also paid us Compensatory Education, which is reimbursement for a myriad of stuff we had paid for that they should have paid for in the first place.

In addition, we file Fair Hearing, another type of lawsuit, against the Regional Center, and receive funding for 12-hours of ABA therapy per week, along with parent training and supervision. By law, the School District is financially responsible for the hours of behavior therapy required by the child that are related to academic tasks, and the Regional Center is responsible for home and community based hours. Thaddeus began an intensive, 42-hour per week behavior therapy program in our dining room, and we started parent training. Hopeful doses of alacrity pulsed my stomach into applesauce.

I felt like I was trying to pull T out of this gaping, sucking, bastard hole of Autism darkness with every ounce of my body and soul, with my left foot braced firmly on the wall for more power and traction, and all of these therapists, doctors, and specialists pulling on my waist in a human chain. I looked at the California public school curriculum and state standards, and I was certain he had met almost none of the targets. The first order of business was to repeat most of Kindergarten, and all of First Grade, I thought. I had taught freshmen how to write like college students, and business students how to critically analyze, but I had no idea about how to teach First Grade. I took another leap in learning to teach my boy, and filed paperwork with the state to officially become a private homeschool with one student, a first-grader named Mr. Thaddeus Stauder. Kinda like eating the entire watermelon in one bite.

Thad's waking hours were parsed into 15-minute increments, and we shoved therapy at him in every way we could. In addition to his packed daytime schedule, a couple of nights per week, while I took Ursula to swim team practice and made dinner, his tutor also came for a few hours most nights to work on T's letter recognition, sounds, memory, attention, and focus. All in the name of Thaddeus getting it together behaviorally, and learning to read, and to pay attention to life. I had so many doctors, therapists, and experts seeing Thad at my house, at their clinics, everywhere, all over southern California for the various therapies to help him, still running more tests to more fully understand the gravity of his illness. Two more therapists, Reanna and Tracy, joined the fun, and we added Developmental Intervention, and Occupational Therapy into his daily mix.

And then, in the midnight hours, Rob and I would sneak around his room, performing biomedical interventions on our son, armed with magnifying glasses and flashlights, numbing his buttocks with Lydocaine, rubbing topical Glutathione on his back, and ultimately, giving him a shot of Methyl B12 in the tush. The methylation system is our body's natural way of dumping garbage, and many kids on the Autism Spectrum have significant challenges properly taking out their bodies' trash. These supplements are a critical part of his biomedical protocol because Thad has so much difficulty detoxing his junk. And if the garbage stays around too long, Thad starts to "stink," our family's dedicated, descriptive word for his yucky, smelly tantrums.

I continue to think about dancing in coconut bras. Someone important once said, when life hands you lemons, shove them in your bra. I agree. Fruit in the bra continues to work for me as a guiding principle.

And while my house is being the battlezone, therapyzone, homeschoolzone, behaviorzone, and desperately trying to still be a familyhome, the rest of the world continues on without us. Very often, what Autism is really like to live with, the financial pain, the emotional pain, the family distress, and the terminal heartache are grossly miscalculated, underrepresented, and misunderstood. And very often, I get mad.

CHAPTER 3

Autism: Slowfood for Thought

AN EFFECTIVE, UNRECOMMENDED way to force yourself to abruptly stop, and reevaluate every aspect of your life is to find out that your child has a pervasive developmental disability. "Pervasive" means that it spans, attacks, and affects academic, physical, social, emotional developmental domains, and it can impact ability for basic communication. If a child has significant deficits on these lists, it is very possible and mostly probable, that you will see that shit fucking up your child's development. All of a sudden, I realize, like a swift kick with a steel-toed boot to the temple, that everything in our family life is different, starting now.

The idea of this invisible force, Autism, gripping my child's soul, his body, his essence, into vacant-eyed noncompliance, gut-wrenching self-absorption, uncalmable temper tantrums, doubled-over stomachaches, him repeating the same phrase over and over for hours and hours, endless sleepless nights, and a crushing, deep solitary sadness that strangles him starts to anger me. In my core, I start to manifest this slow bubbling rage, a need to explode to gain some sort of release to pop this painful bubble of pity, deep fury, and blame. Anger, anger, anger at anyone, anything, anywhere. Everything, everyone, everywhere. Me, myself, and why, why, why?

I realize that I need to redefine, rethink, and replant every aspect of my human existence. To slow it all down, to reconsider, to repot and repurpose every detail that I define as my life. My food, my water, my work and my play, my goals and dreams for myself and for my child, my attempts at advancement and intervention, his skill sets, his schooling, and our emotions. I need to parse out the circumstances that are placed before us, and to determine where Thaddeus and I fit into this new reality. Me pitted and war-torn by anger, Thad consumed by another type of anger, a perseverative madness. I look outward onto my life, and see only black skies.

I am a boiling pot of no water that won't boil. I scald, I burn, I bubble, I overflow, I see smoke and fire inside me, under me, all around me. I meld, melt, and mold into some sort of entity that I do not like, and I do not recognize. I am gripped by terror, by horror, and I fall painfully into the deepest abyss of sadness I have ever felt. My child is alive, and standing in front of me. But, the light is gone from his eyes, as his piercing screams and flailing fists haunt me even when he is asleep or gone from my sight.

At this point, my one and only secret weapon against Thad's atrocious behavior was a can of corn from the corn store, wherever that is. For some reason, Thad continued to be deathly afraid of corn. In hopes of behavioral compliance, I would offer up nonspecific, empty threats regularly that went something like, if you don't stop yelling and kicking the back seat of the car, we are going to the corn store. Or I would pluck a can of corn from the pantry, plop it down on the kitchen table with a grandiose bang, and declare that this was going to be his dinner if he did not eat the steak, squash, and salad that had congealed into a mess on his plate from the long time it had sat there during those most recent protest moments.

A "protest" in Autism Nation fucking sucks on all levels as the child loses control and you attempt to remediate, deflect, support, remain calm, and keep him and others around him safe. It also means your hour, day, or week just took a turn for the worst. Imagine an uncontrollable, outward display of your darkest, most uncomfortable feelings, then manifest it on a physical, emotional, spiritual, and sensory level, multiply that by 100, with the fortitude of a million white stallions with wings, the tenacity of an Ironman participant, the venom of the most dangerous spider, and the fangs of an aggressive snake. Mix that menagerie into the worst 2-year-old's tantrum you can muster in your brain, with the stanch bitchiness of our fair government as they disagree with such certainty and fortitude, and throw a few sentimental items against the wall. As the liquid drips and glass crunches under your feet, stop, step back as a parent or concerned individual, and consider with a contemplative mind and a heavy heart what is happening inside this poor kid that would elicit such a terrible outward behavior. Trauma, pain, confusion, loneliness, boredom, or perhaps a stray thread on his sock, or an unknown person in his midst. Perhaps, as the onlooker, you might know why, and most likely, you have no idea what the trigger was. Welcome to an autistic protest.

In hindsight, I obviously needed some serious parent training on how to manage his behavior appropriately. I did not know what to do, and what I was doing was obviously not working. I was frustrated and sleepy during the day, and flailed at night through intense unceasing bouts of panic, insomnia, and anxiety. The corners of my mind and living spaces were blurry and full of cobwebs. There were dirty dishes and glasses full of nonspecific liquids filling the sink, laundry strewn across the floors, dirty and clean mixed together, me trying to find sanity in small moments like walking to the corner to get the mail alone, or writing a succinct email to the insurance company about whatever the current issue was. Insurance reimbursement went something like this, if he's making slow progress, drop the speech therapy because his improvement isn't fast enough, and if he's making progress, drop the speech therapy because he's improving.

I am the mold, bloat, and rot in a green public garbage can, my soul is full of worms, and my starving mind has no fresh food in sight. My blood is old, brown, stale, and my heart is a vat of putrid developmental expectations, laced with a sauce of confusion that strangles me with every breath I inhale into my tired, sad lungs.

With gentle reminders from my lawyer about complying with the laws that protect and support our special kids, the School District, with a venomous grin, agrees that Thad needs these services, and for their series of their reasons, we end up with two different ABA companies, which is kinda like holding down two full time jobs, kinda like maintaining active residence on both coasts, kinda like spitting in the bottom of my coffee cup and serving it up with a shitty grin, as this new therapy situation gives us two separate behavior therapy teams of between 4-5 therapists each, two supervisors, two sets of behavioral goals for Thad, two weekly team meetings, and a whole lot of reason to drink beer.

I shudder and shimmer with terror each hour, each day, each moment, as mountains of people mill in and out of my house, using my bathroom, texting in their car in front in my house when they arrive early, working with my son in the front yard on playground skills and bike riding, and consequating the behavior that is not deemed appropriate by Thad's enormous therapy team. "Consequating the behavior," means delivering a consequence to the child as a result of the behavior, and is a fancy moniker commonly heard in behavior therapy discussions.

The behavior therapy program that Thad begins is called ABA (Applied Behavioral Analysis), a research-based methodology, therapy, and practice of changing autistic behavior, developed by Ivar Lovaas. Extremely simply put, this method looks at the antecedent (precursor), behavior (dispreferred autistic behavior), and the consequence (an outcome, a reward, or a punishment) of each pulse of Autism that surges in a child's body, and breaks down skill sets in manageable chunks to enable, facilitate and promote learning. A full program clocks in at 40 hours of therapy per week, along with supervision, weekly team meetings, and weekly parent trainings.

One shiny day full of passion flowers and possibility, we commence the get-Thad's-behavior-managed marathon. Bob, ABA Supervisor, sat on my purple corduroy couch the first day of treatment, and told me that we need to get Thaddeus' autistic behaviors out of the way in order for him to begin to learn. I had no fucking idea what that meant. Internal mama vibe told me it was okay to not understand right now, not yet, and to trust. He also asked me what we ate, and if we could do a food tolerance and food acceptance behavior program to help him vary his palate again. At first, I was so freaked out by the idea of teaching him to eat the foods he so vehemently shunned that I could not even be in the same room while they worked on the food therapy challenges. I was so convinced that he had a feeding disorder due to his constant violent outward aggression toward most foods. Nope, that's behavior, Bob would respond.

Meanwhile, allopathic medicine providers, the crafty politicians, those individuals who value the almighty prescription pad over all other possible less toxic methods of health and healing, and the vanilla onlookers try to comfort me into quitting my son, saying that our attempts, our alternative methods, our chosen pathways toward recovering our son are crazy, lunatic, too expensive, and way too time-consuming. Telling a mother to give up on her child is a poor choice at empathy or care. It hurts deeply, and it does not help at all.

Plink, plink, plink, as the water drops endlessly in the bucket. Drops of liquid that respond in circles, in waves, endless outward projections after the small round pebble hits the once placid lake in forever ripples of exhaustion, anger, and fear. I feel feelings that are so hard, so debilitating, so unlike I have ever experienced. I dig deep into my heart and soul for strength, I ask for any and all celestial beings to weigh in on my dilemma, and I ask you, Gentle Reader, to trust my thunderstorm, the crackling heat and pulsing electricity, as I push down into my inner earth and explore my deepest darkest dirt. Rainbows happen after a deluge.

I think about these people who judge Autism Nation from afar without direct experiential trauma or current statistics on the epidemic, and I feel reminded of Plato's *Allegory of the Cave*. The prisoners in a dark cave see only two-dimensional shadows reflecting from the fire's dancing images on the jailcell walls as their only perception of reality. As they understand this as their normal, someone escapes, comes back, and says this is what the world looks like from another perspective, join me in expanding your mind with this new perception of truth. The others are mean and call him a liar because they do not see it. Scared of truth, scared of changing perceptions, they stone him, and they kill him. Our minds will not stretch, they scream in loud voices, we shall kill you instead for blaspheming our comfort into question.

Pumping our babies full of neurotoxins in the form of fake food products, and unnecessary medicines has turned around, and started attacking our children, our future as humankind. Pay attention to the canaries in the coal mine because their sensitive lungs cannot breath. Understand the warning, and plan forth to obliterate the messages of danger, not the messengers themselves.

Perhaps a smattering of empathy, or the intellectual movement toward a greater universal consciousness of compassion could be included in everyone's outward well-wishes of health, as many name Autism parents, our children, our cause, and the expanse of areas in our children's broken bodies that need to be healed, fixed, taught, and remediated to be excessive, expensive, and unnecessary. Oh the time, the effort, and the vast expense to remediate a sick child, they say. Autism is an illness to be treated and healed, we respond.

Those who do not experience this hellride called Autism often onlook, deliver unwelcome advice, shake a thousand tiny fingers of disgust, wear hatred on their shiny normal sleeves, fling damning messages at silent sick kids, and whisper dishonorable wishes at the Autism parents who merely want what everyone else has, their children to walk safely and comfortably in school classrooms and ultimately in life, with the confidence of reliable communication, without fear for their safety, and without fear for their future. Autism families hurt deeply from this unkind treatment, and it does not help us at all. They don't believe what we say, we are castigated, and often ousted from the outside world.

They call me a liar, let him be, he cannot improve, you have failed, you cannot try, you are a bad mother, hey don't worry shit happens, and they throw stones at central parts of the core beliefs of myself. Yes, I brought this child into the world, and I will do whatever is necessary to help him. How dare people tell me Autism is not curable, how dare they tell me to let things happen without intervening, deflecting my attempts at supporting the remediation of my child's illness. How dare they ask me to trust them with his care because I love him more than all of you put together, plus one. Do you realize how much this is going to cost, they ask. Do you realize the long-term implications if we do nothing, I respond. Do you realize the depth of my pain and sadness as I sit helpless? How dare you judge me for something you know nothing about.

They do not understand. These are bumps in our road, those people who block, inhibit, naysay, force, threaten, and push back in our journey. This is a marathon, our people advise us, not a sprint. Slow and steady please, I implore, do not be a bump in our road, I yell, I scream, I whisper, hoarse from despair. Our road is already long enough, strong enough, without your unkind pebbles and thoughtless boulders. Mad, mad, mad, I continue my painful march.

Me mad, me knee-deep in yet another panic attack boiling in my entrails, with a physical need to trip out and get angry on a chemical level, an orgasm of emotion without the usual associated benefits. Bob asks me during our parent training at Starbucks each week how close we can sit to other patrons, a very kind, diplomatic way of asking me, how loud are you gonna yell, Kristin? I regularly respond something like, way, way over there. I really had a shitty week, and I still don't understand how to get him to remember to count and use slow deep-breathing as a coping skill when he gets so mad so fast for so long. Me, with a latte in my left hand, blowing up for the sixty-hundredth adrenaline release of the day.

Like a lizard mother trying save herself and her children from being the snack of a more giant beast, I possess innate fear of a predator attacking me and my babies, and believe I feed off the adrenaline from the "fight or flight" primal brain response as a source of energy. I can't imagine going on with my life unphased, untouched, unchanged by his illness, and allowing him to continue on with these significant deficits unremediated, missing important skills needed to succeed in school, jobs, life, community, relationships, independence, sorta kinda the rest of his life.

All of this weight is pressing hard on my shoulders, burning my hands, eviscerating my mind, grasping my inner thoughts, pulling at my calm, sucking my softparts, beating me like a violent lover, as I continue to offer myself to the cause. I am soft rotten fruit, riddled with maggots and swarming flies. I am pulp and bruises.

I continue to think about how mad I am, and I think about Thaddeus and his mad, our collective state of mad, and I feel so blue. I think about Nietzsche's words and my imminent madness, "Beware that, when fighting monsters, you yourself do not become a monster, for when you gaze long into the abyss, the abyss gazes also into you." I feel terror and sorrow when I imagine being swallowed up by this Autism mouth of loneliness, sadness, and rage. And I feel so scared that madness and anger are my son's way into the world. I worry deeply that we will spin ourselves into an uncomfortable oblivion where we can no longer access anything that appears normal, that place where the beast ingests our souls, that place where we are defined solely as crisp memories of the human experience. I vow to push myself and to push him, a little further, one more day, if only today then okay, I move through our madness toward his possibilities, toward the enormous challenges of his recovery, kicking stones into the abyss, as I hold tightly onto sinewy strings of myself and my boy on a small tight ledge of hope for positive change, and improved health.

Autism is the true conversation stopper. My kid's autistic, and how are you? That's interesting, he doesn't look autistic. Wow, what does it look like to be autistic? What's his savant skill? Is he more like Rainman or Temple

Grandin? No, he's more like Thaddeus, I respond. What does he want to eat? Just cuz he doesn't talk a lot doesn't mean he doesn't know what he wants to eat. Just cuz he doesn't talk a lot doesn't mean he doesn't have anything to say. Ask him.

And then we begin with the Autism taglines, and pat responses. God doesn't give you more than you can handle, as long as he is giving it to you and not to me. Ever notice that the speaker of that particular sentence never seems to be saddled with the same predicament as the one they are harping these empty words towards? A concerned face, you're such a good mommy, I could never do what you do. Yes, you could. What wouldn't you do for your kid? I have the same acrid feelings toward the other asinine phrase regularly flung at me with predicable ignorance, What doesn't kill you can only make you stronger. People, more thoughtfully considered words can actually help with engulfing sadness, and manifesting my death by aligning his health tragedy into a snappy little one-liner is just plain fucking thoughtless.

By the way, I continue, our family's Autism is not a secret. I believe that if the people don't know the "what" or the "why" of our unique family predicament that they will make the shit up. Human nature in action. If onlookers do not understand the stimming, the spinning, or the perseverations, there will be a different story circulating about my child than the actual truth of a very real, devastating, neurological, whole-body disorder, and my unending hopes for his improvement and recovery. I keep others abreast of my happenings in Autism Nation with gossip updates on myself. Sometimes, it has been a bit shocking for others when I initiate this gossip.

I figure if there is going to be a discussion about the crazy things that happen to us, that we do, put up with, pay for, and drive to, it might as well be correct. I say, okay, here is the current gossip on me and my kid, as I concurrently ignore the oh, we would never talk behind your back response. Everyone talks, even me. Even you. I say we are doing the following things to help our child, yes, I know that sounds difficult for us, expensive, and a little crazed. How will I afford, support, and physically be in two or three places at the same time tomorrow afternoon? I do not know. I will try my best.

Hey Kristin, are you guys separated? No, why? Well, I saw Rob with a cute Mexican chick at Thad's gymnastics class, and I was wondering what the deal was. Oh, you saw my husband, my child, and the behavior therapist working on standing in line at the tumbling class? Did you think it was odd that Rob's new hottie was manhandling Thad out on the gymnasium floor, that she continuously asked him to repeat tasks without tantrumming, and that each time he successfully completed a task, she catalogued it in a very thick white binder, I respond. I lost friends faster than an old man loses hair.

Or perhaps, during the shards of early intervention that Thad received, we had a gaggle of developmental therapists who came to our house a few times a week with suitcases full of toys and big bags of equipment, all used in an attempt to engage my boy. Oh, the neighbors inquired, requesting clarification of the role of these people, those people are therapists. We thought that all of those therapists were cleaning ladies. I thought that you must have a really, really clean house because of all of the millions of maids that were milling in and out of your doors everyday.

A few years later, we are homeschooling in the garage-turned-homeschool, with a large whiteboard and many markers, several thick blue mats on the floor, a cool foam barrel to roll in, various swinging ladders, pull-up bars, and a kicking rock climbing wall. Meanwhile, I ask a woman, whose typical kids run mid-session into the space full of toys and perceived child-fun, to leave. Her kid want to play with my kid and his cool stuff, and meanwhile, my child is mid-tantrum in the front yard, as I overtly kick the neighborhood boy out of the therapy experience after multiple attempts to discreetly explain to his mom that his presence wasn't welcome or appropriate in this therapy session. You aren't realllllly homeschooling in a garage with three adults, and one child, are you? Why am I so mean to everyone? Why am I the freaky mother down the street? Can't we just have at least one, relaxed uneventful day? My internal perceptions of my odd existence, and my reasons for why I do what I do continue to bang and clatter into each other, and make messes on the floor. I am an emotional paintball of sadness and fear.

Meanwhile, everyone walks by in their normal life, with a couple of normal kids, a normal dog or two, and, meanwhile, discreetly or overtly stares. Wow, she's a shitty parent. That kid has no discipline, I imagine through the whispers, the thoughts. Meanwhile, I also wonder why is my kid so out of control, as I hold his belt loop so he won't run into the street, and march my noncompliant shriek-ing boy out to the car to go to another day of therapy. Meanwhile, a car drives by full of people having fun, listening to loud bouncy tunes. Meanwhile, a red marker decorates my child's face in the backseat, as his impulse control does not allow him to wait for me to provide paper to his nervous fingers. Meanwhile, my life sludges on like uncooked brownie batter.

When I park in the disabled parking space in front of Target with my jump-ing bean boy, I usually get some nasty eyegaze. She's just trying to get spe-cial treatment, they sneer and whisper to each other in disgust. With specially educated tenacity, I grab his hand and walk. I worry about my child's lack of concern for moving cars in parking lots. I worry about him stopping to pick up a shiny penny as someone texting-while-driving speeds by and hits him accidentally. I worry about him alone and "stranger danger," about a bad man with promises of puppies and candy in his van, and how my child would jump in within moments.

I used to wish that Thad had some outward display of his disability, like a wheelchair, sling, or atypical body feature to explain his odd behavior and man-nerisms. People would then, I thought, believe me when I say that he is disabled, understand the gravity of my words, the longterm repercussions, and the severity of his condition, if his symptoms were to be left unremediated, untreated.

And, I believed by this point, that our special education saga reads better over alcohol, like a story with a punchline, except the end of the joke never seems to come. Half of the time, as I recount our sordid tale, listeners stop and believe that they have mis-heard what I said. Did you just say? As a matter of fact, I did. And yes, pour me another. Make it a double.

Pretending Autism behavior isn't a bad thing, that Autism is something should be celebrated and not remediated, or that it is just a different kind of brain at work and not a serious disorder, is not a gift to the child at all. It is not a cool accessory in our family, a unique plaything, a funky oddity that we tolerate but don't attempt to support and ameliorate through therapies. Maybe it will go away if we pretend it's not there like the ostrich dunking its head in the sand. A two-year-old's perception of reality that if we close our eyes, the bad things dis-appear. I have tried this great plan, and it doesn't work. We celebrate our child, but we do not celebrate Autism. Autism is a cloudy window between me and my boy. Every day, I try to pry that window open just a little more.

Many people like to pretend that Autism isn't weird, and therefore, we shouldn't have to do anything about it. An eight-year-old boy walking around the grocery store, flying a Lego car closely near the corner of his left eye, clutching wooden spoons for dear life, and endlessly repeating the words of a plastic spaceman in a sing-songy voice is weird. So is jumping around the restaurant with flapping arms when excited, or having a light saber fight with imaginary foe in the front yard. It is important to help him in whatever way is needed.

I prefer the idea of teaching him appropriate social behavior versus tolerating weird, inappropriate behavior. If we choose to tolerate bad behavior then there is no reason to try to change it or to remediate it, and with bad behavior comes less academic expectations for the child, with a future to look toward full of no job skills or life options, as they continue to lower the bar on the expectations of my kid's outcome, and I think so much about how to help my boy and his behavior. Some people try to fix the world around him by allowing his Autism to dictate and dominate his interactions with others, and with his environment, but I sorta kinda want him to understand how to live in the real world. Back and forth, Hey Kristin he doesn't have to look at me when he talks to me I don't mind, hey Kristin I don't mind if he sneaks olives off of my salad plate while I'm eating, hey Kristin if he wants to tear up the yard I'm fine with it, oh poor soul he's got Autism, don't expect much, let him simmer in his sickness and we won't bother him in the corner. Allowing him to sit, flavorless and tasteless, in his Autism, and not thicken his broth or season his soup with positive supportive corrections, redirections, or explicit social information makes the soup stagnant, and is a confusing representation of expectations for a boy who only learns currently by direct instruction, and consistent follow-through on behavioral expectations and social mores. Do not allow his autistic behavior to manifest out of your pity, ignorance, or fear. If you do not know, please ask. Please don't feel sorry for him, and please don't feel sorry for me.

And the consequence of this profound deference to Autism behavior in the public sphere can go unchecked with some bewildering results. Thad and I attend an Autism summer camp with me as his 1:1 aide, that summer, and the counselors take a break during the music program. A pleasant, young man with a goatee, and a guitar slung across his chest led the children in various songs. The children followed along with the hand movements he demonstrated.

Yet, when the music called for the young cantors to "throw off their shoes" and walk by the river, within a few seconds, this particular pack of concrete thinkers had taken off their shoes, and were lobbing them everywhere, including at each other. I was the only parent in the room, as thongs and sneakers arc perfectly through the airspace, and the wide-eyed man continues to strum. By this point, another child had commandeered the microphone on the stage behind, him, and was making loud, farting noises into it. The twang of the guitar glinted in the lack-of-exactly-sure-what-to-do-guitarist's eyes. Order was eventually restored. But, seriously, cut that shit out. It's weird.

Me constantly on the phone with beautiful caring friends and family that let me drop bitchbombs into their cellular minutes, bawling, crying, blaming, yelling about anything and everything. Just to help me get it out because unmanaged, festering sadness and anger is unhealthy, and will kill you somehow. Those who stayed with me in the difficult times, those who kept calling, those who kept coming back, those were and are my real friends, when the going gets tough, the real friends stick like cooked spaghetti spirals thrown at the kitchen wall, and the others rinse down the drain like stale dishwater.

Last week, in Trader Joe's, as I tossed packages full of thin sticks of organic brown rice pasta into the cart, I turned around to my dear child wearing scuba flippers, a mask, and a snorkel, chilling next to the cereal. We immediately added a new rule to the docket. *It is not appropriate to wear scuba gear in the grocery store.* He had just come from swimming lessons, and he was wearing a bathing suit. But suiting up for the big dive in front of the granola bars isn't appropriate behavior in the grocery store. Everything must be taught.

The Slowfood Movement, as defined by Carlo Petrini in 1986, honors the practices of traditional gastronomy and food production, considers the food source and creation methods as important aspects, and values the significance of community to the whole food experience itself. I insert myself in this nutritional and social theory as I consider my life outlook, feeding my family in more ways than just food, and the new challenges I face. I knew I needed to redefine the way I understood time, nourishment, and success as I was previously on the fast track to faster, along the lines of I was certain that anything I put my mind to would happen, and if I really really focused on it, it would happen even faster. In our family life, prior to our induction in Autism Nation, the club we belong to but never elected to join, we had big, fat, fast dreams that maybe sometimes did not include as many healthy food options as they should have.

All dreams dashed, and I find myself in my kitchen, amidst large clocks with bright red timers dinging and flashing with visual, and auditory reminders that reinforced, extinguished, or rewarded Thad's behavior. I see the dial moving slowly on my black Excalibur food dehydrator humming on the counter, reminding me to relax my need for speed, as the red triangle slowly becomes a smaller and smaller piece of pie in the next 24 hours toward coconut yogurt taffy rolls. I notice that all of my kitchen jobs, and his behavior tasks have moved into time periods encompassing multitudes of hours or days to complete, a small step like ask for a piece of cracker instead of grabbing took days and days to remediate out of my child, as I saw my homemade yogurt bloom in a vat near the sink, wishing it good night, looking forward to eating fresh vanilla yogurt in the morning.

I read about Weston A. Price Foundation (WAPF) food ideologies, and notice resounding ideas about the importance of quality ingredients, celebrating and savoring the ancient food creation processes, and I gobble up so much new exciting information on traditional food preparation. These unique perspectives on engaging nutrition the way my grandma did propel me forward to begin to read everything I can about WAPF methods, protocol, and beliefs, and I begin to think so much about how to extract the most nourishment from every morsel lovingly raised on a pastured farm. Slowly, as I create and experiment with traditional food choices and ideas, such as loving meat and butter as an extension of self, seeing saturated fats as brain food, and embracing traditional, thoughtful methods in their preparation, I find emotional comfort comparable to a big bowl of beef stew, and I cling to these new ways of thinking like peaches in heavy syrup.

I read about so many diets and food protocols that look toward food as a form of supporting, remediating, and healing the difficult physiological and neurological symptoms associated with Autism, such as the Specific Carbohydrate

Diet, the GlutenFree CaseinFree diet we continue to follow with success, Body Ecology, Gut and Psychology Syndrome, Nourishing Traditions, Nourishing Hope, a mere few of so many ways to think about healing Autism with food, and I continue to think about nourishing the body to nourish the mind.

I contemplate my chicken, sausage and kale soup with its chunky, potato broth as a way to save my boy, to nourish his mind, to help him, and I so like this idea. I will cook for my boy, I will teach him to cook, I will use food to help him regain health and mental clarity. I will teach him the awareness of what he puts in his body as important and significant. I will use food actively in his wellness, as I sit and simmer in my kitchen, ladling my ideas over my soupy mind.

Dehydrating fruits vegetables meats and yogurt became a pasttime, creating different meaty stews and rice casseroles from scratch became a passion, lasagna with kale or swiss chard as the noodles that alternated with the grass-fed beef and warm melty Mozzarella cheese was a hobby, gummy worms crafted from local grape juice and zucchini as a treat, and using beef gelatin as a healthful option and a creative source for all of the different fruits I could suspend in a pretend edible fishtank of blueberry juice and gelatin. Getting Thaddeus to come the first time that he was called, getting Thad to pay attention to the entire question and to respond appropriately, getting him to write the entire word or color the entire picture were the visual and audio feed each day in my kitchen, while I slowly stirred the soup in my cast-iron pot of hope.

I actively participate in my son's healing process by going to the farmstand next door for the Meyer lemons, by sprouting radish seeds for spicy salad surprises, as I begin to create slowfood in my kitchen, a working temple of heavenly morsels of nourishment, made slowly and thoughtfully, masterpieces of bits of thoughtful food in the oven shrine to health, or a sideboard full of hope and possibilities in the form of a flat of local strawberries or a 10-pound bag of Navel oranges, a swirl of whole food bursting with nutrition, broken down into manageable bites, digestable by my family.

I try to use the best ingredients I can find and afford, and I bake and broil for hours and hours, considering the intersections of the ABA therapy and the food we ingest daily, the slow, repetitive, methodical nature of breaking apart skill sets into bite-size tasks that reap great, delicious rewards. I consider breaking down his life into teachable pieces, as I dehydrate persimmons into chewy taffy, and push meaty bones into my crockpot to simmer with thoughtful slow attention. I search out the best people to teach him, to understand him, as I think about this connection between the quality of food, and the quality of life as a method towards his health and my sanity.

In between therapies or on our way to therapies, I drive to a farmer's market for my beans, read more about traditional ways, and search out more delicious food. I think about the special flavors of local CaraCara oranges that produce so much goodness, happiness, and nutrition. Imagining process to be as important as product, and reminded us that product can be good even if it's not visually perfect, I buy local lopsided, unwaxed oranges that taste like heaven. I consider the outward representations of less-than-perfect things that have so much sweetness inside. I see so many round tasteless orange fruits that flood our supermarket shelves, and I search out so many foods and feelings and experiences that I cannot buy at a store. I see these fresh funky local fruits as different, unique, so sure they taste better, and I see food as a hobby beyond Autism. I vow to awaken the flavors on our family tongue, and to awaken myself to a new way of thinking about time, progress, and success, nudging my own isolated, fluttery soul back to health.

I begin to dehydrate my foodstuff, slow so slow, making fruit roll ups with pureed menageries of kiwis and raspberries, grapes and raspberries, yogurt taffy, oranges lemons grapefruits all slowly heated for hours and hours, until the sweetness puckers and the fruit is dry to the touch, as my son practices tying his shoes and reciting his numbers to 20, then 30, then 40.

I grow radish and alfalfa sprouts from seeds, rinsing the gentle shoots twice per day, visualizing new beginnings in these tiny creatures that need to be touched, rinsed, and processed in their states of birth and delicacy with predictable consistency or mold and dehydration could happen, reminding me of the seriousness of missing even just one day of Autism therapy.

I begin to grow crazy weird beautiful mushrooms in a pickle bucket in my closet on purpose, and Thad is charged with misting them with a water bottle as a daily chore. One fine day, we go to the coffee shop to ask for grounds to mix into the sawdust inoculated with fancy mushroom spores, and we set our quiet, secret fungus production in motion. They grow silently in the closet, and we pull them into the light of the kitchen to be diced and sliced into a mouth-watering stir-fry when done, as I consider the myco-remediation of my little fungus, my son, my gourmet mushroom with a cloudy mind and dirty feet, Thad in a dark closet growing into a complex and sunny boy. He is so many beautiful Shiitake, Crimini, and Oyster mushrooms to me. I think about the dark spores that become tasty beauty, and I celebrate mushroom-growing as something unique we do in our normal.

I grow mushrooms in the closet, I sprout seeds in the window, I make beef jerky with flavors from emerald-green herbs sunning in my yard, as various pots and devices sit simmering soaking and slowly cooking different foods in different ways that I have chosen for the gastronomic experience of today. I think how to slow it down so the pace of my kitchen matched the pace of my life and his progress, slow and steady wins the race, I think. Be the tortoise not the hare, as I remind myself at 2 that afternoon, letting the bones simmer to leach out their minerals into the broth, and yes, it will take time. And that is exactly what I have, a big pot of time, as I sit prisoner in my kitchen, as my child slowly plows through his ABA goals in the living room.

I remember exploring the issues surrounding Thad's sudden, mysterious emotional disappearance from our family, also known as Autism, and we went to a family's house whose son was affected by Autism. We discussed the realities and gravity of our son's situation, and noticed similarities. That night, we told our young daughter that this child and her brother might have the same disorder. As we remember, Autism affects all people differently and uniquely. Some people have added complications in their Autism journey. Many suffer "co-morbidities," associated conditions that the person may suffer, such as a dual-diagnosis of Autism and Traumatic Brain Injury, Autism and Intellectual Disability, or Autism and Deaf.

One month later, the boy we visited, the boy we noticed similarities to our son in, died from complications associated with his comorbidity. My girl says, oh, is that going to happen to T too? Crushing blow to the parents. No, no, honey. Different situation, no one is going to die. We swear, we swear. This fuck-up on our part hurt Ursula emotionally, and in retrospect, I had no idea as

I delivered this information to her how big this information actually was. There I was, trying to keep my kids safe, and there I was, failing, again. Ursula was deeply scared, and she asked me about it for years to come, worried each time we went to the doctor if Thad was sick.

Words, how significant they are. What you say about your kid, in front of your kid, is heard by your kid. I don't care how (insert airquote fingers) disabled the kid is, he can hear you. Once when I was prompting Thad endlessly to complete his math homework, he looked exasperatedly at me, and said, "Sometimes my brain isn't fast. It isn't as smart." I need to watch my words with him, and around him. I remind myself again of my need to slow down. Pushing the return key too many times doesn't make the information get there any faster. Pressing the elevator button incessantly, and violently watching the bread bronze too slowly in the toaster per my comfort levels does not support progress or growth. I push my mind to choose meditation, to walk with mindfulness on my breath. A telephone won't ring if you keep picking it up to see if there is a dialtone, cursing in traffic won't make people drive faster, and fervent eyes on a pot won't make it boil any sooner.

Words are power, words are perception. As parents, we have the power, right, and responsibility to frame the Autism discussion. Will he be able to live alone, get married, or go to college? Why wouldn't he? My son is a boy with Autism, not an autistic boy. "Autism" is not a qualifying feature that defines him. It is a prepositional phrase, not an adjective. My words help him get therapy to get his words, to find his words, to connect with his voice once again.

We realize that we need to stabilize the basic physical electrical brain foundations of learning and emotional regulation, and Thad begins Realtime EEG Neurofeedback, a brain-training program designed by Margaret Ayres. Jacque, our beautiful bodyworker, points out the discrepancies in the way his neurons fire. Look, here, she says pointing at the spikes and waves that tell the story of his brain, the Alpha waves are too big and there is too much space in-between, that might be the lethargy we see, and here, she says pointing at a swath of brain pattern that resembled a Bart Simpson crewcut, this incomplete firing here could be the remnant of trauma or illness. Heavy metal poisoning, I inquire. Yes that too, she responds. And his Theta waves are too big, like rolling, loppy, ocean waves, these sleep waves look like coma waves, like experiencing the world underwater. No wonder he has problems paying attention, she says, touching different points on his brain storyboard. We make plans to train his mind to awaken into a tighter, fuller, more consistent state of alert, and we make further plans through EEG training to decrease the potency of the sleep waves that challenge his focus, attention and memory.

We see his brain waves out-of-whack on a computer screen in realtime, and reconfirm our belief that this basic foundation of the neurons firing in his brain must be trained. He begins to brain-train in 30 minute sessions a few times per week. Initially, Thaddeus would be challenged by the sticky glue and the electrodes on his head, as he would sit on my lap in the chair, me pinning his arms, him screaming and flailing during the entire sessions. We plan sessions when others were not in her office, and I watch his brain patterns bounce and move to the intrinsically motivating ding of the machine each time his waves hit the targeted mark, each time his surfing mind successfully rides a brainwave to shore.

Months later, under the continued care of Jacque, we begin an energy treatment called Nambudripad Allergy Elimination Techniques (NAET), created by Dr. Devi Nambudripad, to help his body reorganize, heal, and to train the plethora of allergies out of his system. NAET informs us that the body is interpreting certain substances as poison, as danger. She holds vials of water charged with the electrical memories of things his body perceives as toxic such as mercury, eggs, spider venom, wheat proteins, milk proteins, certain vitamins, minerals and body systems, and various vaccine strains, adjuvants, and additives. We work on emotionally and physically clearing particular items and combinations of items from his cache by touching his acupressure points, muscle-testing and calming and soothing his charged-up, unbalanced system. I am the surrogate in the treatment, meaning that she provides the treatment to him through me, putting my hand on his skin as she works because his compliance challenges will not allow him to do as I request, like hold the vial or touch my arm. Years later, his resistance eventually softens and he is able to be treated by her directly.

Jacque also begins to use NAET to clear my emotional space, my ethereal body, my cluttered mind, of the negativities and blockages associated with Autism, as she begins to heal me along with Thad. She clears my emotional

baggage associated with particular individuals, and upsetting and traumatiz-
ing moments in this experience of getting what Thad needs to be successful.
She tells me that caring for mother is as important as caring for the child, and
reminds me that if the mother in the family is not okay, the family is not okay.

I drink local coffee with raw cream, Jacque touches my meridian points,
swings a pendulum for accuracy, and hands me pieces of paper with damaging words to clear and vials full of electrically charged water to help my nerves
and system unravel. I release, I try, I cry, I promise, I make an appointment for
tomorrow. I remind myself, every day has a tomorrow.

Every journey has uphill trudges, there are warriors who want to bring you
down, and I continue to have the experience of many interactions of, This is
my child and my family that we are discussing and determining the future of, I
say referring to myself, and this is merely your job that you go home from each
night, I say referring to their situation. Your job, my life, and we shall each fight
accordingly. We all act in our given roles, and I begin to parse out the players in
my mind, those for the children, and those against them.

In the summertime, we plant lots of stuff in the yard. In addition, I buy bags
of live ladybugs from Home Depot to stir up the farmy ju-ju and help our crops
produce. Thad loves me to dump them on his head, enjoying the feeling of them
crawling around on his skin before flying away. Sometimes, because he would
get bored of the ladybugs before the last lady had taken flight, he would remove
a sock and swipe the unlucky rest into his sockpuppet hand. Satisfied, he would
hand me a sweaty little white tubesock, full of bright red, ground-in bug death.

And, yes, I was still mad. So fucking mad. Why me? Why them? Why us?
Why him? Why don't people understand? Why won't they help us? Why are they
closing the door in our face? Why are they treating us like shit? Why are they
fighting us? All because we stand by a small boy with no voice, a sweet smile, and
a bottled-up mind? I do not understand, and I cry deep sobs in my pillow, on my
sleeve, and on the shoulder of the occasional caring friend.

I try to practice the art of responding with compassion to the refrain, "Why
don't you just," which I perceive as an irritating conversation starter that really
doesn't have any thought for the receiver behind it. Why don't you just put him
in kindergarten? Why don't you just let him have a cookie made with wheat

flour? Why don't you just give him a break today? Why don't you just let him skip a therapy session? Why don't you just take the summer off? Why don't you just wait a year? Why don't you just wait and see? Why don't you just put him in school? Why don't you just let the teacher take care of it? Why don't you just trust me? Why don't you just relax? Why don't you just let him watch that movie scene again? Why don't you just have another kid and start over? Why don't you just let him hang out and stim in the closet? Why don't you just stop getting so mad? Why don't you just calm down?

People, I see these "why don't you just" words as diminutive, assuming and every "just" you utter at me, is a moment that he loses, an experience that he does not feel, a chapter of life ripped out of his book or placed indefinitely on hold. That little linguistic marker, "just," also belittles the importance that I place on helping my child, and your little "just" digs that knife in "just" a little deeper. And, the first cousin to this stupid phrase, "At least he doesn't (do something that the speaker perceives to be even more fucked up than the fucked up shit he already does)" follows as a close second on deeply hurtful. They say to me, at least he doesn't flap his hands, perhaps to console me. I respond, yeh, see him over there jumping up and down in the corner. He's flapping his entire fucking body.

In cognitive therapy sessions, Dr. Gwen uses watching movies and playing video games to teach him turn-taking, socio-emotional engagement, theory of mind, and perspective-taking, all significant challenges for individuals with Autism, all the while using the joint-attention experience of both watching the screen as a starting point. They practice tolerance to playful obstruction as Gwen adds challenges to using the television successfully, such as the remote being on the wrong channel or out of batteries, as Thad follows a series of written steps to turn the game on or manage the video, as she turns channels, abruptly stops the show and asks comprehension questions about the storyline, slowly softening his rigidity to unexpected changes in his environment. Thad chilling with Gwen, two friends on beanbag chairs side-by-side, learning about life and human interaction with the support of brightly colored images, characters, creatures, tales, struggles and battles on a screen or monitor. I smile.

The Premack Principle, an important concept in behavior modification, asks up to pair higher order behavior with lower order behavior, meaning that we attach the completion of a less preferred task, such as the act of doing the dishes, to a highly preferred activity, such as watching television, the consequence of doing the task is interpreted intrinsically as a reward. Almost like flipping the concept of punishment, in that if you do something wrong, your consequence is a punishment that causes some sort of discomfort. And with this principle, the consequence of doing something you don't want to do will get you something you really want. Genius.

So, Dr. Gwen would ask Thad to converse with her about what his ideas were regarding choices that certain monsters made in a cartoon episode in order to access time on the Lego Star Wars game, she would ask him to solve problems of buttons turned off with the reward of a certain number of minutes of his video, he had to talk about characters he likes and did not like to get access to playing a certain bonus level of the video game. Placing these preferred, and less preferred tasks together helps a child push through resistance towards the targeted appropriate behavior. She addresses his aggressive tones this way, educating him on how to say this-or-that particular comment like a friend would. He works on saying it, saying it with the correct tone, affect, prosody, and eye contact.

Dr. Gwen talks to me about using effortless effort to master the boy, how to teach what is not there and to test what is mastered, as she presses him toward better frustration tolerance, and improved engagement. And one of the most important lessons that she taught me was to be alright with feeling uncomfortable, that everything will not happen at once, how to expand my visceral ability with stress, to accept the challenge of being calm in the face of adversity, fear, and the unknown, to be good with working on his skill sets for days and weeks and knowing that it will not be fixed today but will continue to improve each day, and eventually, slow and steady, and eventually, with our forever tenacity and deep faith in him, this staying power and emotional fortitude will help us win his race.

And I continue to be reminded how so very important it is to choose providers for our children who vibe with the kid, understand our parent groove and intense motivation toward our children, and can access our kids in that special way, laden with expertise, experience, and insight. Dr. Gwen likes Star Wars, and so does Thad. When I first walked into her office, saw a fancily-framed portrait of Chewbacca on the wall, and noticed a light saber displayed proudly on its own table, I watched his eyes light up in friendship. At that moment, I knew that Thad and Gwen were a match. Using video games, movies, and tech to access Thad, fucking brilliant.

When I was in college, I decided to give blood during the first Iraq war because although giving blood is difficult for me, I believed in our country's values and I wanted to support the cause. I say that I am sensitive, that I have rolling veins, and I request that they poke gently and thoughtfully to extract my blood. Then, I am struck repeatedly by a needle in my arm, those who had promised gentle syringes now disregarding the cries of pain rising up from my black and blue arms because the people tell me that it's so easy for everyone else and should be easy for me too. Everyone else went out to drink beer afterwards, whilst I moderately passed on in the sidelounge. It was so easy for them? Why not for me? I imagine this struggle every day as I think about the constant battle, the constant fight for my son. Daunting. Tiring. So easy for others to educate their children.

The gauze ball wadded up in the crook of my arm is a blood orange. I imagine taking the orange and throwing it far up a hill, only for it to roll back down picking up steam, and run me over. A small orange, a big problem, a perception, as I wonder how I can find peace in my tormented soul?

I remember my sweet, innocent daughter watching me trying so hard to not be a bitch, as I talk and explain Thad's challenges to people and providers who do not understand him and his unique needs, and me sounding like a bitch anyway. I feel the physical manifestations of rage, a slow painful syrup of anger boiling from my gut, overtaking my heart, trying so hard to not spew imprecations at those who hurt me and mine, and pushing it down, as I fight unceasing tears, sleepless nights, and empty bank accounts. I am trying so hard to be an example of love and goodness in front of my children, trying hard to not become everything I say I am not, and that I strive not to be, an angry, condescending, ego-driven, mean, mad, sad, vindictive, selfish bitch.

Don't be so intense, my people tell me. How I can be "being intense" if I am not even talking? Physically exuding an ass-kicking vibe, a subtle electrical charge that is emitted by Autism parents when fed Styrofoam platters of bullshit, disguised as appropriate services for our kids. Maybe I won't wear makeup to the next IEP, as I consider a physical solution to my deep emotional heartache and sadness. Maybe my mascara has turned my eyes into black curly daggers of disgust, I wonder. Despair, anger, and fear continue to consume me in the most intimate, damaging, and chronic ways, misery and heartache killing me slowly.

I sometimes feel like Autism is stalking me, lurking, oozing like an untreated, infected wound, like a virus or disease, a bad relationship that won't call it quits, creeping toward me from everywhere, from everyone, in every way. I am standing in the doorway of the taqueria, listening to the women at the picnic tables talking. My kid doesn't talk, he is my first, he doesn't like his toys, and he cries all day, one woman tells the other. I stood there, gasping air with a gaping mouth. I wish someone had talked to me about Autism early on. They start staring back at me as I realize I am staring at them. I want to tell, I want to scream, if he's not talking by two years old, and the doctor is telling you that everything is alright and you know it's not, keep asking, keep looking, don't give up. Trust your mama instinct. Get a second opinion, I whisper to her as I pass. I breathe, and I keep walking, moving forward, trying, coping, breathing.

As I fill out yet another form for the myriad, endless sea of deficits, the problems, the "why" and the depth of his academic, behavioral and social deficits, I come upon this question on an assessment, "Does he enjoy smearing feces?" As an English scholar, I noticed that the question seemed to contain two aspects on the sentential level: one, there was an issue about potentially inappropriate interactions with the defecation he would inevitably encounter while using the commode, and two, assuming said interaction occurred, would it be indeed pleasurable to him? The third and most obvious was, oh shit, I am filling out this form about my child.

Documentation in multiple reports that my child does not smear shit on the walls is positive because applying one's own fecal matter to immediate environmental features is a possible characteristic of Autism. The fact that the report about the autistic child, mine, describes the fact that he doesn't exhibit this characteristic should comfort me in a certain way I guess, but it doesn't. As I told my friend about these thoughts and experiences, she recalled her years of dealing with this difficult, upsetting behavior with her son. Shit-flinging behavior has also been given the visually descriptive term, "crapisode," coined by Kim Stagliano, Managing Editor at www.ageofautism.com, a website I prefer.

I listen to my Autism friend, Melanie, as she cries so many sad tears because sometimes that's all a person needs, to be listened to, not judged, not counseled, not even consoled, just listened to until the water dries up and emotional balance is regained. Just a person to listen, really listen, and not say a fucking thing. Bullshit. No family deserves this quality of hell.

Thad sneaks into Ursula's room in the middle of the night sometimes. Why am I like this? He asks her again and again, through his tears. She lets him lay in her bed. I do not talk about my son's shortcomings and challenges in front of him. He understands. Even if he doesn't talk much, respond or act as if he is not listening, he is. He feels it. He feels different enough. He deserves respect.

And then, sometimes, Thad just clicks on. His personality is intoxicating. Makes me want more, like a creamy dreamy tall glass of sweet lemonade on my parched lips. Dad, what is punk rock? What are those white things growing up from the ground? Gravestones, son. Mom, can forks have brothers? I love the way he sees the world.

As I would thrash and wrestle with my strong feelings and powerful emotions about my child's lack of compliance to my words, Bob would calmly tell me, remember you are the parent. Remember, it is your house, you are in charge because you are the parent, your rules and your expectations are what should happen in your house. I blink, I breathe, I wonder how this could ever possibly be true. I was in charge of my house, I had control of the flow, the existence of my space? Okay, I respond to him. Could you tell me that again tomorrow, and again, next week? Repeat it till I believe it, till I see it, till I internalize it, till I understand it, please?

For his behavioral food therapy, I start making dinner in the morning each day, and we practice eating dinner appropriately every afternoon and night for months, with single food challenges in the morning in various forms, on a very long list that gets check marks and signs to repeat-it-tomorrow, whole apples versus apple slices, peeling juicy citrusy oranges into sections and eating them with our fingers, orange smiles, grapefruit halves, eggplant lasagna, gluten free pastas with various sauces of myriads of colors and consistencies, desensitize, forks spoons and knives, relaxing into the food experience, stuff mixed, stuff touching the other stuff on the plate, napkins used to wipe fingers and chins, green salads with raw vegetables, touching, mixed, touching, mixed, melted, cold, hot, food as a sensory experience, food as a social experience, vegetable soups, meaty stews, baked masterpieces with brightly colored vegetables melting together, touching, melding, beautiful, cup plate bowl mug and plate, food so much food, ending up in his mouth, on the floor, on my shirt, in his hair, in my hair, on our therapists, on the wall, melting, colors, touching, new colors, deep smells, and rich textures. Bonding, blending, and connecting with my child through our food.

Thad would squish shortbread batter and cookie dough, sausage meat fixings and wiggly noodles through his fingers, much to his dismay, as a part of my own homemade desensitization to textures sensory program. I would read about ways of helping him in various domains, such as his tactile sensitivities to various textures. He would do this sensory work in the therapy gym with shaving cream, olive oil, and bubbles. He would work in terms of minutes towards tolerating the scratch of new clothes, writhe through exercises of putting his fingers through buttonholes to secure his clothing, or endure the uncomfortable sensation of a zipper that he perceived as a pulling restrictive torture device associated with wearing pants.

He had so many deficits in so many domains, or areas of development, that I would just pick a few and start working on them myself. He would hoot and holler about sticky, tacky, or gooey stuff touching his fingers, and I would ask him to mix many of the ingredients of our food with those same cute fingers. More specifically, I asked him to slime the ingredients through his hands to desensitize those sensory experiences he so acutely disliked. We went through powdery feelings of rice flour on the skin, the sandy roughness of brown sugar, slick corn noodles soaked in olive oil, and slippery hamburger meatballs with white and purple onions poking out.

I teach him eventually, in the next few years, to grate large chunks of Cheddar and Mozzarella and to store them in large round glass bowls in the fridge. I am thinking about him being a prep cook in a restaurant someday. Does he like this?

Does he do this well? I am always considering what is next, and what kinds of skills we should support. I move toward an even more determined state of mind to help my child. I am resolute, adamant, single-minded, and unwavering in my goal to rescue his beautiful soul from the lonely bitch of Autism.

I must break life down for him, to slow it down, to teach him, to teach him everything about life. I think about Hippocrates' important words, let food be thy remedy, I think about going back to the basics of all foundations of food, and using this as a way of teaching him to learn. We will start where he is. Autism bends and twists him and he does not learn merely by example, by osmosis, by having an innate desire to learn, or independently searching out the information, like everyone else. There are still so many things clouding his focus and his mind.

We live in an orange grove, and thankfully, touching oranges is not a problem to Thad in any way. Although he still would not drink the golden liquid, we would use a juicer for fresh squeezed orange and grapefruit juice each morning, and this daily experience evolved into the term we began to use for practicing skill sets. In our vernacular, working on his academic tasks, food stuff, tying shoes, anything that requires repetition and practice is to get "juiced up." We watch bright orange fluid trickle out of the juicer. It looks like fresh possibilities flowing, it smells like the new hope we all have in springtime, when things are reborn, new, healed, and it feels like a gentle trickle of sweet nourishment and encouragement.

I also begin to bring big bags of citrus, avocados, and locally-crafted beer to Thad's doctors, therapists, and providers as small gestures of appreciation for their awesome assistance, and expertise with my boy. I give them gifts of the flavors of the land around Thad to attempt to describe him to people through their taste buds. Almost like Thad's "terroir," a viticulture term used to describe the different flavors of wine based on different types of climate, soil, and water where they grow, I hand his therapist a six-pack of local beer, and request she do "research" on my son by drinking the beer that weekend. The brewery is half-a-mile up the street, and large onslaughts of avocado and citrus groves fall immediately north. I find myself obsessively trying to think of new and different ways for Thad to understand people, and for people to understand Thad. Again, attempts at little bits of fun, solace, and humor in a very dark life.

As Autism took further control of our lives, a winter storm wipes out the almond, mango, banana and blood orange trees in our yard, and my anger continues to boil. The strong, unceasing winds deplete our calm, our sensibility, and our bank accounts. Slow, slow, slow, everything so slow and languid.

That winter, Thad had an odd behavior of secretly huffing my deodorant in his bed, which was perhaps an emotional remnant to him of sleeping under my arm, at night, as a baby, before Autism, memories of comfort, love and togetherness, whispers of when we showed love to each other without any interruptions. I also used to wear deodorant with aluminum in it, and he has a high aluminum content in his blood which is likely a factor in his Autism. He would lay in his bed with the stolen, creamy white toxic stick, for hours, under the covers in his dark bedcave, searching for solace by humming and chanting pretend words, movie phrases, and sounds to himself, to soothe his sweet soul mired in the acrid solitude of Autism.

Life, being alive, interaction with others, the quintessential human experience, feeling and understanding the emotions associated with friendship, joy, and happiness, playing with a friend, having a friend, love, his life, our world, our family, he was missing it, and we needed to get him back online, remediated, fixed, organized, with some options, some solutions, so he could join us, our family, our world, once again.

Snuggling in, and getting super-warm is a preferred pasttime of ours in the winter. Thaddeus and I like to put on extra-toasty jammies, stoke a roaring fire, make popcorn, pack the dogs in all around us, load up on wool blankets, and watch movies on cold winter evenings. As we nestle into our little love cave one frosty night, Thad asks, Do moms have penises? Burrowing in the covers, he had touched my stomach. I reach down and sure enough, I feel a muffintop hanging out over my sweatpants like a phallus lasso. I love my son's curiosity, his honesty, and his unique perceptions on life, and I am again reminded, everything must be taught and explained to my child. No osmosis, no social nuances, we must practice overt teaching of every part of life, living, and the human experience.

The next day, my friend, Gayle, writes on Facebook that she has a "bun in the oven." I feel shocked because I am sure that my friend is not pregnant, and back in the day, when sorry-for-herself me had a life, announcements of 'buns in the oven' were a definite tip-off that those friends were prego. As a hermit in my own home, makeup-less, freaked out, sometimes clad in the same sweats for days with no contact from the outside world beyond those entering the therapy zone, I am confident that I have been out of the human loop for so long due to the excruciating, encompassing details of Autism that communication in the outside world must have changed, that all language must have morphed into words I no longer understand, and that phrase must mean something entirely different.

One afternoon, as ABA clatters and bangs downstairs, we picnic on croissants and strawberries on my bedroom floor, and I inquire. No, it does mean I'm pregnant, she tells me and laughs. Some language changes, and some stays the same.

CHAPTER 4

An 1/8 of A Grape of Teaching "Normal"

In the 2008-2009 school year, the School District funds most of his therapy program through Mediation agreement between the School District and us, directed by an OAH judge, a result of us filing a lawsuit against the District as they continue to disregard his unique needs. I reteach Kindergarten and First Grade in our home, and family life becomes a crazy therapy zone, as so many of us try to remediate the Autism out of my boy. I transform my living room into a therapy space complete with one student, one teacher who happened to also be Thad's mom, and engage approximately 15 different doctors, co-teachers, supervisors, therapists, aides and tutors hold various active roles in Thad's recovery and development.

I add acute vigilance into my three dogs' family protection jobs because I think they know he is unique, and they protect him and tolerate him in a special way. I put up gates that mount to the wall with bars and I affix locks between the therapy room and the kitchen, the space between the kitchen and the stairs to the second floor, I lock the doors and windows so my boy won't escape from behavior modification therapy and academic instruction, and further secure the house with electronic surveillance, motion sensors and secret codes, all the windows and doors beeping alerts if anyone accidentally or on purpose tries to enter, exit, or make a run for it. All of these precautions are taken so that Thaddeus will physically remain in his therapy space, and to give him a safe effective space for this intensive therapy, a place where we can help him get better, to help him rejoin the world, and his family.

A scary, dangerous part of Autism called "eloping" is when the autistic child makes a mad dash away from you, usually without a purposeful destination or plan, not to get anywhere in particular, or maybe somewhere specifically, or to get away from or get closer to, they were frightened or startled or felt uncomfortable or itchy or scratchy or grumpy in a certain way or did not recognize or remember the people or the surroundings or something else entirely that you are not yet aware of. Basically, the kid bolts for any smorgasbord of reasons, and you better be damn sure you got your jogging shoes on, you saw him leave and know which direction he is traveling, there are no cars coming, all the bad guys in the area are taking the day off, no dogs are out, and no sirens, leafblowers, loud music, or any other unexpected sounds are cluttering the air that fine afternoon.

Hearing these potentially unexpected, unfamiliar yet very common noises in the environment, like shiny, back motorcycles revving or stark, white ambulances speeding by, could cause the child even more distress during the event, and ultimately push the child's levels of anxiety and adrenaline even higher which could cause even more erratic behavior. Yet, these are common noises that happen in the human experience called life every day. Hence, we see that Autism eats at the core of daily existence. Autism makes things suck that really truly shouldn't and don't. Unfortunately, they do because if your child loses his shit in a writhing puddle of boy-fury on the ground because of the unexpected, exploding fireworks from a university touchdown, or the twanging, loud voices from a party happening next door, you begin to hate these sounds of happiness alongside your child.

Clad only in underwear or naked, Thad usually didn't go far when he would escape. I would find him hiding in the bushes around the corner, with the potential wrath of hidden spiders, snakes and coyotes always on my mind. And because we live on the corner, hiding from me on a busy street that has big cars and vans and trucks whizzing by whose dangerous ingredients might include child predators or others that could potentially harm the small naked wild boy crouched amid the Mexican honeysuckle, near the pink pepper tree, armed with a wooden spoon and a little red metal Altoids Mints box full of about fifty small Lego weapons taken out of the various sets, swords, axes, hammers, anvils, all at about an inch long, all made me so scared for his safety, and his future.

At this point, my personal goal in the saga was simply this, I knew that I needed to gain behavioral control over him, my little, sweet, belligerent boy, before he was bigger than me, before he was taller, stronger, and, ultimately, before he could run away without me stopping him, or kick my ass. It was necessary to bring new people into our house, and into our world to help us remediate Thad. Every waking hour, every single day, in 15 minute block increments, I set off on a therapy whirlwind.

And so it began, I set out to teach him the skill sets from Kindergarten and First Grade, school years that mark most of the foundations of academic learning, reading, and math. In September, he could hardly demonstrate any of the California public school state standards. Letters were tricky, capital and small representations were still mixed up and confusing, with sight words as a mere topic of conversation at team meetings, as in "How the hell are we going to get him to sit still for long enough to engage his mind in the mass amounts of repetition that he needs to hold these fundamental reading concepts, that we have yet to even begin teaching him?"

He continued to present with only two demonstrations of emotion, either mad, or not mad. He could still hold onto his mad longer than the duration of most therapy sessions, with a tenacity one might see in Olympic athletes, or monks on the top of a mountain going to their zen, unaffected by earthly temptations or words. Staying there. In that place. He would shriek, lay face down on the ground, take his pants off in public in protest, refuse to do anything even if it was cool when he was angry, go rigid, exhibit atypical body movements, or would ask the same question for hours and hours in a full blown rage usually about how bad or mean Rob and I were to him. He would never recover from feelings or incidents in which he felt wronged, and because of his social communication issues, he felt wronged most of the time, deserved or undeserved. He was so far away from everyone with his anger polluting his relationships, as he would be overtaken by madness, and percolate that mad simmer all day long.

My patience and tolerance toward Autism were waxing and waning, like mooncycles, some days full of determination and fortitude to kick the bitch to the curb, and some days, whatever dark internal forces taking over as I hid behind beer bottles, mounds of confusing denied insurance claims, in an environment thick with fights and deafening silence amongst those with words, and drowning in mountains of unkind letters requesting immediate payment for services not covered by insurance that had been rendered to our child.

Autism pulls the fun out of being a kid as it rips out the significant pieces of development that we understand as benchmarks of childhood, like the life skills lessons learned in the sandbox, having a best friend, wanting to stay longer at the park because you are having so much fun, and memories of storytime at preschool because you were enjoying the class, learning so much, and paying attention. All of these human interactions, school, and life experiences were unfamiliar, scary, and difficult for Thad. At therapy, his internal clock would beep at the fifty-minute clinical hour mark automatically, and on predictable cue, he was asking for me, asking to leave, repeating these requests about every 30 to 45 seconds. Welcome to our baseline of Thad, the place that we look at his academic, language, social, and sensory skill sets and see where we need to work. My eight-year-old had many skill sets of a four-year-old, and some even lower based on standard assessments done at the end of his year in public school First Grade.

In addition to a 40-hour, 6 day per week behavior therapy schedule at home, we spent every day at the clinic working on therapy goals, every day, each day for as long as Thad could tolerate it. It is hard to imagine a child who does not want to play, or know how to play, or know how to relate to another human being over a pile of cool toys. To sustain interaction with another person could literally feel physically painful to him, and maybe could only occur in short bursts initially in the developmental intervention, speech therapy and occupational therapy he received there.

Every day in therapy, he worked on basic language usage and social skills, using his words to communicate instead of engaging in tantrums to get his needs met, he began to work on developing play skills initially with one adult and moving later that year into small group therapy sessions at the clinic as he could tolerate that level of intensity, he began to work on social communication and learning how to handle problems and how to react to the big or little problems, and the reasons why freaking out is never a good idea.

They taught him about appropriate behavior with friends, helped him with his sensory issues through epic awesome swinging sessions on cool crazy apparatuses, and provided gooey, ooey, fluffy, scratchy, soft, hard, slimy, hot, and cold sensory experiences to help him better understand how to tolerate things that might happen in life. And they talked to my child a whole lot about friendship, what a friend is, how to be a friend, why we want friends, and why friends are so important. I saw my boy changing, healing, improving, and then I realized that maybe I was healing too. I learned so much from them, and I began to see whispering billows of hope for Thad's future on a far distant cotton candy mountain.

To facilitate the foundations of social communication, Kelli, Reanna, and Tracy, his therapists there, would sometimes pretend to be too sad or too happy or inappropriately angry or have a party or have a secret or have an issue, and the kids would have to help solve the associated problems that seemed to always occur. They would transform the therapy room into a restaurant or a camping trip or a jungle or a maze, all the time teaching, engaging, redirecting, creating, modifying, and gently supporting various children through playing together, and constantly asking the children to touch the cold spaghetti, to participate in the dinosaur digs in sticky sand, to marvel at the delicate wings of the butterfly and adjust the strength of their touch appropriately, to press the red jello into shapes of stars or ooze the slippery blue bubble mix to help them rejoin us in our world.

Thad developed a special friendship with his Speech Therapist, Kelli, based on both of them being a sorta of "co-bad guy partners in crime" model. Kelli was his very first friend. As Thad's dirty black footprints marked the white ceilings in the sensory gym, he drew pictures of Kelli being eaten by bears, and he wrote mean letter tirades to her to practice his fine motor skills, and he successfully completed the entire Handwriting without Tears Cursive curriculum that year. Happily, his fine motor skills are good, so learning to write in cursive was not a difficult venture. We would work together to brainstorm the ideas he wanted to tell Kelli in his daily correspondence to her, then I would write his ideas on a white board, and transfer them in cursive to lined paper. Thad then would copy it from the lined paper onto a new paper, and proudly present it to Kelli. These letters to Kelli were him finally communicating, and he went through this process every day.

He would present his daily letter, and then engage in human bowling in the hallway with helmets, skateboards and foam pins. A typical day was Thad playfully handcuffed to the desk in the spirit of "Pretend Peril" to help him focus on his letter recognition work, with anticipated rewards of Thaddeus being rolled up like a tight burrito in the clinic's area rug, all interspersed with social moments, meltdowns, mad faces, threats from a short boy, and an occasional smile, tear, or screech.

I felt alone in a sea of people.

Sacia, our spunky, redheaded, second-grade-teacher-by-day-tutor-to-Thad-by-night, worked on alphabet letter recognition. Kelli supported this practice in speech therapy, and I reinforced it in our homeschooling time, and in our after dinner time, and any time I could snatch a moment of his time, to corral his body and mind into the same space. We spend hundreds of hours working solely on letter recognition. He would remember a capital H, and the small s, with predictable accuracy for the afternoon session. A short drive to the clinic and I would proudly arrive, boasting to Kelli, he's got it. She would test his recall of the series of letters that his strutting-around-like-a-peacock mom was bragging about. Yet, in the fifteen minute drive from home to the therapy center, the letters he had mastered moments before had been lost in the steam of his perseverative brain, and Kelli would begin again with the same letters. Again and again. He could not seem to keep the information in his mind for any amount of time.

I begin to think obsessively about his challenges with memory, attention and focus all the time, and I would research and read and research and read theories, criteria, action plans, treatments, and teaching associated with these domains that appeared to be such difficult terrain for my boy, and I continued to realize that I needed more answers, more ideas, more experts, and more plans. I continued to understand the magnitude of this disability, and the levels of faith I will have to push to and through to begin to see that very faint light at the very end of a fuck-ass long tunnel.

Bob does weekly parent training with Rob and with me, independently. He meets with Rob for coffee and orange juice on Monday mornings for an hour, and he meets with me on Tuesday afternoons for an hour before the hour long team meeting that immediately follows. Bob talks to me about busting my expectations of Thad, naming it, the glass ceiling of Autism. He tells me not to let Autism get in the way of believing that Thad can succeed and achieve, and that I should expect great things from him, and that I should expect him to comply and have good, appropriate behavior. Bob tells me that I do not have to settle for my autistic child running the household with his unreasonable demands, and that it was alright for me to be really fucking mad about it, as long as I handled my PTSD anger in appropriate ways.

Bob talks about following through on behavioral expectations with the analogy of Thad's bad behavior as a slot machine. If Thad realizes that he only needs to tantrum for an hour to get his controlling wishes met, he will. The message being that if you keep cranking down on the arm of a Vegas slotmachine, you will eventually get the prize. As Autism parents, as human slotmachines, heavy with quarters that have no value just weight, we cannot concede to impossible Autism wishes and perseverative requests, and if we do, we ingrain the dispreferred behavior even further, which makes that unwanted behavior even more difficult to modify in the long term.

We are also sure that Thad has a feeding disorder, and this is why he only ate a few things, accepted only two fruits and no vegetables on his plate, he could barf on demand, and usually yacked on the table in retaliation. Since we had removed gluten, casein, and eggs from his diet, we are also always concerned about adequate nutrition, and meeting daily allowances for brain and body development. We are looking into therapies to help, we explain. Bob looks at him, then us, and utters, it's all behavior. We are shocked. It cannot be all behavior. Perplexed, flummoxed and in utter disbelief, we drop the discussion with Bob for a few weeks for us to let this information sink in. He could be playin' us for a fool, could it be possible? A mastermind manipulator, Thad had us so well trained into compliance by his atrocious behavior. He would look us squarely in the eye, point "the finger of fury" and threaten "I'm going to get really, really mad." We were petrified of his anger, existing as parents who were so well-trained by the Autism chokehold, applied by the 3 1/2 foot tall drill sergeant.

We ate gluten-free, casein-free, egg-free, soy-free, preservative-free organic food, we did ABA food therapy every day all day, and were actively trying to heal and clean up his challenged intestines, his wonky immune system, finicky digestive system, and busted gut. Thad worked through individual food challenges in the morning session and the afternoon ABA sessions, and then again at the actual dinnertime every evening. The therapists would reward him with Wii time on the television if he ate certain types of food with success. He was required to eat a small amount of the targeted food, and then he would get a large preferred food reward. And if he did not comply, the therapist would eat his reinforcer food, like vanilla cookies or yummy chocolate muffins in front of him. Very much explosive behavior would occur, as Thad would watch the therapist enjoy his snack as a consequence of his lack of compliance to the directive given.

Very often, when there is a targeted behavior that you are trying to encourage or extinguish, there will be a spike in the bad, dispreferred behavior as the therapy changes and softens his reactions and responses. The behavior spikes were even worse when we started parent training on how to successfully get Thad to eat dinner. Rob would slowly throw away pieces of the reward if Thad did not comply with the directive of "Eat your celery." Some days, Rob would come home early from work in the afternoon, and Rob, Bob, a few therapists, me and Thad would battle through a simulated dinner experience, to practice eating the entire dinner on the plate, to practice sitting up straight, to practice not ditching out of dinner to go to the bathroom, to work on not trying to engage family members in movie scripts and then getting mad because the other person was not "saying it right," a particular type of rigid need for another to imitate a sound or a script as he hears it in his mind. According to him, we never got it exactly right.

We simply wanted our son to eat food, to eat enough of the right foods, and to eat the food appropriately. After hours and hours of positive, negative and exhaustive force by our wonderful ABA therapists, Thad would eventually eat the targeted food. Then, I realize that he is ingesting the food like a pill, and not chewing it. Before therapy, he would hold a small bite of a baby carrot in his mouth for literally hours instead of swallowing it. And then he was just swallowing it, but still not chewing it. We backtrack, we review, we chart his chewing, his swallowing, and if he vomited any of the food, including spitting on the table, on the floor, in his hands, or running to the toilet to projectile it all over the seat, and if the targeted food ended up anywhere besides in his mouth on its way to his tummy, he would have to start over with that particular food task.

In the morning, we slowly mastered an extensive list of whole foods, fruits, vegetables, grains, proteins, nuts and seeds, and fats we wanted him to eat. I did not want him to rely on processed snack food products for nourishment, and knew that nutrition and gut health was integral in this model. I also wanted him to be able to eat whole food in its many different forms. For example, he would eat apple slices with the skins off, but we worked extensively on eating a whole apple down to the core. Round and round till you reach the seeds, I would tell him, as a therapist charted his chewing, offering words of encouragement, and stern reminders of expectations during the apple-eating challenge. Then, the apple slices, then sauce, then pie.

I would start making dinner at 10:30am every morning, and every afternoon, around 2pm, we would practice eating dinner, and then ultimately eat the actual dinner around 7pm every night, moments after the last therapist had left. We required him to eat at the dinner table, and we had unique problems with his eating, and with his behavioral compliance almost every night. For example, no matter if he went to the bathroom before or not, he always had to pee during dinner. Then, he would disappear into bathroom for the duration of dinner. Bob says, let him pee in his pants. It's all behavior. We cannot believe we are being flim-flammed by his convincing pee-pee dance, crying, and pleading, as we are slowly trained by our therapists to make him finish his dinner before going to the bathroom. In all of his episodes of the dinner dance urine escapade fandango, we would eventually realize his micturation chortles were fake, and he never went in his pants during the behavioral changes we enforced. Previously, when released mid-dinner, Thad was eventually watching TV, and not going to the bathroom, with his dinner uneaten, with Rob and me destroyed from battle on the couch, too tired to care.

Thad enjoys simulating bombs blowing up in clothing carousels in stores, and hiding and escaping from us in stores because he likes the expressions of worry when others think he is lost. We regularly close down the entrances at various stores looking for him, and add therapist support into simple trips out to the grocery or shopping as his behavior spikes, changes, regresses, and improves. To go buy bacon, to go buy shoes, life continues and the simple things become so difficult as his difficult behaviors intensify and we continue to work on the huge challenge of managing, extinguishing, changing, ameliorating, and replacing aspects of the autistic behavior.

One evening, we tried to get Thad to eat 1/8 of a grape at dinnertime without any therapist support. How hard can it be, right? Eventually, we move into pleading, begging, promising, crying, started with a plate with 6 grapes, 5, 4, 3, 2, 1, then a half, a fourth, and then 1/8 of a grape. Pathetically, Rob and I stood there lobbing threats and promises at our locked-down boy, reticent, and so very sure he would not eat the grape no matter what we promised, or took away. Again, he won. The green shard of grape was abandoned on his plate, and he returned to the television while Rob and I attempted to compose ourselves, admit defeat yet again, and clean up the mess that was associated with trying to get Thad to do something against his will, which was most things. Things on the floor, things on the walls, a knocked over chair and a plant, our deeply saddened souls, and bruised egos.

Bob says that if I threaten Thad's therapist, Karina's assistance to Thad as a punishment for not brushing his teeth on a Sunday night at bedtime that I had better be sure she's on her way over so he knows I am serious. Bob repeats the lesson in my ear, do not threaten consequences without follow-through, do not give 50 chances for compliance, do not be inconsistent with consequences, and do not let Autism wreck you and your boy. And never give up on him, Bob tells me, never.

So many of the foundations of his love for drawing started in behavior therapy. The ABA therapists begin to ask Thad to draw things in his environment in a step-by-step way that starts merely as an exercise in behavioral compliance and following directions, and becomes this rich, fabulous way that he communicates with us. His language comprehension challenges and delays make it difficult for him to describe so many aspects of the way he felt or perceived life. Drawing starts to help him be able to process feelings visually, to help us to understand his perception of events and people, and we literally discovered drawing as a whole new form of communication for him. When he draws, we better understand what are his thoughts and how he is thinking, these whispers of his mind continued to perplex us. His emotions on paper are hilarious with the meanest maddest mouths, eyebrows drawn in thickly-penciled arches, with many precarious things happening, usually involving bombs and shark attacks.

The fluid human arts of perception, how life appears to us from our own unique viewpoint, and perspective-taking, the ability to see another's point of view, were being taught to him on paper, and it was so interesting to watch him move into having an opinion or a perspective or a preference, even down to the color of someone's eyes. When he was young, he worked briefly with a green-eyed speech therapist. He was amazed by the color of her eyes, and he would talk about how much he liked and wanted green eyes frequently. When he started drawing, he always drew his brown-eyed self with green eyes, and anyone else he really liked had green eyes also. But, if he did not like you for any reason, your eyes happen to be green, and he was drawing you, the likely outcome would be brown eyes. Only good people get green eyes, he would tell me when I asked about his preference.

To help him describe his feelings, to work on flexible thinking, and to help him work on processing his perspective of what had just occurred, he was directed to begin his drawing tantrums and meltdowns. The pictures provided insight on how he felt that people just incessantly bug him to "do stuff," and how he is basically an innocent victim in the fray. He drew so many pictures of himself tantrumming because his therapist asked him to read louder in the back of my black Prius, and as his mom buys big round oranges from the farmers in the grove, and the sun is so hot, complete with a yellow burning flame inside. Me driving around to various neighborhood farms to buy deep-purple blueberries, bright yellow butter, and long ears of green corn. Cornsilk flying, Thad and Andrea battling in the back seat, no, start over, put your finger on the word, louder voice, nope start over. Thad draws and draws these experiences, see here is my fight with Andrea, Mom, he says. *Battle royale* in the backseat, in the kitchen, in the yard, Andrea, Karina, and Alex always battling him, girls always with pretty hair, boys always with elaborate facial hair, and everyone always drawn with very mean eyes, the world according to Thad. Thad was all about drawing mad, mean eyes. And not because he was an innate angry person, but because this state of being mad was his porthole into the world.

He was taught in small increments how to draw a house, and then directed to draw himself at his house. He drew a house, and said I'm inside, see that little window. He draws and writes his love for those who teach him with masterpieces of therapists falling out of the burning plane into hungry sharks as a request for friendship, or a Wii game representation of a teacher or tutor with elaborate facial hair and the maddest eyes as a true Thad compliment. Once, he was stung by a bee and he drew a picture of himself reprimanding a swarm of bees with a stern, wagging finger and the words, Do not sting boys.

We had to teach him the process of how to have a unique idea, a broken down process of minute steps, showing line-by-line skills and teaching expectations, and then require him to try his hardest, and to use his best effort, instead of half-assing it. He was taught to care about his work, and to do his best. Initially, when only the therapists could keep him in line and I had yet to gain "behavioral control" of him when they were not around, he would draw concise thoughtful pictures with them, and then with me, use the smallest smidgen of effort he could muster and purposefully not do his best. We worked through these issues of behavioral compliance, as Thad pleaded to me to not tell his therapists that he drew a "bad picture" (a.k.a. low-effort) because he cared what they thought, me not necessarily yet, but them for sure. Caring what others think about him, yes I will take that.

And then, so happily to me, sitting down together and drawing became a way that he and I could hang out together. Sitting, chatting, and hanging out are very challenging demands on him, something that was done more in therapy sessions than for relaxation because he still was challenged by the tangled wires of communication in his body and brain. But, hanging out with him drawing about his day at the beach, or his enraged thoughts about his most recent brawl with me, or using smelly markers to sketch the different vegetables, or dangerous representations of Lego guys climbing mountains, or his perspective on why it was so unfair that he could not have another cookie, or to let me know that he was excited that Christmas was coming with so many pages of brightly colored trees, or that he was really scared of bees with graphic depictions of attacks was so satisfying to both of us. Binders and binders of his drawings, a long conversation I have stacked in my office of his conversations with the world, with me, and with himself.

There are so many holes in my yard, from the wreckage of the winter storms, no money to replace them, and the backyard is a wasteland. Thad begins digging fairly large holes in the back and front yard. I fall in one, and twist my ankle. I ask him why he is digging holes. He doesn't know. I think about functional behavior. "Functional behavior" is an Autism term tossed around regularly. Basically, we think about everything that people do, they do for a reason, some sort of merit. Lining up objects, repeating movie lines nonstop, flapping fingers in front of the eyes are all nonfunctional. These activities, in a way we spend our day is the way we spend our life kinda way, serve no purpose, and we all strive for a certain level of meaningful engagement in life within existence.

I hear Bob's voice in my ear to make all behavior functional, whatever the thing is that I want him to do, or he chooses to do. Thad digs random holes in the backyard because he feels a special affinity to garden tools at this junction, and the garden spade is a cool addition to the cadre of stuff he kept with him at all times to soothe and amuse him. I tell Thad that every time that he digs a hole, I will put a tree in the hole, and he will cover the hole with dirt and fill the rootspace with water. "Why do I have to be the gardener?" My inner bitch screams, because I cannot afford to pay for a gardener anymore. Because this is your job, I respond. Everyone has a job, and this is yours. During the day, you work with your teachers and therapists, I explain, and your weekend and evening job is to plant fruit trees. Mom, I'm not a gardener, I'm a farmer. Fair enough, you are a farmer, I say.

Using his physical engagement as a way of focusing his mind, I begin to think about how we can plant trees, we can pick the fruit, and how we can make stuff with the fruit from the trees. We plant various types of fig, mango, lemon, orange, grapefruit, and guava in the yard. We work on movement sequencing, sensory challenges, motor planning, vocabulary, frustration tolerance, mood control, and coping skills all within this task of planting an orange tree in the backyard.

We consider how to dig a hole in thoughtful sequential steps, and with therapist support, we are able to manage appropriate hand placement, and comfortable body postures for digging a hole with a shovel, we consider sensory challenges of the feel of the heat from the sun on our body, the bugs, the sweat, the dirt touching parts of our body, sequencing the movement of putting his foot on top of the shovel first and then pushing the tool down into the ground, hand placement for garden tasks, and the vocabulary for the different plant and shovel types, verbs, so much frustration tolerance, fucking rock in our way, coping skills, so many fucking rocks in our ex-orange grove space, old dry riverbed, chock full of rocks sandy loamy yard. And by the way, we don't throw rocks at moms, dogs, sisters, or friends.

My response to Bob's assertions that he will teach Thad to ride his bike or tie his shoes is regularly, Good luck with that, as he sets his sights on things I've tried and tried to teach Thad without success, me firmly believing those defeat-biased stories based on my previous failed attempts that these are skills he is not capable of learning. Bob unteaches these distortions, and Thad learns to tie and ride. I continue to practice not being scammed by my child. Bob critiques me as I parent in real-time some days, to support the challenges of Thad's behavior. To give me strategies to handle and teach and expect better from him.

And sometimes, during parent training, I would have tantrums behaviors moments, rainstorms of difficult emotions, me crying, big fat droplets empty from my eyes, sitting at my table as big fat droplets from the sky splatter onto the red roses outside the kitchen window. You know its not supposed to be like this Kristin, Bob would remind me as we sat in my kitchen, Thad with a 24-hour EEG turban on his head checking for seizure activity in his brain, ABA behavioral therapists present to support him not ripping off the nodes that are glued to his skull to take data on his brainwaves, and me fielding a new fresh round of legal issues from the school district. I am so grateful for my people who support me, as the waves of depression sometimes consume me, as I try to give up, to give in, to admit defeat, and sometimes the sadness would just pour out of me like bloody cranberry waves.

Carl Sagan said, "To make an apple pie from scratch, you must first create the universe." You must teach the foundational skills first or there is no way a person who is perseverative about the temperature of his feet, and continuously, incessantly replays a scene from Harry Potter in his mind can focus on the intricacies of a conversation with another person. We teach our boy the foundations of "normal," the fundamentals of being cool, being chill, hanging out, how to not sweat the small stuff, and to be okay with change. We explain, role-play, discuss flexible thinking, relaxing into the moment, attempting to coax him to release the chokehold-grip of control he craves in his environment and from the behavior of those around him. Normal left on the 8:30 train, People. We must start at the very beginning, at the foundations of normal. I must build up his roots so my sweet flower can grow.

I sit in my front yard during the southern California wildfires of 2009, watching the flames skip and jump the ridge, licking at the trees and burning the hills. I can see them from afar, and wonder about the idea of "normal." A cartoon tells me that, "Normal is just the setting on a clothes dryer." Is it normal to see smoke and fire from your front yard on the nearby mountains? Is it normal for a child to tantrum for hours when asked to clap his hands, eat a bite of food, or to put a red peg in the blue board?

Mom, can we have fires in September, he asks me, returning from the restroom unattended, as I figure out quickly from the ash on his fingers, and aroma on his clothes that he was burning paper towels with a votive candle in the bathroom of the fancy hair salon, my grey hairs sprouting as fast as I can cover them.

Fantasy versus reality, and delineating real and pretend, especially in cool comic-book moments, feels particularly scary and omnipresent because we never know if a certain violent moment might accidentally lodge in the wrong place in the Autism brain, stir some shit up with the impaired sense of danger, and take it to task with the difficulty in impulse control. One day, we thought it was a good idea to let Thad play a first-person shooter game because that is what kids his age do sometimes. The next day, Thad started setting the house up like the inside of the video game, with plastic axes and ropes in the corner. My death was impeding, and Gwen says, no, he cannot play these games safely because parsing fantasy from reality remains a safety concern. I recount to her, he loves the Zippo lighter app on my phone, and pretends to burn everything down. Just like he would probably do if I handed him a real lighter. Same difference to him.

But, the outcome of burning down the house with a real lighter versus an iPhone app would be markedly different and dangerous. Same as if you kill someone in a game, you press 'reset.' In real life, we are finite with no "reset" if someone hurts us to the point of death. These thoughts stay with me, chilling my soul in morning hours like an old cup of dirty black coffee by the bedside.

My creative side waves loud and proud that spring as I begin to paint the inside of my builder-grade white house in the very brightest colors I could find to help him pay attention to the world. Maybe the pay-the-fuck attention purple in the dining-room-turned-therapy-space will rouse him, I thought. I follow up with good-fucking-morning riveting blue in the hallway outside our bedrooms.

One of his behavior programs addressed the inappropriate way that Thad responded to his sister referring to her parents as "Mommy" and "Daddy." Thad did not like that, as he told her to shut up, continuously correcting her that we are only "Mom" and "Dad," and tantrumming if he heard any different, he was so mentally stuck on this detail. To desensitize this odd behavior, Rob, Ursula, Bob, a collection of therapists, and I would walk around the house saying, Where's Mommy? Did Daddy just call you? What should we do with Mommy and Daddy today? Days and days, on and on, desensitizing, documenting, pushing him, as he screamed, banged chairs and slammed doors to ease the uncomfortable feelings he experienced from unsealing his bottled-up state, uncorking his perseverative, controlling existence.

Things that his perseverative mind interprets as drugs continue to challenge us. One day, Ursula calls for an emergency evacuation at Target, as we crest the toy departments on the opening day of Toy Story 3. I watch the Buzz Lightyear syringe plunge deep into his veins, and his eyes begin to glaze. Buzz, he mumbles, drools, and leaves us again. Mom, we are losing him. We exit double-time. We did not purchase what we went in for, as we continue to avoid the things in his environment that stimulate autistic behavior.

Thad has his first successful birthday party at the clinic, at age 9, with a few boys from therapy that he quietly invited, and his therapists. In the previous years, all parties ended in disasters, tantrums, and a few of the years, we just said happy birthday and that was all because he did not like to call attention to himself and he did not want any presents. Sadness fell on us each year on his birthday because celebrating him was so difficult, and he would not allow it. Thad's directives for his party were to whisper the happy birthday song, for everyone to wear superhero capes, and to have goodie bags that looked like bombs. That birthday marks the year of the nose cake. At that particular moment, he had been highly focused on the different ways to draw noses, so, per his request, we made a gluten-free nose cake complete with 2D and 3D noses. If you ever want to make a 3D gluten free nose, mix powdered sugar, melted butter and vanilla for a fun, malleable, edible experience.

Autism is a thing that has kicked our collective ass up and down the street repeatedly. We work hard on many aspects of its wrath multiple times per day, every day. No vacation, no weekends, no breaks. We have never experienced something so huge, so daunting. We all were working so hard, and it continued to be a giant mountain we continued to climb. We see him progress, and it still feels so painful and slow.

Even before we had a formal diagnosis of Autism, I knew in my heart that something was not right. How could my boy not look in my eyes? How could my cuddle push him away? Why was the silent, faraway gaze over my shoulder, through me, past me, toward infinity his response when I whispered, "I love you, son" in his ear? I tried to begin my own variety of therapy to help. To practice the art of eye contact, we would have staring contests for candy prizes, starting this game with staring contests at each other in the mirror because direct eye contact was too physically painful for him. I would subtract the difficulty of using actual words when we would practice the body language of social communication, and the subjectivity and unpredictability of humans. We would practice looking at each other, gesturing as if conversing, and saying blahblahblahblah to not burden our practice of socially interacting with actual language at first. I took pictures of him demonstrating the few emotions he could identify and demonstrate, happy sad and mad, and we studied the features of his face together, trying together to crack this unwritten code, communication.

Thad would tape Ursula's toiletries and makeup to the bathroom sink, set booby traps for her with the tape and pretend bombs, and hide her collection of rubber ducks as attempts to socially engage with her. He would then forget where he hid the ducks, she would trip over the tape in the threshhold of her bedroom door, and arguments and screams would begin. Then, she would teach him social skills on the Nintendogs DS using games about raising dogs, teaching him how to know when the dogs are hungry, how to buy and open dog presents, how to not to let the dogs pee on the lawn or eat trash, and how to buy a new dog and name him. They would engage in sibling warfare if he used up all the virtual dog shampoo by washing the same dog over and over, or if he bought the dogs a series of funny hats and did not have enough tokens left over for any two-dimensional food. She continues to be the best big sister ever.

We continue to manage his diet, with the word "diet" signifying what he eats, not the unfortunate, modern spin on that word defining what a person avoids. I witness all the hijinx in life that Thad can muster with his deep craving and deep allergy toward jelly-filled candy, an unbalanced brain craving for this chewy drug. He convinces others who don't know to allow him to eat those brightly-colored chemical snacks, and as an Autism ninja, he is laser-focused on getting access to the allergy-producing gummy treats and one day, he smooshes several stray jellybeans on the floor in the supermarket checkout line into the bottom of his shoe with the idea of scraping them off in the shadows and eating them. Fast forward to his future school placement, I intercept Thad's plans of eating the glued gummy treats acting as nuclei off the cell membrane project on back wall, and I thwart his designs of eating a friend's dropped lunchtime gummy worm from a pile of dirt and pencil shavings after school one day. He cannot be believed or trusted to monitor his own food intake as so many substances still jack his brain into hazy madness, mercury and aluminum whispering encouragement to his lack of impulse control, telling him to just forget about moving forward because sideways or backwards is always an option.

By now, we are so poor from being bled dry for cash by Autism, and the lack of coverage by private insurance and Medi-Cal, that Rob, along with his full time job, begins to teach extension classes at the university to supplement our decrease in income and our increase in medical bills, as we turn in our shiny leased minivan and start to share a single beater car. Autism is kinda like driving in a broken-down jalopy with a busted heater, down a two-lane mountain road in the snow, rain, and fog, holding on all of your money, coins included, in your left hand out the window, while eating a drippy hamburger with your right, and taking a productive shit in your chonies, all at the same time.

Thad tends to regress in his language and academic skills sets around Halloween each year. We think it is perhaps because the days are getting longer, and there is less sunlight to stimulate his foggy brain. During these years, it used to be when the So Cal mountains were ablaze. School was out for a few days each year during October for the high levels of dangerous particulate matter in the fluffy-with-ash grey air, mandatory bandannas over the mouth and nose for trick or treating, and you could see the fires skipping around the mountain ridges from our front yard.

Kelli would come to our house sometimes, and her and Thad would lay quietly on adjacent pillows on the capital L of purple corduroy couches and discuss again and again why he was mad, how they could solve these problems, if these were big or little problems, and they would together silently wade through mires of his defiance and nonfunctional behavior.

Kelli was his emotional anchor for so many days during that period of regression. We would arrive in the waiting area at the clinic, mad. He was always mad. Mad, or not mad. Those were his two emotions. We worked on his mad face, and non-verbal body language, such as when a person steps backwards and looks at his watch and we understand they must go without using words to tell us. Very often, he would use a "mad face" to try to engage with others, and quite often, it was an inappropriate gesture and was not perceived as an attempt of friendship, although it was an attempt at communication.

Imagine if all facial expressions looked the same to you. If mad and confused and sad looked the same. If a person could not conceptually understand the feelings of guilt or remorse, and much less read them in the expressions on another person's face, communication might feel very difficult and confusing. Imagine if you did not see it. You could not interpret or understand those important human nonverbal communication messages. This characteristic of Autism is called mind blindness, the inability to read the nonverbal communication and social clues of another person. Mind blindness can affect people with various levels of severity, like all possible characteristics and symptoms of Autism. Another reason why Autism is so tricky to appropriately treat, the aspect that each autistic person presents, and their varying profiles are so unique and different.

That year for Halloween, Thad dressed like a haunted house, made from a bathroom outhouse costume, with little white ghosts made from Kleenex attached by red string. This costume choice was met with gleeful cheers from his parents, as for the previous three years we could only get him to wear his Buzz Lightyear pajamas each Halloween, even if he had a really cool new costume. Each tissue ghost had a smiley or frowny face with a bright red marker crafted by Thad. The yarn ghosts blew around him as he moved, and it was the perfect costume for a boy who was easily anxious in crowds. If overwhelmed, he would stop, put the house structure down on the ground, tuck in, and hang and hide for a few minutes to regroup.

We experience challenges with his lack of impulse control as the Halloween decorations go up on the outside of the house. Rob spends two hours unraveling and securing a ten-foot-wide spider web over the bright orange lantana bushes and the white trellises in the doorway, and finally, a big scary spider is dangling in the air above our doorway. The spooky masterpiece is complete. Within moments, Thad goes outside and cuts the spider line. As it falls to the ground with a satisfying thud, he questions if Dad will put it up again. When asked why he cut the rope, he replied that he wanted to see what would happen if he cut the rope, would it fall?

Kelli and Thad hang out in her office working on segmenting sounds, happily pretend-handcuffed to her desk, and Reanna would tape five spelling words printed on small cards all over the walls ceiling and climbing equipment, yell go, Thad would run as fast as he could to get words, say them and stick them on the cabinet as spelling curriculum, and he would practice social communication through drawings of Kelli being eaten by sharks, and correspondence to Kelli that started as page-long threats in cursive, and eventually became daily letters to a friend, with excerpts like, Hi Kelli, Do you like dogs? I like to play in the snow. Snow is really cold water. I melt in happiness seeing my boy communicate.

Sacia and Reanna would smear shaving cream on the mirror in our downstairs bathroom, and write alphabet letters in the goop with Thad. They were building relationships with him, they were building his confidence, and they were making a big fucking mess. Do you mind that we are destroying your bathroom, they would ask. Anything to bring my boy back, I would respond.

Falling down the deep rabbit hole of confusion, Rob and I still sit shrouded in PTSD, Post Traumatic Stress Disorder, as Bob labels the feelings we have. Loss, trauma, damage, emotional heartache, fear of his regression, the unknown. "The Dark Days" when Thad was 3, 4, and 5, still freak us out to the point of neurotically avoiding contact or mention of eggs and Buzz Lightyear, like a soldier checking doorways or under his car for bombs. Is it normal for us to be petrified of eggs and the movie, Toy Story? Grocery store runs always determined a path that did not cross the egg cartons. Even as Thad progressed, we worried that one day we would wake up and be back in that place. Could we call it hell? Never been there, but I imagine it's close. Dante's Inferno talks about hell as the place so far from your beloved. A sealed-off child, that's hell on earth, a depth of sadness hard to fathom, pressing day and night on my soul with feelings that I am his only hope, and that my perseverance, my fortitude, my strength, is the only thing that will save him, the only things that will ultimately help him of the darkness.

Karina will sometimes ask me why I did not disclose to her that Thad was exhibiting this-or-that atypical behavior, or not doing something that he is capable of doing, scamming us, working us, whatever. I answer honestly, because I did not realize it. When you are in the epicenter of the storm, it is hard to see all the buildings crashing down around you. His quirks, odd blips, autistic behaviors, and goofy mischief were so entrenched in our daily routines, so engrained in us, so much a part of our existence, that I did not see or realize the "atypicality" of it. We were so well-trained into compliance by our autistic child, and his finger of fury.

The driveway was sweaty with flashcards and lack of compliance one day, and Thad threw down with one of the biggest tantrums of his history with Bob. Basically, Bob takes away Thad's video game, Thad has a mondo meltdown, Thad writes an extremely mean letter to Bob, and Bob is so excited. Once upon a time, Thad did not turn down the volume of the television when Bob asked. After the third request, Bob walked over to the television, removed the Clonewars DVD, walked out the front door, got in his car, and left. Thad had not complied, and Bob leaving with the CD was the consequence. Thad and I looked at each other, as we both could not believe he had done that. Two hours later and knee-deep in one big fatty of a tantrum, I am on the phone yelling at Bob, Thad screaming behind me. Thad still remembers that moment. He threw a tantrum that day with things I care not to mention flying around my house, and a level of upset that should never be subjected to the human soul.

Then something amazing happened. Thad sat down and he wrote a very nasty letter, an entire college ruled page long, yeh, about how angry he was, how disappointed he was in Bob, and demanded respect from Bob with his written words. Then next day, Bob looked at the letter, and said, I'm framing this and putting it on my wall. I am so proud. My job is done. Thad had appropriately demonstrated emotion, he did not shut down in the face of a controversy, and he told me with his words directly and exactly how he felt. I was elated. My behavior therapist beamed. Thad's behavior shifted, and things started to improve.

When Thad did not want to do something, he would have a behavior. "To have a behavior" in Autism Nation could mean a variety of things from recently busting a hole in the living room wall to laying stick-straight, face down on the floor of the supermarket and refusing to move in line, or obsessively repeating a word phrase or sound, or punching someone or something, or incessantly picking a scab past bleeding, and might involve particular superhero costumes, clothes, foods, characters with levels of perseverative precision that grip and mangle his brain. There are lists and lists of behaviors associated with Autism, each one unique to that particular child. As they say in the trenches, if you have seen one child with Autism, you have seen one child with Autism.

A unique Autism behavior that my child displays is that he will incessantly compliment people, in order to get them off the task of teaching him something. A *non-sequitur,* a clay pigeon, an avoidant behavior, his charm is his behavior, and a distraction in the most innocent, devious way. He would typically have "pretty girls" as therapists, and be flirtatious and coy with them. He is a handsome boy and would flutter his long lashes at them. The girls would giggle, and think he was so cute when he said he was too tired to work. We would laugh when we finally realized this as a behavior. His therapist, Andrea, would say that she would be tricked by Thad, left there at the table by Thad, him at the TV, her still holding the unfinished homework, with flushed cheeks and a pumped-up ego after Thad had complimented her into submission.

We meet Carol, an amazing Audiologist, who tests Thaddeus and delivers a Central Auditory Processing Disorder (CAPD) diagnosis. She used behavioral stressed listening tests to assess a child's auditory processing skills as well as their peripheral hearing system. She had to engage Thaddeus to provide reliable and valid test results. Carol spent time to explain to me the difference between peripheral hearing, how the ear mechanism works, in contrast to how the central auditory nervous system processes and recalls information. She encouraged me to ask as many questions about the process and the test results, she told me that there are no stupid questions, and encouraged me to ask about all the things that I did not understand. Thad was difficult to test, and many of his standardized results carried red flags of "interpret with caution" because the behavioral expectations were still so difficult to manage. She tested certain parts of listening and hearing profiles multiple times for the sake of accuracy, and I continued to understand the importance of positive, trusting relationships with Thad's providers.

Thad had to take several tests including hearing two words being said at the same time, listening to single words being said with background speech noise and multiple people talking, listening to two sentences that were said in each ear and being asked to ignore one and repeat the other. The test results indicated that part of Thad's listening and learning difficulties were related to disordered auditory processing and a mild high frequency hearing loss in the left ear. Annual follow-up evaluations would track the improvement as a result of intervention, maturation of the auditory nervous system and educational instruction, she told me

Carol recommended that Thad would be a good candidate for the Fast Forward program, the programs "Seeing Stars" and "Visualizing and Verbalizing" Lindamood Bell Learning Processes' multi-sensory reading programs. Carol Atkins recommended that Thad would be a good candidate for the Fast ForWord auditory training program as well as learning using a multi-sensory reading program such as Lindamood Bell Seeing Stars and Visualization and Verbalization programs.

She also indicated that classroom adjustments were necessary including preferential seating, teacher repeating directions at least once using the same word order, and use of a personal frequency modulated (FM) auditory trainer. She explained that having Thad wear a personal FM receiver that looks somewhat a hearing aid without a microphone and his teacher wearing an FM transmitter that included a pick-up microphone would reduce the effort to listen in the classroom. Use of the auditory trainer allowed him to hear the teacher's instructions without as much interference of background noise.

The FM trainer pulls the voice of the person speaking with the transmitter to the foreground and increases the signal to noise ratio so the background noise is less amplified. In addition, the teacher does not have to hold the transmitter and has complete use of both hands. Thad was continuously troubled with figure-ground situations that interfered with discriminating directions and or instructions accurately when the background noise was as loud or louder than the teacher's voice. There was a sound field auditory trainer already used in his classroom, sorta like a PA system in the class that amplified the teacher's voice through speakers within the classroom. This supports helped him although Thad continued to have significant confusion in figure ground, the ability to differentiate sounds of importance, and ambient background noise (i.e. the hum of the classroom computer, the incessant tapping of a classmate's pencil on the desk, and the voice of the teacher coming into his ears at the same level of importance and volume, proved confusing if not properly parsed out).

When homework would get challenging, as we sat at the kitchen table, after he went through the normal compliments of eyes, hair, clothes and smile to me, we would then move into Thad tossing out a second round of compliments regarding my pretty elbows or fantastic eyebrows or exquisite shoelaces. Wow, the homework must be hard tonight, Rob would comment from the kitchen island whilst making our gluten-free, egg-free, casein-free, soy-free dinner.

And, for a long time, the sound of a ringing phone would make Thad screech and cry because all sounds seemed to hurt his sensitive ears. Eventually, he tolerated the ringing but would not answer the phone, and he would only speak to Rob or Ursula on the phone after I had answered it. So, I decided to spend one afternoon teaching him to answer the ringing phone. He had many concerns surrounding the interaction between the interlocutors, such as the anxiety of not knowing who it will be on the phone when you answer. Rob called him approximately 100 times one afternoon so we could practice. What if it isn't Dad, he would worry. It is, I would reassure. His anxiety would skyrocket each time the jingling of the phone started, but slowly, it took less time for him to answer it. Each time, as the phone would initially ring, we would discuss that for sure it was Dad, and okay to answer. After about 20 rings, he answered the first time with me swearing up and down that it would be Rob. Eventually, after that productive afternoon, we were able to move forward with him using phones.

We go to Gayle's wedding one sunny Saturday, and Thad eats a bunch of covert gluten and casein off of the reception buffet, all kinds of breadsticks and mysterious crackers and dips and blobs of purple frosting from the wedding cake. His autistic behaviors skyrocket, and Autism rears its ugly head. He tries to inappropriately hug some boys he doesn't know who rebuff him, and then he gets upset about the color of Rob's tie, demanding that Rob remove it in the middle of the reception. Thad has a big poop attack in the bathroom, and we leave early.

Meanwhile, as we work on skills such as walking up and down the stairs appropriately, ways that a person can calm down when super-mad instead of hitting or running away, and Rob, also lovingly referred to as the Stool Hunter, spends a portion of every month or so taking Thad's shit to the post office to send to doctors with the poo either floating in a mysterious chemical cocktail to preserve clues that might help us understand what is mysteriously attacking him, or on dry ice. I imagine that it is a rather awkward exchange to hand a box of frozen shit to a postal employee, both of you acknowledging with your eyes to each other what is happening, the human biohazard skeleton glaring under the uncomfortable gaze. I imagine that saying, "I send all kinds of shit through the mail," could be understood in such a different way now, taken so literally with auspicious undertones.

We also use very sensitive doctor labs when we mail the fecal treasure troves around the country and all over the world in our endless quest for answers to the mysterious, revolving symptoms that present challenges and deficits in our child's physical, behavioral, and emotional health, and his ability to communicate. Labs that commonly take insurance are not specific or sensitive enough for the levels of Porfirin, or amounts of Methylcobolamine needed to correct the imbalances in his system. We tend toward labs that do not accept insurance, or that insurance will reimburse partially with a superbill, and usually a whole lot of bellyaching on our part, in various forms such as denials, appeals, and escalations.

Our bank accounts shrink, we get more answers, we start more biomedical protocols, and I see him getting a little better, sometimes infinitesimally small but somehow, someway, almost every day, a little bit more emotionally with us, in our world. Every moment, every hour, every day, I feel glimmers of hope, and experience throatpunches of disappointment.

CHAPTER 5

It's Good & It's Cold & It Starts with An "I"

WE MOVE FORWARD and fall back in his progress like an endless clock stuck on the same time, daylight savings, fall back, lightness to darkness, day to night, spring forward, my child's mind turns on like the brightest ray of sunshine one day then turns off into emotional blackness, then on again, then off again, fall back, spring forward, 1 to 2, 2 to 1, 1 to 2, endless cycles, so many hours of deep work with him, therapy, trainings, meetings, and little inches and tiny soft whispers in his process, of his progress.

I realize he has significant problems with his comprehension of the numbers, 0, 1, 2, 12, 20, and 21, all possible combinations of 0,1 and 2. A binary nightmare, the baseline, the whole computer memory shot, and oh so deep was the confusion at 0,1, and 2. The numbers 0, 1 and 2 haunt me in my sleep, as we clock therapy hour after therapy hour working the numberline, counting, touching the numbers, making the numbers we touch match what we say with our voice. We set out to retrain the confusion between 0, 1, and 2 as I dream of counting in my nightmares, number recognition hours and hours, counting myself lucky, counting my blessings, counting on you, count the cookies, Count Dracula, and me counting on a break.

When Thaddeus started at Lindamood Bell Learning Processes (LBLP) for intensive academic remediation in the spring of 2009, he had been out of public school for close to one year, and homeschooled seven days per week in a 1:1 intensive home environment. We had worked daily, hours-upon-hours on intensive alphabet recognition and phonetic work with gallons of therapists, teachers, and myself before he started LBLP, which provided some language foundations for the amazing work he was about to execute. Since 2003, he had not had a single positive learning or academic experience in a school environment. So, we take him to LBLP, and they teach him to read. Plain and simple.

When he began at LBLP, I was concerned that his sporadic attention levels might not be able to sustain the 50-minute concentrated bursts of focus required. I was concerned about his sweetly manipulative, extremely effective task-avoidance techniques, and how instructors would recognize this behavior and effectively power through it. I was concerned that he would be too difficult for the teacher to figure out, and that he would be asked to leave the program. I worried about his compliance to adults, and introverted behaviors that he claimed as tired. Most of all, I was starting to become extremely worried that he really couldn't read. I did not want to believe the School District's hypothesis that he would never read. Yet, the task of teaching him to read still seemed so daunting. Multiple therapists and I had been working with him 6-8 hours, 6-7 days per week for an entire year, and we were only at the alphabet, the most simple phonemes, and CVC words. Was he truly mentally retarded, like the school district hinted repeatedly, and I should just face the facts and give up?

Then we met Anne, Center Director, and Maria, Thad's Supervisor, at LBLP. They took time to understand Thaddeus' unique needs, and used creative methods to get him excited to learn. Academics, homework, and any type of the learning of anything that resembled schoolwork had previously been a constant battle, and Anne and Maria made Thad feel smart and motivated. He would run laps with them at the break to fortify attending behavior, they were conscious of his interest in camping, animals, and surfing and engaged him through these interests in many ways, including a pretend fishing trip on the patio for having a "smart-boy body" during sessions. Maria would successfully pull him out of scripting behaviors, and she did amazing parent training with me. Anne was always available to answer questions, and coordinate with me. I felt a sense of calm, respect, and trust in Thad's teachers at LBLP that I had not experienced in a long time. Thad is so lucky to have them in his life, I would think daily.

That summer, we took out Thad's first academic loan, a type of college loan, so he could have a change to maybe go to college someday. So he could maybe have a bright future. But first, he needed to learn to read. At LBLP, his academic skills sets increased by years in months because my son finally had the tools, and the confidence.

Four hours per day, five days per week, for months and months, I drove the 60-mile commute one-way to Pasadena, and along with beautiful bursts in his academic prowess, we watched his self-confidence grow. I hung around during the ten-minute breaks between sessions, and I would monitor him, encouraging play with other children. Initially, he would sit next to me outside and snack on his lunch, eyeing the children around and not interacting. As time progressed, he began to engage in conversations with staff and other children, read bathroom doors (BECAUSE NOW HE CAN!), and declare his independence that boys do not go into the girls' bathroom with their moms.

We continue working with Jacque doing NAET and EEG brain-training a couple of times per week in the afternoons, and each morning, he powers through the LBLP "Seeing Stars" program to strengthen his decoding skills, and eventually, the LBLP "Visualizing and Verbalizing" program to support and teach the important skills of visualizing language, and reading comprehension.

We join the cult of Lego, and I begin to use Legos to teach him so many skills, such as frustration tolerance and patience, slowing down to review his work, staying focused and paying attention to the task, and the sequencing of getting the things on the "shopping list" in the corner of the page first and then putting it together. I also particularly love how most Lego characters provide two types of emotion on the front and back of the head. A character will have a I-am-chill-and-driving-the-boat face on the front, and the oh-shit-I-am-about-to-be-eaten-by-a-shark face on the back of his head.

We act out social situations and dangerous situations with the Lego people, and twist their heads around as the appropriate emotions occur in the story. His spatial reasoning and understanding is stellar, and he does harder and harder Lego sets faster and faster. I am so proud of his fantastic abilities to build and conceptualize these three-dimensional masterpieces, manifesting his smarts in fantasy castles, beach houses, farms and quirky zombie-monster towns. He develops so many hilarious and unique ideas with Legos supporting his process.

In addition, Thad attends Speech Therapy at the university, we meet a soul-surfin' brutha Audiologist named Dr. Keith, and him and Thad became surf buddies. Dudes are Thad's thang, and Keith is a big cool friend. One Halloween, Thad showed up in his office with tattooed shark bites, and wearing ace bandages. Keith and Thad had a long, serious sit-down about the shark attack, and how Thad was so lucky because he barely made it out alive. The light in Thad's eyes shone so brightly as this big friend, this surfer boy who liked him, spent time with him in his world.

I ask Dr. Keith to give Thad a hearing test and a Tympanogram. We are challenged by fluid buildup in his ears that sometimes becomes infected and sometimes not, and that sometimes affects his hearing, and sometimes not. With a marked history as a poor test taker, Thad goes into the sound booth and I expect that I will be joining him there soon in a menacing method toward his compliance. I sit next to Keith outside of the soundproof box, watch Thad doe-eyed do all the testing, and then Keith gets him to do some extra more difficult tests just to push him a little. Typically, I could not get him to repeat a single word or push the button to say he heard it without physical prompting from me next to him in the booth, and there was Thad listening and repeating words as Keith hid his mouth to increase the difficulty of the task. Repeat after me Thad, baseball, hamburger, playground, Thad does, as he keeps asking Keith how he is doing, Thad's conversation skills extent, because he likes Keith and really wanted to know how his friend is.

One day, we go surfing with Keith, Thad and him tandem on a board, and they have a massive wipeout. Keith claims, the biggest in his life, as the surfboard breaks in half and pops out of the wall of water with substantial force. Both surfer boys are unscathed, and Keith, although freaking internally, remains calm and plays the wipeout as cool and no big deal. The learned response he got from Keith of "no big deal" and "we can recover from wipeouts" became strong metaphors for Thad. I took pictures of the broken surfboard and the two cool dudes post-wipeout flashing surfer pride hand gestures, which gave Thad a conversation starter in his binder, and he wrote the story of the wipeout that accompanied the pictures of the busted board.

We continue to search out good providers that make sense to us, who understand our child as we do, and we meet Dr. Susi who does an Occupational

Therapy (OT) assessment on Thaddeus, and begins to treat him monthly. Susi's gym, as Thad would call her clinic, had so many squishy balls, nets and swings, so many foam pillows and blocks to create sensorial experiences to heighten arousal or soften agitated systems. He would work with her on crossing the midline, throwing beanbags into specific piles while swinging, and she taught him strategies of how to listen to his body.

Dr. Susi teaches me so many important things about Thad through parent training for home OT issues, such as mastering the art of buttons and zippers, tolerating the scratch of new clothes, ideation and sequencing in social situations and conversations, postural control, core strength, and discussing the millions of emerging puberty questions I had.

Thad and Susi had a certain sweet coolness between them as she required him to look at her and answer her questions about his day before accessing her gym, he was verbally defiant and he complied with her wishes, the only time I have ever seen a person defiantly drink water, my dear Thaddeus, in her gym, and he would practice self-regulate using so many cool balls, and other spiky, smooth, soft, hard tossable gizmos to calm his sensory imbalances.

And Susi taught me to find simplicity in what always seemed to be so complex to me. I would arrive worried to death that he would never master the art of wearing a belt because the climbing rope smooth belt he wore was always cranked down too tightly and hiked his pants to his armpits. I describe the life-or-death situation to Susi, and she simply says, how about get a belt with holes to impede the impulse of too tight crank-downs. I breathe relief. I arrive worried one morning that his fingers are in his nose way too often for common courtesy, and we have a booger-awareness sensory session the next month, accessorized with a big bowl of green snot made from jello and granola. Genius, I think. They read social stories about when it is appropriate to dig for nasal gold, and how to ask politely for a Kleenex.

We continue to work with Jacque using NAET to clear the bad vibes of heavy metals in his body. As a surrogate, I feel the same visceral feelings he does during the treatments. For example, as she walks toward me with the vial of mercury, I feel all the lifeforce energy leaving my body, and when her two fingers delicately push my arm to test the strength of the allergen, I bend in half like a deflated balloon or a broken baby-doll. As she approaches me with combinations of eggs and aluminum (Part of his Autism cocktail is the big vaccine bomb with many of the strains grown in eggs), I felt an immediate, uncomfortable sense of something aggressive coming toward me with the intent to hurt me. I felt unsafe and scared suddenly, acutely sapped of my energy by an enemy with those vials in my presence, although I consider Jacque a dear friend. I could imagine how Thad felt inside his body, and in the presence of these very damaging allergens. We continued to work on my mama fear for her boy that was manifesting outwardly still as anger, and I tried to breathe through my worry, to calm my soul by opening myself to the challenges and unseen opportunities in our collective unknown.

Hyperbaric Oxygen Therapy (HBOT) is often used to decrease brain and tissue inflammation in Autism populations, and many other sensitive groups. Large metal chambers sit silently in a room, where a technician puts a spacesuit hood over his head with a long white vacuum-cleaner-like tube snaking back to a tank of pure oxygen. So Thad and I plunk ourselves down in the chamber together to be pressurized, a feeling similar to being submerged in the ocean or up in an airplane with popping ears, to force healing oxygen into his sick tissues. In five days, we dive ten times, twice per day, sitting and watching the world through a window marinating in a vat of rich O2. He watches movies on a white device, and I compose sad poetry with teeny pencil marks, and angry ink jabs the pages of the books I read and read and read, as we sit in the tank together for hours and hours and hours, oxygen pressing his sluggish cells towards wellness. I read a book about *wabi sabi* (the Japanese notion of finding beauty in imperfection), and I write haikus about my son in the book margins.

Big, loud responsibility
For small, quiet child

Tired brain and eyes in books
Finding freedom from illness
Self-doubt

Breathe in springtime
Shiny clean air
Hyperbaric spaceship

We spend a week diving in a hyperbaric oxygen chamber, and I meet Dr. Robyn, Developmental Optometrist, who is doing an informational talk one night on the Interactive Metronome. The Interactive Metronome (IM) is a system that helps train and organize the body's timing. Simply put, IM is a computer program that trains the brain's "internal clock" and supports challenges in attention, memory, and the mechanics of social skills. For example, if we consider all of the timing involved in a conversation, all of the non-verbal, all of the reading of social cues, when you talk, how I respond, and the movement of my hands and your mouth and the way we step forward or back or gesture in disbelief, joy or disgust, and now imagine laughing when you shouldn't or allowing an uncomfortable pause in the conversation just because your brain and body are still catching up, or misinterpreting cues from the other speaker. The back-and-forth turn-taking of a conversation challenge many people with Autism because this internal timing system is disorganized.

When I met Dr. Robyn, my mama instinct knew she was part of Thad's recovery. We went to her office to be assessed for IM, and his timing was in the significantly disordered range with numbers that did not support this intervention at that time. Dr. Robyn suggested vision therapy, and gentle IM training to work toward doing the IM protocol of three times per week at one hour of attention each go. We trained for one to two hours per week for the next two years in Vision Therapy (VT) to prepare his body to learn and tolerate the IM protocol.

Behavioral Optometry asks us to separate the abilities "to look" and "to see," addresses eye-teaming, tracking words on the page, working on speed, fluency and memory through a series of fun engaging activities in the clinic. He would bounce on the trampoline, work on memorizing items in sequences, find holes in his vision field to fill in, and work at home on so many remedial vision-based computer programs that they monitored remotely. Robyn would tell me that Thad had huge potential, and continued to remind me of how smart he is as she showed me the slow progress he made as he sat and worked on coordinating his gaze, reading the entire word, the entire paragraph, the entire page, as he jumped and bounced and pointed and thought and remembered and played and said and tried with his therapists, calling them all his beloved Eyeball Girls.

As Thad mastered a series of playground sports at home in his ABA therapy with relative physical ease and some challenges with behavioral compliance, we pined to his supervisor over the lost rockclimbing days. Happily not lost, Rob started doing ABA parent training at the rock climbing gym with Thad and the therapists. Put on the shoes, tie in the rope, compliance, compliance. Climb to the blue hold, compliance. Compliance, compliance, climb back down. He was a great climber, just not too interested in complying with adult directives. He clocked a few healthy tantrums in the gym that summer. And eventually, thanks to the pure awesomeness and determination of Rob and the amazing therapists, Thad was climbing specific taped routes, and occasionally scaling across the ceiling attached to a rope. And he was pretty damn good.

One day, he begins to freeze his toys, so many small figures and animals suspended in plastic bowls of ice in our freezer, and I experience a brief moment of normal. I used to be amazed when Gayle's kids would freeze their toys, although I admit that it did seem a little strange as I watched, then Ursula did it also, and I realized that this is what kids do at this age. Okay, I get it, enjoying the shards of normal glistening in my mind. Thad freezes his stuff. Oh shit, his therapists said. So normal, I respond, hooray.

I feel so much inspiration, motivation, and joy at the sight of my boy reading as spends morning after morning at LBLP. Mom, is this my new school? I hope so, he continues, because I only want to go to school with people who are nice to me. His special LBLP teachers there made Thad comfortable by being cool and mellow. They allowed me to set up scenarios in which he needed to ask for things to build his social skills and self-confidence, such as asking for a parking validation stamp on this card, a signature, ask what time, what thing, when something is going to occur. There was a bulletin board of pictures of the teachers and students on the back wall, and he was so happy to see himself included on the student bulletin board. Mom, I go to school, he said proudly.

Tears form in my eyes as he begins to visualize words in his brain, and I hear positive words from intelligent well-trained clinicians about how well he is doing. These supportive words can do wonders for Autism parents. Rob says I come home each day, and I appear happier, more focused, more engaged, just like Thad, because the success he feels, we all feel. A quality of family osmosis that feels just great. I thank the therapists for believing in my boy, and for help-ing him see that learning to read is attainable and fun. I thank them for looking past his unique challenges and capitalizing on his unique strengths, I commend them for bringing my son back to academic life, and for giving him the confi-dence and tools to feel smart. We understand from LBLP that Thaddeus needs to learn to visualize his language, and we work on him picturing the words he reads, very challenging oftentimes for autistic people.

Lindamood Bell Learning Processes (LBLP) is a language-learning, read-ing and mathematics comprehension methodology developed by Pat Lindamood and Nancy Bell, and based on Allan Paivio's "Dual Coding Theory (DCT)." Simply put, DCT delineates visual and verbal information each as unique ways of accessing mental representations of a word or idea. For example, we could think of the word "tree" and imagine a picture of a tree in our head, along with the orthographic representation in letters, T-R-E-E, both retaining the mean-ing of that thing with green leaves and a brown trunk. LBLP does not assume language skills and supports at all levels, offering intensive programs that begin at basic sound formations, through consonant, vowel, and word-blends decod-ing, and all the way through visualizing and verbalizing language in reading and math. LBLP protocols develop brain connections, creating and strengthening neuronal pathways in the visual and verbal language areas of his brain. There is so much truth in this model as a way to support the comprehension challenges of people with Autism.

Happening upon so many pieces of the jumbled puzzle I work on constantly, I began to learn about some very interesting holes in Thad's perception, that the way he was "seeing things" might be why he was missing significant pieces in comprehension, and I grab this new information as a place of hope. Considering his responses and the comprehension pieces that he missed or glossed over, the teachers and I realize that he is not even acknowledging certain parts of the story he just read, and that we are not even at comprehension as the primary issue we are working on just yet. We must dig further into the foundations of his thought to figure out where the basic repair needs to occur.

In addition, we ascertain that based on Thad's belief system regarding his black-and-white, oh so concrete dogma of what boys and girls "are" and represent, that we have a problem with colors. Hmmm, so Thad believes that there are "girl colors" and "boy colors," following the lines of the stereotypical colors associated with each sex, girls are red and pink, and boys are blue and green, and on and on. So, according to him, only things of this color can be associated with something he perceives to be male or female, which can also include examples of him telescoping his world views of our blue camping tent being male because him and his dad sleep in it.

Simply put, girls wear pink, and boys wear blue. But, if he reads about a girl in a blue shirt, he does not dispute it and say, no, she must wear pink because she is a girl, he will simply not acknowledge it, the information will not even enter, and the rest of the sentence or paragraph about this fictitious creature of a girl in a blue shirt has not even entered his mind. We begin teaching him that it is acceptable for colors to be universal with boys and girls.

We also discover that he has rigid male and female ideas on numbers (boys like the number 5, and girls like the number 3), directions (boys, right, and girls, left), and a variety of other significant global details that can easily make or break understanding a story, or cohesive idea creation. For example, if he reads that a boy who plays baseball breaks his left hand and therefore cannot write his homework assignment, it will be dismissed because a left-handed boy does not conform to his belief of left-handedness as a boy attribute, and therefore is disregarded as significant information. And we begin to offer him stories to read that directly challenge, and overtly teach that these characteristics can apply to everyone.

We also figure out that he sees things outside of his immediate view computer-screen sized, and we begin to use a tape measure to check the size of all things. When he sees a picture of the refrigerator, when he sees a mental representation of a refrigerator, and then compares himself in size in relation to the refrigerator, a fridge is this big on a piece of paper, crossing the midline of his brain with these exercises, as we try to bring the understanding of size into his burgeoning ability to visualize words and language.

How can he visualize the moving language about the vast expanses of heat and zebras in African savannahs, or the wide open sky of Montana the morning after the blizzard when everything is crisp, white, and silent if he cannot understand and feel this description of size, and attaching this greatness to the magnitude and immenseness of the words? If he understands the rest of the world, those things in life that he has yet to experience and everything outside of his immediate view as screen-sized, how can he be drawn to language in the way that sometimes we are seduced into books that provide us so much internal motivation to find out what happens next in the bar fight at the wharf in 1898, or the outcome of the serf on the stretch of feudal land?

His own foggy self-awareness was further complicated with his lack of "theory of mind," a deficit commonly associated with Autism's impediment of disallowing individuals to understand that others have opinions and perspectives different from their own, and be emotionally okay with it. His sensory-processing challenges, and awareness of his own body are impacting his ability to demonstrate value with his own body (i.e. how big I am related to the car or the tree), and we begin to get his body involved in the learning process by measuring things and comparing size, feeling the difference as a way to access somatic systems of learning this important perceptual information.

Mom, I am thinking of something, Thad said, as we braved the afternoon freeway traffic on our way home. Yes honey, what is it? I thought, perhaps we would discuss one of his current interests, dinosaurs, sharks, and camping. He then threw me a curve ball. It's good, and it's cold, and it starts with an "I." Guess what it is, Mom. You are engaging me in a word game? He made me yell in happiness when used abstract language for the first time ever in his life to inquire. I had never heard him utter a word-based joke, riddle, anything like that before this moment. After a quick swerve of the car and a few happy skips of my heart, I responded to him.

After years of my son telling me that he was stupid, a fool, boring, and could not learn to read, he looked at me one morning through his long lashes, over his breakfast bowl, and asked, Mom, am I smart? He smiled as I said yes, my boy, you are smart. Even though I regularly praise him for being smart, this time he internalized my response because now he believed it himself.

Isak Dinesen says, "The cure for anything is salt water--sweat, tears, or the sea," and that summer, we decide to return to the water with Surfers Healing. Izzy Paskowitz, the founder of the fabulous, non-profit organization Surfers Healing, realized the calm that the ocean provided his son, and decided to share his discovery with other Autism families by taking Autism kids out for a day in the waves in fun surfcamps all over the world free of charge. We cheer for every one of the kids who rides waves that day because the emotion of our children's successes is so palpable, so overwhelming. You don't even need to know those other parents personally who stand next to you on the beach as you cheer in unison, with sandy toes, a camera, and such hopeful eyes, because you can imagine their life as yours.

This beach event was our first experience of uniting with other Autism families for something happy. Usually getting together with Autism and disability as a unifying factor is sad, and we talk about how to fix, we talk about the deficits, and how to cope with our life. But, Surfers Healing is pure celebration of our children, our families, our essence, our mojo, and it is happy, joyous, and love in action. Aloha Izzy for changing our boy for so much good.

A pack of handsome sandy surfers, who fill our ears and hearts with so much yes, so much hope, who tell us, yes your child can do this, yes they can participate, no it won't be too much, take our children out to catch some waves. They are a kind, selfless tribe who made an indelible mark on my child's learning that summer.

I meet Doc Paskowitz, patriarch of the large Paskowitz surf family, as we happen to have neighboring towels one sunny day in Malibu at Surfrider Beach. He talks to Thaddeus about surfing, and he talks to me about how the act of surfing represents so many of the social skills necessary in the human experience. A brilliant, kind man, he tells me about how paddling out to a wave involves crawling on all fours, pushing, pulling water through our fingers of development as we grow and mature. He then tells me that we develop our social skills in the lineup waiting to catch a wave, etiquette and balance and maneuvering our way through life and through people as we surf forward toward our shores. I am amazed at the clarity and truth in these images, and I find such wisdom in Doc Paskowitz's important words:

> *There is a wisdom in the wave*
> *Highborne and beautiful*
> *For those who would but travel out*
> Mahalo Doc for this important conversation.

The serendipity of the summer season swishes my skirt, squirting a symbiotic salve of salvation on my sadness of self and soul, supposing symbolism toward something sweet in the sea I seek swimmingly.

Thad would be so excited, counting each day until his next surfing gig, and always, that morning, his anxiety would start banging its big black gong and he would trip out and protest until we got there. The anticipation of wanting to surf so bad always morphing into an ugly case of anxiety, and we developed a support for this situation that seems to befall us. Each surf morning, we would frontload him with the bad news of the requirement of him having to surf 50 times that day. He would bargain and bargain with us through getting dressed, breakfast, and during the two-hour drive to the ocean, he would whittle the requirement down to 6 or 8 surfs, we would pull into the parking lot, and we had to get him on the board immediately. Once he surfed the first time, all the anxiety washed away, and he happily surfed all day. His favorite surfbreak is at Tourmaline Surf Park in Pacific Beach, known in Thad-speak as the beach with the "white bathrooms and soft waves."

Thad rode with Nick one morning at Surfers Healing, and they wiped out. Thad was very frustrated because he liked Nick very much, and he perceived their wipeout as his failure. As we walked back from the break, Thad told Nick about his frustration with wiping out as equalling Thad not surfing well, and how he was so mad. Nick began to explain to Thad that wiping out while surfing is all part of the surf experience. He told Thad that part of learning to surf is wiping out, and how very often, the wipeout can be the best part. We always are challenged by Thad's resistance to practicing something toward mastery, and somehow the message from Nick, "a cool dude surferboy," that practicing something to get better at it is a cool thing to do, and that part of learning something, like surfing, is practicing, and also "wiping out" (a.k.a making mistakes as you learn and practice a skill, or not having full mastery of whatever you try and being emotionally alright with it).

Swells of Thad's motivation to learn push my emotions in so many ways, and I dance on the sand in delight. I have so much gratitude to Nick for these words that Thad understood, for this conversation that changed his thinking, for this day of baked sunshine and swirls of possibilities, for this moment that cracked open Thad's world in so many beautiful illuminating ways because he began to see practicing skills as something that he might even be willing to do without a fight.

The man standing next to us on the beach that day is strutting around like a proud peacock as his autistic son stood and crested a wave with the whoosh of crowd applause. You gotta force 'em to live, he exhaled to us, endless smiles falling off his face into the wet sand. "I want to feel like this every day," Rob tells me after a day of watching Thad and so many other sweet children succeed at riding waves. Oceans of blue, green, and brown eyes glisten in the salty spray, the waves crash all around, and my heart backflips in love.

The next day that fine summer, we board a boat that cruises us through the Pacific Ocean for a few hours onto Santa Cruz Island in the Channel Islands, a paradise that lacks cars, fast food, and the grime of city life. We camp there for four nights, cook food on a little propane stove, and roast marshmallows in a firepit. Where does it all come together for us? Commence family bonding to occur at the campsite where he responsibly cuts potatoes with a pocketknife, and my little reader started listing the names on the cans of food. Smoked oysters? Mom, where is the fire?

We see and smell ocean for days, and we are healed in a certain way. Wild foxes native just to Santa Cruz walk around our campsite, I breathe in the salty incense of musty caverns, tourist boats, ice plants, and curly mist, we snorkel and hike, we meet neurotypical (sans Autism) boys with knives and he wants to be friends with them. They make tridents and spears from sticks, and Thad smiles and participates in life.

My nipples are pomegranate seeds poking through the wetsuit. I pull on my rubbery booties and hood, and I plunge myself into the red, tangly kelp forest near the shore. We were sure that Thad had one snorkel session in him because the sensations of pulling a hood over his head, and feeling wet rubber on his skin would be poorly tolerated the first go, and he would adamantly refuse if we ever tried to get him to suit up again. We waited until midday to ask him to put on the wetsuit and get into the water to snorkel. He has always liked the ocean, sealife, picking up rocks, finding creatures, and being in the water. But, the added security and necessity of the rubber wetsuit, hoodie, boots, and gloves in 55-degree water was something we were sure was going to be a bust.

So very happily, I was so very incorrect. He remembers the names of all the islands we saw and asks often to go there to snorkel again. He wore the full wetsuit with a hood, booties and gloves multiple times without issue in our stay. He was engaging us in joint-attention above and below the water surface, and he was drawing everything he saw on smooth white pages that fluttered around his knapsack. He is so loving to all, so engaged with us, and this vacation is the best we have had in years. I love to be this kind of wrong.

Two weeks later, I see the glistening sweat of a boy laughing in the back seat on our way to surf lessons one afternoon. He was being the little brother who was bugging the shit out of his sister, writing her annoying letters in the car, poking her ribs in jest, driving her crazy with inane questions, and acting just like any other bothersome little brother. Tears of joy charge my cheeks, and waves of love pound my heart.

Keep trying, I remind myself. Last month, I tried to win a surfboard in an online contest. I submitted under entry number 548, and wished myself good luck. Subject: Why I need that sweet kickin' surfboard. Here's why:

WAVES OF LIFE

I am a mama with a purpose to connect with her child. Thaddeus has Autism, and surfing changed his life. Learning and the unknown are challenges for kids with Autism. He surfs the waves and now rides life with a new confidence. We use "wipeouts" as a metaphor for him--to help him understand that trying something new is fun, and that learning is a win/fail process. We talk about how "wipeouts" in life are cool, and all part of growing and learning. I need that board to help me teach my boy about the awesome world we live in.

Wipeout! I didn't get the board, But, I got to think about Thad and how he learns, and how I will continue to teach him about the world using whatever tools life supplies, currently a surfboard. I keep pondering Thad's recovery, research and more research, and I keep trying new things, new ways, and I keep believing. I do not have every step planned. I follow the "mama instinct" so often. Sometimes, I see a website, or hear a person speak, and I know that that person or intervention is a part of his future. I just know it. As the masters say, "Always trust the gut. It knows what your mind hasn't figured out yet." I pursue a service or a provider or an experience to fruition, and believe that, "If I leap, the net will appear," as a point of emotional stability when I feel these strong urges for my son's care without a definitive plan on the details. I visualize my son's wellness daily, and I try to talk about happiness in the present tense. I actively strive to see my family as happy, now, and our life as good, now.

In the words of Swami Satchidananda, "Life is change. Learn to surf," as I attempt to be fluid, to be grateful, accept life's challenges with grace, and to see change in the waves of life as an opportunity to learn and grow. I believe it. It's part of my recovery plan for my son, and for me. Breathe. Allow calm to wash over me. Let the universe align. Let go. Trust. Be peaceful and be thankful. Say thank you, and listen and forgive. I try to feel all the feelings washing through me, I try to love, and I try to see the message from the universe to me. Waves, sunshine, clouds and boats glisten in the distance, shimmering on the horizon, my goal of his recovery, as I continue to paddle, to stand up, to fall down, and to get back up again. I can do this, I can do this, my internal mantra, a mental filler for the endless waves of therapy, hours of commuting, waiting, hoping, and wondering.

Never give up, I say to myself over and over. And then I try to win another surfboard in an online contest, and this time I do. I win a cool board for writing the following paragraph on my feelings toward Clay Marzo, crazy amazing pro surfer on the spectrum, and my opinions on if he will do the World Tour:

Clay Marzo may or may not win contests, and he may or may not do the World Tour. Although, I am biased to believe that he will do this and more. In addition to his insane accomplishments in the surf world, he will make history as a man who, "because of" or "in spite of" a complex neurological disorder, will make re-invent the sport, re-define "normal," make magic, turn heads, crush expectations, inspire an entire industry and hopefully, the world. My 9-year old boy is diagnosed with Autism, and he too perseverates on surfing. Doing it, talking about it, drawing it, watching it. This weekend, he paddled out and rode a wave alone for the first time. He felt so smart and proud of himself. He loves to watch Clay do his crazy, cool shit in his movie, "Just Add Water," and our family continues to draw inspiration from him, his family & his path in the world.

Your name will be written in the stars, Clay.

I explain to people who meet him that Thaddeus is a smart boy who learns differently from most kids. He is very aware of when he is right or wrong, and strives to please in certain ways with certain people in certain moments with certain reinforcements and certain supports in place. He has a wonderful gift for drawing, he has a sweet singing voice, and his abs are rock-solid. A 24-pack, we say. He learned to dance salsa through ABA, and skates ramps at the local skateboard park with ABA support. He comments, "Hey, that boy doesn't have any hair" whenever he sees a bald man, boys without hair as a new obsession, and got over his extreme intolerance to his father wearing rash guards at the beach through extensive hours of behavior modification regarding Thad's feelings toward Rob's beach attire.

He likes knives, guns, and swords like any other boy, flashes his pretend claws at others when angry, and really does a great job in most experiences involving water. His focus and attention to the gestalt, the detail, the connection, the inference, the social referencing, the main idea, the question and the response to whatever he is being asked to listen to or respond to or participate in is very hard, and he perceives anything that he thinks is schoolwork to be very difficult.

The rigidity and the perseveration of Autism is often quite difficult to moderate. For example, fast forward a few years in this story to when he spent an entire year throwing up all the time, with me and his teacher endlessly trying to figure out if it's a legit illness or avoidant behavior. Sometimes the vomiting and doubled-over pain was real, and sometimes he would barf or claim imminent vomit to avoid tasks. He was a physically sick kid with a behavioral disorder that made him act in odd and irritating ways that if left unremediated could become potentially dangerous and damaging behaviors as he grew taller and stronger.

And a deep need for sameness continued to persist in so many ways. That same year, Thaddeus threw up in my coffee cup once because he was nauseous during that morning therapy commute. My cup was empty and available, and it was a better option than the floor. So, the next time he needed to vomit mid-commute, I was ready. I had another Tupperware bowl on the floor, and directed him to barf in the tub. He refused because he only wanted to puke in my coffee cup. I still had a full cup coffee and a long commute ahead, and I was not interested in sacrificing my black gold to the morning tantrum. Heavy so Cal morning traffic intermingled with a freaking, about-to-barf boy who was yelping about the need to puke exactly where he had puked last month had the peculiar mouthfeel, the uncomfortable effervescence, unexpectedness, and tang of icy acrid early-morning pissy toilet water reverbing on the back of sleep-warmed thighs. The only place to puke is your coffee cup, wailed his perseverative, heavily-metaled mind as I tried to save my java from the barf. The dry heaves begin as he starts to vomit onto his lap. Immediately, I pull over, dump my cup, and he has a barf fest in the caffeine dregs.

Thaddeus is an 11-year old cartoon character, loving, snuggly, rigid, bad guy and good friend all at the same time. He will tell Rob that he is "dead meat" if he messes with me, and he has gallons of blonde wild hair, and so many wishes that his 2 big brown eyes could be "one brown--one green," like the surfer Anne Marie, in the movie "Blue Crush." Thad engages others socially by pretending to cut off their arms, with drawings of them being thrown from burning planes and subsequently devoured by sharks. He is particularly happily enraged when his older sister pretends to "eat him" with a pretend knife and fork. He will ask others to replay fight scenes from movies endlessly, and neurotypical (opposite of 'autistic') peers tire of this game eventually, especially when he refuses to incorporate their ideas into the play. He wants to play with the other kids, but many times he does not know how to join the game, how to sustain the interest of the other kids with him, and very often, he ends up playing alone.

Thaddeus continues to regularly cause me concern regarding his perceptions of safety. Like engaging in the following conversation with me: Hey Mom, do you know where the lighter is? Mom, you say, no. No? Oh, don't worry, here it is, as he whips a green Bic out of his pocket. How the fuck did he get that? So little perceived concern for physical safety, and so much pretend peril always with cartoon outcomes. I will slash off your arm and eat it. You will barf it back up, and then screw it back on. We have a fuzzy, tenuous line between what is real and what is pretend, and Thaddeus is not left unattended.

He begins to describe the people he sees by referencing crayon colors for their skin tone and race. Will I go see a new teacher on Monday, he inquires. Yes, I say, you will like her. Oh, he asks, is she brown or peach, referring to her skin color. The roots of his drawing interest grow deeper into his sandy loam as he air-writes things to describe to me when no paper is available, makes humorous observations about offbeat details in social situations in his drawings, and finds that bringing a pad of paper and a pack of markers to a table with kids is a good way to stir up some possible friend opportunities that doesn't involve a big bunch of language. Drawing silly pictures amongst friends is a cool, socially appropriate way to hang out.

Thaddeus tells me today that he aspires to be the man at the Aquarium of the Pacific who cleans the tanks and talks to the kids about fish through the glass when he grows up. Being in the water is a very positive sensory experience for him. He has a sensory disorder that makes him constantly seek sensory input for his vestibular system. He usually looks like a Mexican jumping bean or freshly popped corn. He operates with an on-off switch, and when he is working hard to hold his body core upright, he will bounce around like Tiger, or feign deep sleep when asked to do something he does not want to do. When he is in the water, he is at peace. He has balance.

He tells me that he is turning 20 on his ninth birthday because he is desperate to sit in the front seat of the car. The legal age to sit in the front seat of the car in California is 12, and he understood the number 20. Thad has a language comprehension disorder that sometimes interferes with his ability to correctly understand information given to him, and challenges him with social interaction, academic skills, and self-confidence.

Abstract language must be modified for my concrete listener also. He hears it all in black and white terms. For example, last week, we went to a new restaurant in town. Rob asked me if the restaurant had "gluten-free dishes," and Thad inquired if we would be eating the actual plates for dinner. And as they were packing clothing for a camping trip one fall evening, Rob asks Thaddeus what he wanted to sleep in. Um, a sleeping bag, Thad replies.

There is also questionable accuracy in his opinion if he is hurt, sick, or injured. Sometimes he cannot feel whatever visceral sensations are coursing through his body due to his sensory disorders. We had to get his nose x-rayed one day due to repeated nose poundings. That morning, he had misinterpreted the social and verbal cues from a boy winding his foot up for the big goal. He cried when the wallop occurred, but soon after he was not bothered although two shiners glistened under his eyes. Later that afternoon, he fell face-first onto the hardwood floor in the kitchen, as I cooked and he acted like a ghost. The no-hands-used-to-break-the-faceplant scenario was due to the fact that he was swooshing around on the wood with a blue nylon sleeping bag over his entire body, on upside-down and zipped up. He came crashing down on his nose, as he tripped over a dog. His nose was swollen and looked sore. One of the ways our body lets us know there is a problem is the visceral experience of pain. I hurt, therefore there must be a problem. Again, Thad wasn't sure if it hurt, if he hurt. We are constantly looking in his ears for the same reason, his inability to locate or verbalize pain.

Finally he learns to eat salad and secretly, we think he honestly likes those dark green leaves, organic extra virgin olive oil, squirts of lemon juice from local trees, chunks of fresh garlic grown next door, some tomatoes maybe still warm from harvest, various nuts and salts and flavors, intertwined, here, now, so many local foods and flavors speaking to his soul. He kinda feels like he has a reputation to protect in regarding his theory that all teenagers, who he positively identifies with as a group that he is part of, all do not like vegetables. Although he does eat a variety of vegetables daily in many forms, he still actively insists that he does not like vegetables, and that never, never does he ever eat salad. Even if he's currently chewing on a bittersweet lettuce leaf.

Yucca Whipleys bloom again that summer on my back hill, large, creamy white ice-cream cone cactuses that I rename the Due Process Cactus, a dig at the circumstance of their blooming cycle that falls in line with the unfortunate twirl of legal battles we seem to be engaged in with the school district. Each year, the passion flowers spurt forth on the fence in the fall, usually when Thad's new services commence or are freshly funded to continue. Then the cactuses get sharp and prickly in late summer, and those huge white dicks penetrate the blue desert sky when we are being fucked once again. His academic life follows the seasons of the yard, as I sigh from every pore in my being, breathe pieces of saccharin sanity into my world of madness and promises, and continue my pleas for his justice.

Sometimes, I feel my situation is larger than life viscerally, and I continue to believe that my motivation for educating others about Autism is that I do not want other families to go through the living hell that our school district has put us through. Having an Autism diagnosis is tough. Remediating a child with Autism is tough. Yet, having an organization that is supposed to educate my child appropriately stand firmly against my family throughout his Autism remediation process, and being directly slammed by that entity who is supposed to help us, not hurt us, really fucking sucks. I breathe, I cry, I hope, I listen, I am silent, I plead, I dream, and I am awakened by the slightest hum of life as I while away sleepless hours considering a different way, a method or protocol that I had not thought about or tried yet, ways to help him, to heal him, to pull him from this confusing, layered disorder.

By law, my son is entitled to a special education that allows him to access the curriculum in a meaningful way, and the local school district is mandated to provide this remediation and support. That fall, through another Meditation spawned from another lawsuit, in a bright room thick with lawyers and a judge, after six hours of negotiation, debate, statistics, unique needs, reading and reread-ing goals and opinions, fore-thinking, foreshadowing, talking, waiting, talking more, waiting more, remembering, reminding, understanding, helping, see-ing, concentrating on my breath, breathing into my belly, waiting, and then, we should, what if, can I, and then, waiting, and finally, at a hard wooden table, in a room with all walls and no windows, one morning, one afternoon, one day, two weeks into the 2009-2010 school year, Thaddeus is offered an appropriate school placement, and appropriate related services in Speech, Occupational Therapy, Audiology, Counseling, and Extended School Year effective immediately. I sign on the dotted line.

Sometimes I am aware that my odd existence is an odd existence, and some-times I don't even know the difference.

CHAPTER 6

Zen on the 210

THAD TELLS ME that my uvula looks like a penis. We had been working on a Lego alien abduction set, and the spaceship beams a cool, eerie red light. We look in each other's mouth with the light, as I say thank you to him because I believe that this assertion was delivered as a compliment because it is boy-related. At our house, Thad openly disses girls, girly things, and actively hates the colors red and pink, girl colors. He likes boys and not girls, likes this and not that. Rigid, and very black and white in his thinking. Yes or no, up or down, black or white, never grey. I am a boy and I like boys and hanging around with boys and doing boy stuff, therefore I do not like girls. The color grey of nuances, social inferences, nonverbal gestures, and body movements are lost to him. There are multiple meanings happening in conversations around him. And still, the only perspective he manages to see is his.

In the fall of 2009, we secure a Second Grade placement at a Non-Public School (NPS) that focuses on intensive intervention for children with Autism, specifically with speech and language disorders. A "Non-Public school" is not a private or a public school. It is a school that specializes in intensive intervention in a specific area, and it is a public entity. The school, Speech and Language Development Center (SLDC), follows a "Reverse Inclusion" model, which means that he will be educated in a classroom taught by a Special Education teacher with neurotypical (*sans Autisme*) kids in the class.

"Reverse Inclusion" is unique to this school, and is the opposite of Inclusion, the practice of adding Special Ed kids into a General Education classroom. Classroom Inclusion is great in theory because the kids with Autism get to interact with neurotypical (*sin Autismo*) peer models in a neurotypical (**Без аутизма**) classroom situation. Often, inclusion happens for most Special Ed students in public school environments in nonacademic enrichment classes like music, art, physical education, and assemblies. Unfortunately, inclusion happens with varying levels of success, can look so different in multiple environments, must be managed and modified actively and constantly for successful outcomes, and has varying levels of expertise driving the subjective bus of appropriate.

At SLDC, all the related services are provided on one campus. He will be educated where he receives therapy, many of the kids in his class will be familiar peers in therapy sessions, all of his teachers and therapists will co-treat, and talk to one another about Thaddeus in real-time. Thaddeus will become a part of a classroom for the first time, and he will be a member of the campus community as a whole. People will greet him when he walks by, because they know him and they like him.

In his new classroom, there is a small staff-to-student ratio of 1:3, so he can receive the intensive academic remediation that he needs. The OT comes into the class to work on handwriting and fine motor skills, and then whisks various kids to the OT clinic on campus for deep sensory work in the ball pit, a swimming pool for fingers of dried beans, the zip-line, the towers, heavy foam blocks and barrels, as the children negotiate through obstacle courses of blocks swings nets and slides. The school is knee-deep in Speech Therapists, Audiology and Counseling services, Adaptive Physical Education, the classroom has an FM system (a type of classroom PA system that amplified sound) to support attending behavior, there are neurotypical (*nicht Autismus*) kids in his class all-day long to model appropriate behavior, and all of these specialized services are coordinated and provided on one campus. Did I die and go to heaven? Nope, I hit the freeway in rush hour each day, and happily and joyfully drive to Buena Park.

SLDC has a unique model of teaching that presumes the child is intelligent, interesting, has unique ideas, and the teachers are charged to compliment their unique needs with individualized instruction. But, the campus vibe itself there is different too, unlike any other feelings I recognize previously. When I walked on campus, I knew that this school was for my son because the energy in the air was deliciously unique, and there was an encompassing sense of calm, like a continuous virtual reassuring hug confirming that everything will ultimately be okay. Rob felt it too, and he wanted to know if there were tertiary crossing underground rivers, any spaceship landings, or unexplained vortexes that had occurred there recently, to explain the unique energy of the school. We walked onto campus, and we all knew that this school was his next step.

Thaddeus exhaled, relaxed his shoulders slightly, stood in line with the children, walked into the class, and told me that, "that boy," his future Teacher Jeff, seemed cool and that he would be open to spending his days at SLDC. Thad and I began to drive there every day, five days per week, 66 miles one-way, and I quickly realized that even though it is far from my house, I was actually driving less because before I was driving all over creation for individual services before, and now I was experiencing a coordination of care, a vibe of calm, a connectedness to a community of like-minded people, expertise in his school environment, and a so strong desire for engagement from Thad. And then, I exhaled too.

I began to experience the IEP concept of "Parent Participation" in action at SLDC. "Parent Participation" is the parent's right to meaningful engagement in a child's educational plan, something I had only dreamt of prior. When I was asked what I thought about his IEP goals and if I had any input, at first I thought the Vice Principal was kidding. My only prior experience with getting my parent opinions, concerns, or even potentially good ideas heard regarding my son and his program usually involved resistance from those mandated to pay, as I would sit flanked by my lawyer, my husband, and a series of outside providers who worked with and knew Thad, and who would support what I had to say, helping me to help those I speak to understand my words about my son.

Thad successfully settles in to become a true member of a classroom, Room 905, a blended Second/Third/Fourth Grade classroom with Teacher Jeff, and the magic of learning begins. Thad begins to do some serious work with some amazing results, and he starts his first experience of being successful in a classroom environment.

Teacher Jeff figures out that a usual behavior management protocol of reducing recess minutes, or taking special things away in class for dispreferred Thad-behavior will not work with Thaddeus. My boy's staunch ability to say no, deeply mean it, and not really care about what he was offered or deprived was attempted previously and ended in classroom failures. And his new teacher understands that he must be a friend first to Thad for behavioral compliance, meaning that Thad would take direction from Jeff and "do stuff," like actual academic work, because he liked his teacher as a friend, not as a rule-enforcer. Taking away minutes of Thad's recess because he was noncompliant, him sitting by the sidelines, removed from the social interaction was his previous game-plan, and was exactly what Thad wanted to do during recess, not participate.

The Teachers and Aides actively engage in supporting Thad and others who were challenged by recess, a period of the school day recognized as difficult to many kids with Autism because of the vastness of unstructured time, the confusion of unclear objectives, and the fact that it was very difficult to keep him in continuous engagement with others on the playground. A free-for-all-recess plan doesn't work for Thad because he tends to get overwhelmed on a playground and shut-down emotionally. Many of my trusted providers tell me that taking away minutes of potential social time it is not an effective way to appropriately support Autism kids on the playground, and that taking recess minutes as negative reinforcement is the sign of a bad teacher, non-flexible thinking, and it is a non-creative, dispreferred teaching model.

I watch my boy work on spelling a series of words correctly with Jeff as he bounces on the trampoline one day. I see Thad attempt to cloud the learning environment with *non sequiturs*, questions leading to nowhere, wiley avoidant behavior, as Jeff pushes these behaviors out of the way, his keen focus on Thad's comprehension and engagement. Jeff is like a lighthouse guiding the boy through a fog, a mental mist that the Autism was pumping into his head. No Thad, he says. We are going to show your mom that you know how to spell these words, and then you may go play on the swings. Jeff exemplifies the idea of, Be the friend first, Develop mutual respect, and Show the child that you generally care about him as a nudge toward behavioral and academic compliance.

Jeff shows Thad and me that Thad can successfully learn difficult words, and retain them in his memory with focus and practice. Jeff does not believe Thad when he tries to divert his teacher's attention away from the task, or claims it's too hard. Jeff also demonstrates the important concept, Do not reward a lack of bad behavior, as in you will get time in the classroom store for not engaging in autistic behavior. Jeff expects good behavior from students as a baseline, a normal, an expectation, and then rewards and praises kids who are on task, respectful, and have good behavior. I internalize this idea, and work on practicing this at home.

A few other grateful mamas and I create a club we call "Teacher Jeff Room Moms for Life," Elizabeth, Sonia, and me, so grateful, so amazed that this type of excellence in teaching does exist. Teacher Jeff, we are with you forever, call on us whenever, and we are always there with you in gratitude, so much gratitude.

In the wild world of Thad, the ultimate compliment is if Thad draws you, and the staff at SLDC is constantly being sketched as we continue to work diligently toward engaging my boy. Teacher Jeff and Horacio, a classroom Aide, decide to get into Thad's psyche by making silly jokes about his name, as Thad particularly likes to get pretend-enraged as a form of engagement with others. He became "Thad-i-mus," from Horacio, as a goof on the word "Thaddeus" to instigate a minor brawl that would in turn make him pay attention through anger and irritation, and Jeff would always refer to him as, "Thad Stauder, rhymes with chowder." Thad was pretend-furious, and fully emotionally engaged when they would call him these names. And, of course, evil mom that I was, I was in on the deception. He would tell me, Mom I don't like it, I don't like when Jeff and Horacio make jokes about my name. I would say, fine, make a joke of their names to joke at them back. Playful joking, a form of emotional engagement.

Thad sat at the kitchen table extremely focused that evening, on his task of rescuing his name from the torture his teachers inflicted on him when he was in his head, spacey, and not following the lessons. He drew a ban sign over himself swimming in a bowl of fish-infused soup, no more Thad Chowder, he exclaimed. On the second page, he drew a depiction of his teacher as a small yellow fruit and titled it, Jeff Lemons, a play on his teacher's last name, and Horacio became "Ha-mushio," a mushroom with a face. He presented these drawings proudly to his teachers, he promised to work on paying attention, his teachers no longer made jokes about his name, and he began drawing so many representations of field trips and special moments he felt and experienced in his classroom.

Teacher Horacio got Thad to play with him by engaging him in some rough physical play that looked odd from afar, a small boy literally climbing all over a teacher on the playground, and often other teachers and aides would interpret Thad and Horacio's grandiose physical interaction from afar as an "autistic meltdown" and regularly ask if Horacio needed assistance with this perceived to be out-of-control child. Horacio was accessing Thad emotionally with "trash-talk" and fake fights, starting the communication and relationship from a place of Thad's interest and tolerance, starting from where Thad is. Horacio and Thad modified "Chase," Thad's favorite playground game, as Horacio chased Thad to engage him and then he would pretend to steal his nose and run away because missing body parts was not something that Thad was about to tolerate so he would take off running after Horacio to get his nose back, demanding that H screw it back on.

Teach it, teach it, practice it, practice it, repeat, repeat, check comprehension, we work, we remember, we remind, just like when Horacio and Thad spent multiple days dissecting why it is not appropriate to wolf-whistle at a lady, although Thad saw it in a Tom and Jerry cartoon and understood the cartoon notion that if you see a pretty girl, a boy must whistle his approval. Black and white, yes or no, on or off, up or down, as concrete as the staircase we climb each day.

Over the years, the classroom is populated by fantabulous important support staff like Bobby, Cynthia, Katrina, Lynne, Yaneth, Renee, and Karina, who all give Thad the friendship, the reinforcement, the academic assistance, and the overt social direction he needs, and they deliver these lessons in a way that make him feel smart, cool, and capable.

Thad is so lucky at SLDC to have so many awesome people getting into his business, and Thad's team of service providers are drawn and redrawn in particular scenarios depending on where they fit into Thad's pantheon. It is so interesting to watch how he connects and interacts with each one of them. Dr. Jerry, the OT, is a super hero in a cape very often, and Sara and Karen, Speech Pathologists are the bad guys, who, according to him, terminally "bug him" about "whole-body-listening," and are always asking him to "do stuff," like pay attention, or work on the task at hand. Trish, his other Speech Pathologist, is a best friend, who like Teacher Jeff, Susan, and Dr. Jerry, all primary "good guys" in Thad's school-life cartoon, could do no wrong. Sara, Karen, Mary, and Horacio, all playing active "bad guy" roles, as each role that Thad gave to each "character" in his "story," acknowledged his recognition of that particular person in a particular way, and their relationship to him.

Thad only acknowledges people he cares about that he has some emotional stake in, a hopeful advance from not being able to emotionally engage with anyone at all at the commencement of his years of intensive therapy until now when he now has a series of people in his emotional storyboard. Simply put, according to Thad, you are a "bad guy" or a "good guy," yes or no, black or white, concrete thinking at its finest, as both are the highest of compliments in Thad's mind. Bad guys are just as cool as good guys, according to Thad. I find that notion to be legit logic, as bad guys have always been preferred in my house by both of my children.

Trish works with Thad on words, such as bat, break, and sample, that have multiple meanings and can mean multiple things in multiple contexts. She wears a particular pair of black high-heeled shoes to work that Thad find to be irresistible, and I request that she always wear them on Monday and Wednesday for behavioral compliance with Thad. For some reason, he is enamored by the shoes, and Trish and him get so much accomplished when he wears them, so she does. We figure that he is putty in her hands wearing the soles that get at his soul, and I request that she never get rid of those shoes that Thad likes to draw and to discuss. There is a drawing on the wall in her office of the beautiful perseveration of her shoes advertising a social skills workshop.

Thad has drawn a series of his therapists and teachers who will present, all with non-descript, rounded cartoony shoes, and then there is Trish, who has a pair of elaborate foot coverings in the picture. Her shoes are a periscope, a ladder, a crutch, a support, a rope ladder into his mind. And Thad is able to get real with Trish, as they are friends who hang and play on the playground equipment to connect, as Trish delivers powerful doses of speech therapy amid the play, not allowing Thad to disengage as he goes up and down the slide, back and forth on the swings, and around and around on the equipment, a level of care unique to our school that engages my child so successfully. In addition, Trish takes no BS from him, a no-nonsense relationship, and Thad respect the hell out of her. Thad complies with his teacher who is also his friend, as I envision positive movements toward inner calm.

Trish and Thad work on him paying attention in spite of the fact that sometimes he doesn't understand the words that people are saying to him, developing an awareness that he needs to comprehend what the message is before he does anything else. Previously, he did not care if he understood what people said to him, and this challenge was amplified with his expressive-receptive language comprehension disorder. Basically, didn't get it, didn't care. Trish set out to change this breakdown, and she teaches him strategies for communication repair. For example, they worked on "verbal obstruction," to get him to care that he did not understand what someone said, as Trish would ask questions with a covered mouth, or use unknown vocabulary, or words that did not make sense.

They also worked on managing, understanding and responding appropriately to "impossible" requests (Please count all the clouds in the sky), unreasonable directions (Touch the moon with your fingers), and how to respond to distorted information, vague information (How many are there, without a direct referent to the question), unfamiliar information requests (what does "adjacent" mean?), They looked at how to manage and respond to information requests that are too lengthy (Tell me this and that and this and that), and unreasonable requests for unknown information (How many words are in the dictionary?), as Thad begins to care about the fact that he doesn't comprehend many of life's messages, verbal and otherwise, as he and Trish work to help him move forward in various ways of communication repair, strategies for when you know you didn't understand the message and you seek to.

Trish tells me about a fight they had one morning, as they tend to regularly bicker and banter a bit like old friends. The sentence card reads, Vegetables come from a store, true or false. Thad says, false. Trish responds, true. Thad is adamant that his food does not come from a store. This assertion is true because the vegetables we eat comes from a farmer's market, from the weekly vegetable box, or directly from the garden itself. At the store, we buy dried pasta, toilet paper, and clothing. But, not vegetables, this notion perhaps derived from my maternal indoctrination of the importance of local, organic, and seasonal. Or perhaps because his prior experiences and perspectives remind him that Monday is CSA day (Community Supported Agriculture, the weekly vegetable box), and that we frequent Farmer's Markets as the larder runs low. They discuss, they each tell opinions, and although Thad understands that others may buy veg at the store, he doesn't. Therefore, he is correct that vegetables come from the garden, not the store. Trish tells me, I laugh, and I feel strangely comfortable with my son's behavioral defiance regarding his unwavering beliefs of the origins of his dinner.

SLDC is a unique program because it is the only non-public school I know of with a wine cellar. And the staff and parents have excellent taste in wine, and oh so many corks. One of our brilliant Autism moms noticed that the repetition and precision of lining up and gluing wine corks on boards was mentally organizing, engaging, and soothing to our kids in its need for exactness with the rectangular pieces twinged in varying degrees of pink and purple grape. The children then draw pictures that are framed with the cork art, and the masterpieces are used for school artwork and gifts, and fundraising purposes.

Thad's art decorates the walls of his therapists' offices in colored paper and thumbtacks, and brightly-colored representations of his understanding of social skills are framed in cork and hanging in the speech building halls. Drawing, always been part of a home curriculum, begins to happily spill over into school, and continues to satisfy so many aspects of communication for him and with him that we crave in our home and in our family, but lack due to Autism.

In the Speech building, across from Trish's office is Sara's office. Sara is Thad's other SLP, Speech Language Pathologist, at SLDC. Sara is one of the mischievous bad guys in the wild, cartoon world-according-to-Thad. They develop an elaborate ongoing joke in which Sara waggles her finger at Thad in a pretend-disapproving way, Thad gets so lip-licking hungry, bites off her finger, swallows the digit, and then eventually Thad returns her finger to her by screwing it back on, barfing it up, or pretend-punching himself in the stomach as the finger flies right back to Sara's outstretched hand for safe keeping until the next faux brawl. Sara informs me that sometimes she will be walking the campus with outside professionals, see Thad, need to stop and engage in some finger-munching behavior, as the wide-eyed adults look on. Just engaging my people, says Sara knowingly, smiling as she and Thad bid farewell until the next battle.

Sara is a walking lesson in social skills and friendship to children whom others less awesome and less skilled might have labeled "unteachable and unreachable," a particularly lame phrase bestowed on my boy early on. As children all over the campus flock to her, high-five her, sign "hello" with their hands, she tells me that all behavior, all attempts, all expressions, nuances, fists flying and sloppy cheek kisses are forms of, and attempts at communication. She explains to the kids, and models Social Skills Expert, Michelle Garcia Winners,' "Expected versus Unexpected Behavior," as an overt teaching tool of explaining the norms of social behavior, and how others might be confused, alarmed, or worried if someone demonstrates unexpected behavior because it is out of what we perceive as normal in society.

Thad has IEP goals associated with the volume and prosody of his voice, and Sara works his whisper voice into a more amplified state, saying to him, if I cannot hear, it doesn't count, and you must repeat the answer. He is taken to task on his voice volume, the melody (prosody) of the words, and the difference between a "talking voice" and a "fighting voice" which seem to still be one in the same for Thad. Sara reminds Thad that there must be a beginning, a middle, and an end to a story or a conversation, and shows him strategies to use in case he is not sure or at a loss for what is next, and how to get the social interaction back on track. And then, he rubs his hands menacingly at Sara with full eye-contact, salts her finger, and takes a bite to both of their joy and anger, ah engagement with a friend.

She teaches the "communication tap" as a way for children to appropriately and respectfully engage others, and she teaches the children to be a "social detectives," by looking and learning about nonverbal gestures and body language as clues for what a person is trying to tell us without words. My son adores Sara, and draws endless pictures of his favorite bad guy, the highest compliment from Thad.

One day, Trish and I go into Sara's office with Thad to deliver a bag of oranges from our local grove. Because every moment is a teachable moment and because it was necessary to leave a note, Trish asked Thad to write a message to Sara on her whiteboard so she would know who was leaving her citrus gifts. He thought for so long and came up with the following:

"To Care, I put oranges on your desk. I hope you like them. Love, Thad"

The exciting thing about this important sentence written by Thad in orange marker on Sara's board one day in January is that I felt that he has captured the philosophy of SLDC, a true mecca of language, social skills, love, and deep respect to our children, in one concise sentence. First, we see that he spelled "Sara" phonetically, meaning he sounded out her name and came up with "Care," which is also "Sara" written phonetically. He was learning how to communicate orthographically which he has been working on for many worksheets, he knew the phonological symbols that pressed the sounds S-AIR-UH out into word form. "Sara" and "Care" can be pronounced the same. We could not acknowledge to him that it was spelled wrong because then he would continue to spell it wrong out of blatant defiance, a symptom of Autism, which was understood and accepted by his mom and his Speech Therapists, as we pressed on in his learning.

So, we ignored the misspelling of her name temporarily, and felt excited that he had written a sentence that demonstrated social awareness, and acknowledgement toward to others' feelings, as he writes, I hope that you like them, written to her about the oranges, demonstrating emotion and care. Trish had to prompt him to add his name because he did not realize she wouldn't know because he had just written the message to her.

Thad enjoys drawing ban signs, no smoking, no shoes no shirt no service, no llamas from a particular movie he likes, and other things that are dispreferred or illegal on signs. He begins to draw ban signs in the margins of his pictures, like an autistic protest on paper. For example, I tell him during drawing to un-capitalize the "B" mid-sentence. He says no, does it anyway, and adds a small ban sign on the side with a banned small "b," demonstrating his defiance toward my dislike of his enjoyment of unnecessary capitalization. Small ban signs decorate his art to Sara, circular indirect compliments toward his very special friend-slash-bad-guy.

Sara tells me a funny story about working with Thad on a game of "Emotions" telephone in a social skills group one day. The line-leader looks at Sara's face as she demonstrates the targeted emotion, and then the children are to pass that emotion, that face, down the line. Sara begins with "surprised," it moves down the line of 8 children, and it ends with a "mad" face. Sara is confused at the end result of this pass, and begins again with a "sad" face, and again it travels the line, with the last child demonstrating "mad" once again. Sara is perplexed, where is the breakdown, she wonders. She begins with another emotion, and watches each child. Thad is mid-train, and changes the "surprised" look to "mad," as Sara realizes that Thad was the one changing the look the prior times. Not because he was being defiant, but because he did not recognize the other emotions that were being demonstrated in facial expressions and his repertoire of nonverbal emotional expressions was impaired, and Sara realized this to be an area that they would learn together.

Thad was so lucky to have yet another bad-guy in the Speech Department at school named Karen, and he was so happy that he was taller than her, reminding her I'm-taller-than-you daily. Karen is part of one of Thad's weekly social skills groups, and he loves to be particularly enraged at her and blame her for many things. Once he drew a series of pictures of how he had envisioned himself so very wronged by Sara and Karen, as they secretly shrunk themselves and stowed away in his backpack to come to his house to bug him further about "Whole Body Listening," an attention strategy that gives each part of the body a job to do when paying active attention to the conversation. Thad was constantly reminded about making his body look like it was paying attention to the speaker, and this repetition obviously bugged the shit out of him. Hilariously, he drew himself, innocently opening his backpack, looking down, first aghast, and then super-furious, to miniature versions of his therapists yammering on from inside a dark backpack about engaged body parts and bright, focused eyes. In the culminating event of the story, he plucks them from the backpack, and puts them inside a little door he has drawn. I won, he says in a talk bubble with an elaborately drawn smug grin, I showed them not to bug me about Whole Body Listening anymore.

Another drawing series that was quite humorous depicts a summer event that he recounted in drawn form with Thad, in a bathing suit, engaging in water-play, one summer afternoon on the playground, and somehow Thad got it in his mind that it was time to go to Speech. He left the sprinklers water balloons and squishy wet balls, and ran to the Speech building, no towel, no shirt, dripping wet, in a bathing suit. When he loudly and wetly arrived in the building, he exclaimed, I'm here to see Trish, and Karen requested that he dress and dry off first. How dare Karen interrupt, as he angered and pleaded. All I want to do is see Trish, he shrieked, benign and fully innocence in his intentions and sure of

Karen's unruly plans for him. Karen exited the soggy urchin from the building, and he went home that night to recreate his impression of the wronged event on paper. He drew an innocent boy, Thad, walking, only wanting to see his friend, Trish, and Karen, peering evilly out of the window, waiting to bust him. Him, red-cheeked, flustered, with heavy red circle of embarrassment and anger on his cheeks, and Karen being the biggest, meanest meanie in the world for asking him to get dressed and dry off. Be a bad-guy, be a friend, as all the players in Thad's world have a defined role. Pretty girls, bad-guys, can-do-no-wrong-friends, and then there are those who are not considered, indifferent, don't matter to him and he overtly makes it clear where everyone falls in his model.

Dr. Jerry is Thad's ultimate superhero therapist who engages Thad through obstacle courses in the OT gym, card games with friends that include specific instruction on how to chit-chat with a friend. He asks Thad to work on unexpected, unfamiliar touch by using bumper cars that challenge him because other children in the soft, round amoebas on wheels are unpredictable, playing scooterboard hockey, making up and doing obstacle courses, working through physical mazes in the gym individually and with a friend, and working so hard on strategies he could use if someone or something touched him unexpectedly. In his past, Thad would feel upset when others would bump into him at school accidentally, or do something physically in his vicinity that he was not visually prepping or emotionally planning for. Dr. Jerry worked with Thad to desensitize this hyper-arousal to unplanned-on stimulus. Thad feels very protective of Dr. Jerry, and feels very worried one bummer day when the OT gym floods from faulty pipes. Thad draws the gym underwater, complete with some fish sharks and turtles in the ball pits, and squid on the slides. Thad is wearing a superhero cape, flies in, saves Jerry, and Jerry is sooooo grateful to Thad.

Thad would fly through the air from rope-swings that landed him in piles of cushions, pillows, and foam blocks in the OT gym in order to regulate for reading class, he would ride bumper cars in the walkways, play scooter board hockey with his classmates, and work toward appropriate maneuvering through social situations found when engaging in playing a game, such as winning, losing, accidental touch, sharing, smiling, agreeing, remembering, and planning. Indifferent hand dominance for many of his tasks and being ambidextrous were challenges, as we continue to favor the left side for all tasks because that was the hand he ate and wrote with, Jerry explaining to me the importance of hand dominance. They would play card games as a way of practicing hanging out and social conversations, he would have to negotiate how many barrels to fly over, which kind of swing, and would they slide or climb the rock wall first. All discussions, all words, eye contact, body language, social skills-laden events in the sensory gym that pushed and pulled Thad's muscles, some out of dormancy, and some into compliance.

Dr. Jerry's voice was terminally set to the dial "soothe," and I always felt immediately calm, so confident in his vast expertise, experience, and I would stand in awe as he directed Thad to do physical tasks in the social skills group, individual therapy, and in the OT gym that I had never seen him do, such as elaborate jumps, dives, and bounces through nets, cylinders and rope-swings. He provided so much good direct parent training to me also, as a Neuropsychologist and an Occupational Therapist, he could explain Thad's developmental breakdowns, recommend solutions, and help me problem solve thru his challenges with planning, new idea creation, and ideation.

Susan is the fabulous counselor that supports Thad's participation in Cool Kids Club each week. The group overtly work on social skills incorporating metaphors, movement breathing and relaxation into the social experience, in a crazy-cool, relaxed environment run by a *simpatica chica*. She is a friend to Thad who speaks to him through visceral awareness of language, as she would challenge the children use various methods of expressions of feelings, pushes in self-esteem, and talking openly about conversation, social challenges, being a friend, giving a gift, delivering a compliment, receiving a criticism, with grace, courtesy, and emotional calm.

I'm not doing it, his response to all things, so staunch in his conviction of previous noncompliance with crossed-arms and a downward gaze, morphs into a vocalization now that he's not doing it, while he does it. Compliance at school begins to happen, as various teachers and therapists figure out ways into Thad's world.

Dr. Mary, the super Audiologist, would sabotage the FM system on purpose, or purposefully forget to put in batteries, and it was Thad's job was to report that his system wasn't working. The idea was that he had to notice that he wasn't getting the information, and he had to care to advocate toward the repair of the broken system. We were constantly trying to figure out why he was not paying attention. Was it because he could not hear, was not paying attention, was choosing to not pay attention, or had fluid build-up in his ears, or some other reason we had yet to consider or discover? Environmental, Autism or physical symptoms, the constant conundrum of why his attention waxed and wanes daily. Dr. Mary would give him regular tympanograms to see if there was fluid in his ears that may or may not lead to an ear infection, and that may or may not be a contributor to his lack of attention. Perhaps he was not attending because he could not hear due to fluid, perhaps he could not hear because the FM trainer needed new batteries, perhaps, perhaps, as we focused on him understanding that he needed to do something about it if he did not comprehend the words.

His related services and classroom experiences melt together in a delicious educational experience, like bright yellow grass-fed butter on warm sourdough toast. Like salted caramel, as the opposing flavors that, at first blush, might seem counterproductive. Ideas like "You must feel the words to own the words" flutter through my mind as I see him taking social risks, and trying to begin to try to begin to try to begin to try to engage with classmates.

He draws pictures of wine for the school fundraisers and golf event flyers. He typically doesn't draw the hues, nuances, or variations of color in his pictures, but interestingly in drawings of wine, he does. He practices drawing my hand on a wine glass, a corkscrew, a bottle, and each time he fashions a glass of Merlot, Syrah or Cab, there are the pinks, reds and purples that he sees glinting in the glass. It is a unique circumstance because usually he only draws in new ways that he is explicitly taught, no one taught him the subtleties of the colors of a glass of red wine, and he does it every time he draws wine. Perhaps a foreshadowing of his hopeful future as an artist or a grape farmer.

The Principal of the School, Dawn, remarks to me one day, oh Thad tied me up on the playground today. I am horrified, mortified, and begin an apologize-a-thon. No no, it's great Kristin. He was "battling" Horacio (a.k.a. interacting and socializing a la Thad), and it looked like he was having aggressive behavior. I came over to find out what was going on, and Thad pretend-tied me up to the swingset. He was focused and engaged and using a bunch of language. It is so important that people not only understand that he wants to communicate, but that they understand the way that Thad communicates. Such a good day at school for him, she tells me. Amazed at how lucky my child was to be in the presence of Special Education greatness each academic day, I thank every deity I can muster and think, we need more Administrators like her in Autism Nation.

Thad has a long list accommodations and modifications in the classroom that make it easier for him to access the curriculum. In an IEP, an "accommodation" is loosely defined as a physical or environmental change, such as extended time on test. And he also has "modifications," a change in the expectation of the task, such as simplifying materials. I read online that, "*accommodations* level the playing field while *modifications* change the field you are playing on." For example, in math homework, an accommodation might be that the child gets to use a calculator to do the work, and a modification might be that he only has to do the odd numbered problems when the rest of the class was assigned the entire page.

During large group instruction, he wears a personal FM trainer in his left ear to amplify the voice of the speaker, usually Teacher Jeff, who wears a microphone clipped to his collar rockstar-style. The FM trainer supports Thad's challenges with attention and focus by decreasing ambient background noise and increasing the speaker's voice, known as working in figure-ground. In addition, there is a classroom-wide sound-field FM system that broadcasts the teacher's voice over a classroom PA system. This is helpful because voices of instruction are louder, and quite necessary when the teacher writes on the board and children cannot see his mouth as he speaks.

Thad uses a sit disk, a round plastic pillow with nubs, to help deliver sensory input to him when he sits without a need for him to fidget, twirl, or flap his arms, his pencil, or his legs. He takes a sensory break as needed because he has access to swings immediately outside the classroom. He continues to eat a particular home-cooked diet to support him, and I leave gluten-free brownies in the freezer. He is still working on knowing to say, "No thanks" to gluten-filled stuff, and when birthday cakes arrive for classmates he is able to still participate in the fun, and eat food at a social event.

For most kids, recess is the best part of school, and recess is extremely difficult for Thad. Most kids think, recess is cool because I can do whatever I want. Yet, for Thad, he did not know exactly what he wanted to do and chunks of unstructured time for him are daunting, and left unsupported, he will choose to be alone and walk the perimeter of the playground. Happily, at SLDC, recess is not break-time for the teachers and aides, an unfortunate scenario that seems to be common in public school. Lunch and recess are times that my son needs significant adult support to access peers and practice social goals.

His teacher would frontload plans with Thad for recess, and provide varying levels of support depending on the day. Thad could pick three ideas from an array of possible playground scenarios, chose a friend and make a plan before recess, he could join an organized sports activity, he could practice getting a hit or goal or a point and the feelings of any associated emotion that comes with it, and sometimes he would work with a teacher or aide to review the rules of the game and the social expectations.

"Find a friend" became the daily mantra for Thad's recess time. If you don't, I will find one for you, Teacher Jeff would inform Thad each day at noon. They worked on choosing appropriate playground activity, compliance toward game rules and adult expectations, took baselines on how many conversational turns he could engage in with a peer, discussed how it feels to win or lose a game, how it feels to be picked for teams, how it feels to be on a team, how to shout encouragement to friends, and to be consoling if others didn't win or make the basket or were tagged out. Every day, all day, little bits of social communication in real-time with a jumprope, a soccer ball, a friend, and a smile.

Thad participates weekly in two social skills groups at SLDC, Cool Kids Club and Afterschool Club, both with the focus of how to be a social person in the world, as each group reinforces a series of particular highlights in aspects of unique communication, sensory, and emotional issues. Cool Kids Club, run by the Speech and Counseling Departments, focuses on emotions and feelings, self-esteem, being a friend, having a conversation, "I feel" statements, and affect regulation. Afterschool Club, run by the Speech and Occupational Therapy Departments, focuses on social communication interactions, functional skills, proximity, the mechanics of conversation and communication, problem solving, whole-body listening, and walking on the tightrope to understand levels and subtleties of language.

And, of course, there were so many hilarious occurrences in each of the groups as the children work on and work through issues. For example, during the Christmas holiday, Afterschool Club decided to have a party for fun, and to practice the skills of having a party, giving and receiving a gift, showing gratitude for a gift, saying thanks for gifts that maybe one might not necessarily like or want, and other aspects of holiday fun that can be challenging for people with impaired social skills. I learn about the party and I feel concerned about Thad eating too much sugar or some sneaky gluten, and I resolve to make all the food for the party. This is great for us because everyone will eat the same thing, and Thad's food allergies will not be an accented anomaly at the party. I make a shitload of GFCF diet-safe food, and display it pleasingly on the table. Thad has a wrapped gift within the parameters of the $10 maximum budget that is suitable for a boy or girl, and I am sure that this party will be a great social and learning experience. I am also sure that I have considered all wild cards as parties are usually a challenge for us, and I feel I have prepped the situation so thoroughly for success.

The therapists ask the children to describe the brightly wrapped boxes that they each want, and everyone begins to open their shiny treasures. To my dismay, my son gets a gingerbread house set, all brightly-colored, so full of sugar, gluten, and preservative toxins, and I realize that gluten can also assault our lives in the form of a Christmas gift. Fuck, I did not consider that. He looks at me sideways as if to say, haha, I got this big no-no for Christmas at school, and since he got it at school as a Christmas present, that must override mean Mom's low-to-no-sugar and no-gluten rule. I see his eyes glimmer with the possibility of inhaling that large palace of sugar and preservatives, as I concurrently see sugar-plum nightmares and holiday bellyaches in our near future. A large tantrum ensues, and continues to churn at a healthy clip during our multi-hour car commute. Hours later, at home, he's still angry at me for taking the gingerbread house away because moms don't take boys' Christmas presents away, and eventually I trade him the toxic house for a new Lego set.

The next year at Christmas time, I ask the therapists for a "no-food-in-gifts" policy to remediate last year's experience, and everyone agrees. Again, I feel like I have mastered this Christmas party business. No chinks in the armor here, and again, I happily make a pile of food for everyone at the party that is safe for Thad to eat. He has his wrapped, unisex-appropriate, non-food present to share, and we are set. I am sure that I am invincible because I am confident that I have considered all the variables for his success at this party. He opens his metallic-green present with a red bow, and my eyes of horror view a big shiny game of Buzz Lightyear checkers. Again, we begin the conversation of how he cannot have it because it is Toy Story, which makes him mentally stuck, and his pleading words of justice that he gets to keep the allergen because he got it for a present escalate.

Again, the therapists and I try to impart the subtleties and nuances of why he cannot have the present, and I prep for the brouhaha ride home in the car, an imbroglio of misunderstood words and social communication with a solitary, continuous volley of "You took my stuff. Give it back." and "Why can't I have it? It's mine," bouncing around in my rush-hour-traffic impaired car. I think about how "Thoughts become things," as the way he manifests his allergens towards him, and I learn to be a little more flexible with myself and I do not own this experience as my failure. I chalk it up to merely another learning experience for she who is called Mom. As we drive and drive and drive.

The cellphone structures on California highways are cell towers trying to disguise themselves as landscape features, a nice, but don't-look-twice-as-you-speed-by entity. Although, if you do happen to look, what you see are gawky metal junipers, or a lanky palm with oxidized leaves reflecting the sun from a shiny silvery trunk. As I speed by for endless days, I think about these towers as a metaphor of blatantly hiding the Autism epidemic out in public. Hide the problem, hide the kids, and considering all the while the truth that we must put them somewhere. They've always been around, we just never noticed before, they say trying to assure the masses. Out in the open to desensitize the magnitude, maybe disguise the appearance, fudge the numbers, maybe change the criteria of what it means to be a palm tree on I-210 freeway in Rancho Cucamonga. Perhaps we don't talk about it, and just let them watch us from the side of the road as we drive past them in our normal lives. Perhaps because metal trees have no words, their silence is acceptable, even welcome. Maybe no one will notice. Well, some of us do. Especially when the awkward juniper is our child.

Sometimes the freeway is clear and we get there quick, and sometimes cars don't move or overheat, sometimes we hear about a wreck a few miles up or a pileup on a parallel freeways that has rerouted traffic right into our path. Vehicles sitting motionless for miles and miles, for hours and hours and hours. Imagine a neuropathway inflamed from Thimerasol, and a spelling word sitting in that mental traffic for infinity. Perhaps the car has a flat tire, busted drivetrain, crankshaft, steering column, or perhaps the car runs out of gas. Have you ever seen a couch in the middle of the freeway, or a cardboard box, or a flowing piece of saran wrap or old carpet? Imagine one traveler moving without obstruction, and now envision the biggest wreck you have ever seen or hopefully not, experienced. Do we all get there at the same time? Do some of us never even make it?

Imagine this traveler as an emotion, a thought, a unique idea, an interjection, an inference, or a consideration on the topic being currently discussed. Now, imagine our babies' brains. Is there a freeway delay so significant in their brains that even those who get out to walk never make it because the distance is too far, and the warps and whispers of Autism derail and displace normal movement and development like the troll under the bridge dislodging safe passage, brick by brick? Does anyone help the stranded traveler, or do we look the other way still focused on our own ultimate goal of getting there on time?

A wreck! Dare I venture another metaphoric moment among vaccine injury and our immune system, the ability to learn and relate to others flavored with Autism alongside a horrific accident produced by reckless driving and careless concern for other travelers who share our road. Wounded bodies and personal belongings smeared on an LA freeway, soaking in the guilty connections between the injuries and deaths of individuals and thoughtless, selfish driving. A backup for miles of the commuters who drive by and witness the bloodbath. I was late for work due to traffic, and I am calling into work dead due to a wreck. When does the information finally fucking arrive? Does it arrive ever? I cannot seem to remember my 3 times tables in math because I have an uncomfortable amount of mercury in my brain fucking shit up. Obviously, no connection.

I think about driving each day as my personal Zen practice, my place to find internal balance and calm as I watch my breathing, my posture, and my thoughts, relying on the masters, considering the journey, the moments, the realities, the secrets, the sacred texts that combine to make my existence, my reality, that swirl together to create my life. I convince myself that 66 miles one way is not far because it is so worth it. I often drive in silence for the multi-hour commute focusing on breath, watching my thoughts, and the way I manifest the future with conscious attention to my intentions and my words. In reality, sometimes, I speak to my friends and families in various time zones because our 7am rush hour commute works nicely with fast-forward East Coast coffee breaks, sometimes I listen to the news or to music, and I share so many in-between moments with others who have choppy life schedules like my own.

I engage in overt meditation while I drive and Thad sleeps on the way to school. I practice Zen on the 210, sitting *zazen* with my meditation cushion, a moving-car driver seat, with my focus on the alignment of my spine, and the distance between my black Prius and the white Jetta in front of me, the dusty landscape truck with the wonky wheel to my right, and where the next entrance to the carpool lane opens. I concentrate on my breathing, even, slow, complete, sweet deep-belly breaths to calm the internal frazzle that often spikes as I sit in silence for hours and hours of daily Orange County rush hour traffic with the crush of LA traffic spitting venom in my face and a terminal construction *klusterfuck* in the dusty expanses of the San Bernardino County freeways. I find connection in the dust, the construction, and the sense of loss and love on the freeway, as I traverse three counties every morning and afternoon, driving and searching, forever searching for my boy.

I have phone dates with friends during my drive time. My friend, Steve, is from Florida where the 10 Interstate snakes from my coast to his coast. I drive "the 10," unique California-specific vernacular for that particular freeway, in an I-drive-the-10-to-the-57-to-the-91-to-get-him-to-school-every-day way. He questions, Why you gotta call Interstate 10, the 10? He pokes fun at my California-cool-speak, as I did not say that when I lived in Ohio and now I do as a California resident. We pick up language by the osmosis of being around others, how the intensity and effortless beauty of so much language is imbued. In addition, he understands me when I refer to "the 10" because although he uses different words to describe that same expanse of concrete, his flexible mind understands and assimilates my words as they relate to his words. We also talk about the band named Phish, over my Bluetooth through the car speakers, and Thad believes we are terminally speaking about the fish in the ocean, chiming in accordingly on how he wants to see some fish too, perhaps at the aquarium this weekend.

Driving in the car solo with him is still a challenge as he battles with me about obscure topics, and threatens and accuses me of everything under the sun, found and unfound, during our commute of hours and hours. I realize that this is utter bullshit, and I begin to attempt behavioral control tactics while I drive. I also began to scripting the script in the car and at home, scripting Thad's endless movie reel script in order to make him stop, copying his mad face to show him what it looks like and how it feels to be scowled at. Get rid of it, he'd shriek, referring to my unkind grimace in his direction. Not until you do, I respond, not backing down to Autism. We battle out in mad faces, stink eyes, and engage in excessive pretend bomb-dropping in the front seats of my car. Joyfully, barreling down the freeway, rush-hour-style.

And then today, I am accosted by a few naysayers who seek to debate me without my permission about the vaccine-Autism connection. I fire out a few choice statistics and words regarding my reality, and their overt ignorance on a topic that they obviously know nothing about besides the media hype to CYA those who are hurting so many children to make a buck. I just wish that the amount of venom, the amount of energy, attached to this issue could be used in more positive ways, that people could harness that level of fear of the unknown to do something positive for the affected kids, and ultimately, take steps to assure that this health crisis and madness stops. We must focus on healing our sick children, we must delegate enough dollars and the expertise so desperately needed to improve our warped healthcare and education systems, we must clarify and modify the confusing and incorrect media representations of health and wellness, and we must gather up our damaged families in support, kindness, and assistance.

During morning social time at school, we begin to work on Thad telling the truth about what he reports happened at his house last night versus reporting what he wished had happened. Hey Kristin, I didn't know ski resorts are open in September in your local mountains, Jeff comments to me after school one day. Oh, they aren't. Why? Hmm, Thad reported to the class that he was skiing in Big Bear all weekend. No, that is probably what he wished. We cleaned the garage this weekend, and ate homemade spaghetti. From then on, Jeff would consistently check in with me regarding Thad's assertions of his happenings and whereabouts disclosed each morning during social time. Separating fantasy from reality is always a consideration when we receive and provide him information.

And because we tend to steep Pretend Peril into most things that happen with Thad to engage his interest and attention, sometimes he can appear to be fibbing while telling his perception of the truth. A subjective interpretation of what happened. For example, one blustery winter day, I found my voice on the Room 905 classroom speaker phone for clarification during classroom social time. Kristin, Jeff inquires, Thad is telling us that he ate "dinosaur skin" for dinner last night, and we wanted to check in. Well, I begin to explain, we roast organic kale under the broiler with coconut oil, chopped garlic, and sea salt. It tastes great and looks similar to dinosaur skin. And because Thad vocalizes with so much certainty that he doesn't eat vegetables, and because it might be cool, dangerous, and gross to eat dinosaur skin, the dish is named accordingly.

What grade is he in had always been a perplexing question to me, limiting almost, as I consider answering with a multi-pronged account of how many years he has been in the system, or how many actual years of elementary school he has sat through, or what level he is in reading or math, or maybe socially, or what his numeric grade versus age and why it doesn't exactly match and how he has academic and social goals that span many years of remediation and development as I look at him, sitting "like a friend" in the front row of Room 905, a placement where he is developmentally, academically, socially, and emotionally being stimulated, challenged, supported, remediated, and healed, and now, exhale, now he is officially in Second Grade in a real school, and he is truly part of a class.

We relax into his appropriate placement, and I spent long moments convincing myself that my 66-mile one way commute to his school that traverses three counties and crushing daily traffic was not far. I knew it was far because it is, but felt all right about traveling so far because I could see palpable progress in him daily. Breathing fully and deeply into his healing, his wellness. Each day after I drop him off, I go swim laps to strengthen my body, and do yoga to untangle my inner mental-parts. I feel calm that year, his Second Grade year, and I think about things that I can do to move forward in my personal healing because he is now appropriately supported.

I think about ways to heal my family as a whole because him finally getting into an appropriate school placement is a sigh of relief, and the program goes until Sixth Grade. We are working together with our School District, I think. They finally understand, and we can all be at peace because Thaddeus has won. He has found the place that will support his differences into wellness, his strength will be restored, and his lovelight and happiness will again permeate our world. We will smile toward each other about that time in the past when we had disagreements with our School District, but only because back then they did not understand, and now they do, and he is doing so well in his placement.

IEPs are annual events, and we return to the table with the School District at the end of his glorious Second Grade year. We are thrilled because Thaddeus makes notable progress in Second Grade for the first time in his academic life. He has an appropriate classroom placement with a teacher who understands his strengths and supports his differences, an appropriate amount of related services in Speech, Occupational Therapy, Audiology, and Extended School Year, and he is taught and cared for by doctors, teachers and therapists who understand how to turn Thad's wheels and keep his engine on track.

Based on his wonderful academic and emotional progress at SLDC that year, and the new layers of happiness we see playing with the corners of his mouth, we are shocked, saddened, and loudly disagree with the School District's shitty offer of FAPE for his Third Grade year to leave SLDC and return abruptly to a School District catch-all Special Day class with a smattering of services, their argument being that because he is making progress in his placement at SLDC, he should therefore leave. I cannot believe my ears as they offer up this large carafe of bullshit, asking us to hold our cups closer so they can fill them to the rim.

Knee-deep in Thaddeus' Third Grade year, one day all mistletoe and holly and Santa and reindeer, as lawyers send so many faxes back and forth and back and forth through a series of holiday seasons involving pumpkins and turkeys, we drop our children off at the airport to fly with my parents to their home in

Ohio for Christmas. The School District had filed Due Process against Thaddeus that fall, and Rob and I will stay in California a few more days to handle our legal tangle for appropriate services for Thad, and eventually we will join our family for holiday cheer. Rob and I were hoping to have time to process the situation, to breathe, to plan, to figure out, and to try to regain some emotional balance, perhaps even taste the unfamiliar flavor of calm on our tongues.

Travel in an airplane is a preferred activity to Thad. He likes to fly, and to go visit his relatives, but very often, his Autism blips him back into submission with perseverations on the plane, he can experience difficult behavioral challenges that feel enhanced for all onlookers on 6-hour flights cross country, and I worry about him successfully boarding the plane without my support. Alivia, my Autism mom-friend, advises me to get a doctor note that will allow me to escort him to the gate through security, and to pre-explain any confusing Autism behavior that can and is very frequently misinterpreted across the country with other autistic individuals as suspicious behavior, or something illegal amiss. And for me to bring him through security with my high behavioral expectations placed on him, and deposit him directly onto the plane, and then leave will work. Once on the plane, all will be well. While walking through metal detectors around armed guards, he will ding every "exhibits odd behavior that requires further investigation" bell for Homeland Security because he particularly loves weapons, and enjoys scripted movie language that includes graphic references to those particular implements of destruction.

We get through airport security successfully with a doctor note that explains Thad's Autism, and why it might be challenging to get through security without behavioral support from his mother. It advises the officers not to touch the boy who would squawk and tantrum from a stranger's unfamiliar touch, to ignore any suspicious behavior such as his incessant jumping, odd utterances, unusual body and eye movements, and a particularly intense "weapons" perseveration. The letter further advised that the endless scripts of "I have 723 guns, 42 smoke-bombs, and a tornado in my pocket" should be ignored and not treated as terrorist behavior by a boy who harbored his current preferred weapon, a 1-inch long plastic anvil, in his front pants pocket, left side. We were actually stopped the previous year as the airport security detained us because the officers saw the suspicious piece. We all had a good laugh when they found the teensy-weensy offending item.

In the same airplane safety letter, Thad's Developmental Pediatrician, Dr. Diane, particularly and explicitly requests that no stranger touch my child, citing the very high possibility that it will push him into aggressive autistic behavior that negates unfamiliar touch in a particularly escalating, fuming, overt, all heads-turning kind of way. He will tolerate unexpected physical touch, and be moderately behaviorally compliant with me usually if I stand next to him, and add stern words of potential consequences for inappropriate behavior. Usually I just ask to handle the challenging parts of his behavior myself out in the community as I understand his bells, whistles, and triggers because I comprehend his nuances, and his shades of understanding. As this airport experience happened to coincidence with the happenings of the Underwear Bomber, all parties at airports were on hyper-awareness mode, with heightened emotions toward anything at the airport that seemed out of place, amiss, different, which could ultimately mean terrorist activity and total world implosion, so ready to trip out and apprehend the villain, the perpetrator, the bad guy, the bouncy child, in a split second.

For example, when he had to get a set of ear tubes put in, I requested that I join them in the operating room through the anesthesia process with the justification that I could encourage the acceptance of the touch of doctors as they prepare for surgery in his midst. I was so happy that they heard the gravity of my words, and I was so relieved when I was invited to scrub up, put on a stylish blue Elvis jumpsuit with matching booties and accompany my boy into the bright white operating room. I stayed there until his eyes went sleepy, until he was successfully sedated, with my face moments from his, telling him it's okay, that he must relax his shoulders, his feet, his fists, that Mom is here and I will take care of him, that the doctors are friends and they will help him with his hurt ears. I could imagine him possibly resisting the gas-mask, getting scared or confused, squirming shrieking and kicking at the multitude of strange faces and lack of Mom, him possibly punching people out, as I sit and try to read a rumpled magazine in the waiting room, head churning, wishing they had listened to me.

That early morning at the airport, I was happy that his current IEP goal of being emotionally okay with unfamiliar, unexpected touch, in the form of bumper-car games in the OT gym or by being felt up by an airport security cop prior to boarding the plane, was in alignment with national security requirements, and I felt that his personal weapons mantra that holiday season celebrated a certain joy and confidence in the right to bear arms. Perhaps some Social Studies in our ever-present homeschool curriculum. Or maybe this is me talking pure bullshit with just one too many holiday drinks under her belt to consider or comment on any type of goal with honest sincerity, and appropriately low snark levels.

I am confident that I have thought of everything to make this airplane ride a successful experience for all, letters from doctors, extensive discussions of appropriate behavior and airplane safety, gluten-free food, extra games and warm socks, so sure that I have gotten my children safely on the plane to Grandma's house, and that Rob and I will embark on a three-day respite from Autism to combat our deeply tired eyes. Instead, as we drive back home from the airport, in all of 20 minutes, a big mobile asshole comes out of nowhere, sloshing tequila in his veins and shining no headlights, barreling down the 10-freeway, circa 5am on a Sunday morning, and he totals my spine and my car. If my kids had been in back, they would have been very injured or worse, and we would have experienced a difference outcome. My children almost harmed again, me deflecting their injury and remaining a partial casualty of life, a stupid representation of the walking wounded with seven permanently-damaged herniated discs, a totaled car, so many months of therapy ahead, and a chronic back condition.

My babies barely miss being plowed by the drunk motherfucker, and I think, how could I again almost let them fall in danger's way? Most other people can drive their children to the airport to visit the relatives, and give the parents a break, oh not us, so not us. I offer myself to the cause, as another slow slice with danger comes out of nowhere fucks my world once again.

Chapter 7

Her Hand Stirs the Broth

Autism is like cooking a big pot of soup, hand on the ladle, yum it's almost done, and abruptly someone pulls the area rug out from under you, the soup is on the floor, hands and heart are scalded, there is no dinner, the child is crying loudly, banging his fists on the counter freshly enraged, inconsolable from the unexpected crash, and my soul withers into dust as I realize the Autism nightmare is not over. As that winter, we become an example of a school district suing an autistic child for needing more remediation services and educational support than the school district is willing to offer.

I have a reoccurring dream that I cannot scream, maybe how my subconscious mind imagines it feels to not be able to talk. I see various things that are scary or emotionally uncomfortable in my dream, a drowning child, me naked in the grocery store, bullets, angry tigers or thieves, danger or injury too near me or those I love. In every dream, I see something upsetting to me, I try to tell, cannot, and eventually I try to scream. My mouth won't work, and my dream-eyes and my dream-heart are full of fear and emotion. I scream to tell, to alert, to ask for help, and no one hears. Always, I either end up waking myself up from the sound of my own voice as it screams, or Rob will wake me up in my restless fury from what I imagine sounds like a muffled wails. Same dream, he asks. Yes, I respond. Trying to get off my ethereal emotional cliff, I wiggle my jaw, surprised at the ease my conscious mind can process Rob's question, and my quick, automatic response.

How easy it is for me to talk, I think as I try to allow sleep to take me once again, but this time hopes of restful slumber fail me as I anticipate with flocking anxiety our impending court case with the School District. Gluten-laden pizza and Starburst candy become centerpieces of his legal case, and our Due Process lasts eight long days with a judge, lawyers, and so many witnesses in the form of doctors, therapists, teachers, and me, the parent.

I listen to the testimonies of experts about his needs, I think about my parental concerns, and I feel the bitch-slap of this financial burden hitting me hard. As the lawyers and judge question, cross-examine, redirect, object, sustain, and overrule words and considerations about my boy, I wonder if the California taxpayers realize that they are funding this push against the autistic child too. Shut those fucking parents up. Be okay with sub-par, celebrate the average, and don't make waves or we will tsunami your ass. American Citizens, you are on the hook too, as so many state and federal agencies use state and federal dollars to aggressively fight to prove our children don't need the services that they so desperately need, instead of using that money to help the families pay for these important services.

In many cases, a special education lawyer is necessary to help parents navigate a confusing legal system, to translate intense parent emotions and concerns into viable words, expectations and requests, and to assist public agencies in compliance with laws that protect children with disabilities. Sometimes, the word "lawyer" misleads, and one might reflect on incorrect stereotypes. But without legal representation in our journey, Thad's life trajectory and future possibilities would have been very different, and far more limited.

I swear that I am telling the truth, the whole truth, and nothing but the truth, and I say things under oath in the Due Process, such as:

I have the highest hopes for him. I think that in his program now, he has superseded so many of the things that I never thought he'd do. And I am very, very proud of him, I am so proud of him. And the thing that is so great now is that a few years ago he used to tell me he was stupid, and a fool and he wasn't smart. Now, he's smart, he feels smart and he tells me that he is smart. And you know, that motivation to learn, that motivation to get up in the morning? He finally has it. He now has his own alarm clock that he sets and follows, and this is huge for us. He picks out his clothes the night before. He is thinking about, he is anticipating what's going to happen tomorrow. His longest day is Wednesday because he has his social skills group, Afterschool Club. For my child, who was deathly afraid to step foot in a school a few years ago, and now his favorite day is his extended day? I mean, to me, that is amazing. And so yeh, as his mom and as his advocate and as his friend, we spend a lot of time together. I see him growing up, and I see him growing into a smart, strong, confident boy.

I believe that there is a reason for everything that happens in the world, and that there are no coincidences. I believe that each life experience that we encounter is a teachable moment from the universe to us, and that if the message is not understood, whatever it is, it gets louder and louder. A difficult idea to stomach as I find myself regularly in a swirling vortex of crap, screaming, I'm listening, Universe, what's the big fucking message?

Although delineated by law as the right as Thad's parent to have meaningful participation in the decisions that are made about his academic well-being, my opinions and wishes always seemed to be received with suspicion or not at all. He will not just get better, he will not just learn, and he needs support in all of these domains, I say. I am accused of wanting my child to have an appropriate education. I am accused of wanting him to succeed in life. Unnamed others thought that perhaps it was an ego pump, yelling, fighting, and that perhaps I might, in some twisted way, enjoy spending my time writing strongly-worded correspondence to state and federal entities about my son's disability and their lack of compliance in supporting his rights. No, actually, I am deeply jealous of parents whose biggest worry for their children's schooling is a B- on the Algebra test. Being in a fight with the best friend, that he got home too late from prom, or other normal conundrums like which extracurricular activities to chose because the kid wants to be involved in everything are what I crave in my human experience.

A series of shitty things occur in the courtroom those days, and butterflies drink my sweat with long cylindrical tongues as I roll around the dirt in my garden and sob. Popping kumquats between my fingers, imagining a different life, a different body, a different outcome. My psychogenic lachrymations flowing, I sit under the fig tree, gusting my sadness into hot drops on my knees, wondering if people going crazy know they are going crazy, or just jump right in and never return.

And then, in honor of totally feeling sorry for myself once again, I indulge myself in a little more misery prose:

The School District are Cannibals of my Family Life
they feast on a Salad of Postcards
of Places we will never vacation due to Therapy Bills
Nuggets of the Braces on my kids' Teeth we cannot afford as Croutons
thick, beefsteak slices of my Heart, still soft and beating
they gnaw on our Family Finger Bones
Rob working six or seven days per week typing endlessly
Thad with a tripod grip, Ursula with Opportunities of Normal flying away
me ground into a fine peppery dust that burns our Family Eyes
sprinkled on top is Thad's Urine
shipped to Paris on occasion to find something lurking
that we might remediate to
heal our Boy

Take a swallow before you speak, Mark tells me the next evening after one of the particularly long days of the legal proceeding, motioning toward my frothy mug of hops and calm, before you start issuing universal ultimatums in loud defeatist tones, drink the elixir please, because I know that you know that I know that you know you will never give up. Okay, are you ready? No, probably one more swig of local craft beer goodness is necessary before you answer. Okay, wipe your eyes and blow your nose, okay, ready, okay, breathe, okay, one more breath, all right, are you ready, now tell me the words I know that you feel. My hands shaking, my heart deflated, and yet another moment, day, year, life of Autism hardship sits like a ton of bricks on my mind. My friend sits with me in comfort and strength. So, what is your answer Kristin, Mark asks with a kind heart and a serious tone. Yes, you are correct, I agree. I will never stop fighting for my son. I will never give up, I say.

Once upon a time, I had an invisible IEP that got lost in the sauce, and I continue to believe that a mother knows her child the best. A mother's love, care, and concern for the well-being, happiness, safety, and success of her child is an asset, not an impediment. In addition, after a child exits the education system at age 22, only the parents are left sitting at the IEP table, and we should be prepared. Sadly, I never prepared for so much hatred and resistance against me for advocating for my child's right to an education. Thaddeus has a civil right as a citizen of California and the United States to be educated at public expense. I am a taxpayer, and if my child needs extra help to learn, I was certain that whatever my kid needed, he would get. Because that's what happens.

And again, to release my boiling internal pressure and stoke my soul-fire into compliance, I begin to analyze a few of the special education acronyms that bounce off the walls of my brain, and nestle in my psyche like unwanted crawly bugs that itch and bite. I consider the term FAPE, Free and Appropriate Public Education, a law that supports access to the appropriate education that all citizens are guaranteed, and wonder inside about the true meaning. Perhaps, FAPE might mean:

FUCK AUTISTIC PEOPLE EDUCATIONALLY

as parents strive to *Find A Proper Education* while *Fighting Against People's Egos* with a certain *Fortitude Against Paltry Experiences*.

And I wonder about the IEP process, an annual meeting of the minds regarding the child's academic, social, behavioral, and sensory performances over the previous year with thoughtful suggestions, plans, aspirations, and brainstorms for the upcoming year of more ways for the kid to catch up, keep up, and close the gap might get mixed up in the swirls of snarky words that continue to soften and percolate my brain-drain about these heavy, painful issues, and think:

IEP=IS EDUCATION POSSIBLE?

As,

I eat pizza, but I expect problems.
I envision pain, and I entertain platitudes.
I engage people, as I enter purgatory.
I emulsify prayers, and I elongate promises.
I espouse priorities, as I emote profusely.
I erupt precision, and I energize people.
I explain previous, and I expound possibilities.

So many families touched by the Autism experience have similar or worse challenges than us getting an appropriate education for their child, and it is a very serious problem. Of epidemic proportions, we might muse. The amount of effort that I have had to put forward just to get my son properly educated and to get state and federal agencies to honor his civil rights is enormous, and the amount of energy, money, and trees who died in honor of the cause is phenomenal. I literally have an entire office full of paper associated with getting Thad just through Elementary School. At our next IEP, I will talk to my School District about his Middle School placement after a Mediation agreement that lulled and nulled our communication for the three-year duration. I hope that we will listen to each other, and come to an appropriate agreement for the appropriate, continued remediation of Thaddeus, a civil right that he is entitled to as a resident of California, an American Citizen, and a human being.

I search for an allele of joy in my mental genome one day, and I can find no happiness except for the act of painting the inside of my pantry the colors left over from painting Thad's bedroom. I celebrate my children's independence by allowing them to paint their rooms whatever colors they desire. Thad has chosen dark green walls, a bright ocean-blue closet, and an orange-cremesicle door. When he tells others about his slumber space or draws his room with bright beautiful colored-pencil lines and shades, the teachers usually think he is kidding. What kind of parent would allow that?

Taxguy says our income tax flags that we have a 300% lower than normal car payment (a.k.a. people with our income typically drive way nicer cars with higher car payments), and 300% higher than normal deductions for out-of-pocket medical and legal expenses. Fighting legally for your kid and medically remediating your kid is a deductible expense. Although we are taxpayers in a public school district, we are US citizens, we have private insurance and Thad has Medi-Cal, we still end up paying for most of his services with our own money. And that fucking sucks.

Vaccines don't cause Autism except when they do. Meanwhile, as we plow through our lawsuits, I request all of his medical records since birth because I aspire to use Homeopathy as a next pathway to consider in his recovery. As I look through the thick binder of his medical life, I see the vaccines label stickers with cryptic numbers that determine the ingredients, the scribbled notes of Nurse Triage at 2am, the nights and days after the Autism cocktail was dispensed, mom frantic, crying child, fever, Thimerasol, rash, vomit, MMR, Prevnar, Varicela, second call logged, third call, a cool bath, some toast, applesauce if he can tolerate it, currently on antibiotics for ear infections, two sets of PE tubes, aunts and a cousin with seizures, not significant, the next day, a boy with a spider bite at the Urgent Care, aluminum ajuvenants, vaccines grown in eggs, mercury, mom yelling, so many questions, confusion, sweating, sweating, lost. All the feelings rush back, and kick me into an emotional shitpuddle on the floor. Kinda like standing with packed bags for the cruise that no one told departed yesterday, as I stand alone, hopeful turning into sorrow, without an umbrella drink, with bags packed, and only the cockroaches are able to muster.

I meet with Mark and Dawn on the benches in the school garden because Thad has a fever and cannot stay in class but I must stay to talk because I go to court on Monday to fight for my child. I de-heat my feverish kid with a strawberry smoothie, and tell them how nervous I am about being the first witness on the stand at Thad's Due Process hearing. Dawn asks me, what do you have to do with an offer of FAPE? Madness drains. What do I have to do with FAPE, I consider this question very carefully. It is merely their offer to me. It is not my reality, and it is not my truth. All of a sudden, I am not a lightning rod of anger anymore. I exhale.

Mom is still stirring that motherfucking soup, a continuous batch, a terminal brew, slowly, so slowly, trying new things with him, with me, and mixing it up endlessly on all fronts. I begin TFT, Thought-field Therapy Techniques, an energy medicine protocol that asks us to tap acupuncture meridian lines to relieve physical manifestations of stress, anxiety, and sadness, with Jacque. After you break down, you must rebuild, as I work on my lack of self-esteem and self-worth as a parent in these energy medicine treatments, and I fortify my role as his mom through the thoughtful precise tapping of my points. I add energy and subtract rage from my emotional equation, as I sit and listen thoughtfully to my body's internal dialogue. In addition, I try to understand the wordless messages from Thad's constant erupting skin issues, as I poke and drain his painful boils, as I lance his skin, and dispose of the oozy toxic sludge dripping onto cotton balls from his bumpy sore thighs. I think about the skin as the body's largest excretory system, and give thanks that whatever goop, that has been trapped in him and that has been trapping him, is finally being released.

And then, one fine fall day as I drop Thad off at school, I learn that my son doesn't know how to pee appropriately in public. I had always thought we would not delve into remediation of that part of his development because toileting and articulation were the only two areas of his development we were on target with. He has always been quite private at home about his bathroom activity (i.e. easier to tell if Dad was taking a shit at home than if Thad was), he openly enjoys getting naked in the backyard and peeing on the plants, and he is also quite proficient at depositing #1 and #2 in the woods.

Kristin, we have to talk, Teacher Jeff says. We chat regularly, so this statement I perceive as oh no. Okay, what's up? Well, Thad doesn't know how to use a urinal, and prefers to sit-down pee in the stall. When he is directed to use the urinal, he drops trow to his ankles, pees, and then shimmies over to the stall to get a square of paper which he uses to daub himself dry, he tells me. Kristin, he doesn't do the final shake, Jeff declares with a look of moderate male horror. I imagine his two handfuls of cute boy-butt cheeks shining in a fluorescent bathroom haze. I think about his lack of "stranger danger (i.e. be scared of the bad guys)," and imagine him in a public bathroom alone. I think about appropriate social behavior, and his personal safety as a reason to jump all over this adventure. Like flies on shit. Shit in the outhouse. And by the way, don't sit on the urinal. Only stand in front of it.

Well, I contemplate to myself, he sits down on the toilet at home, and I am his social model in the public family-style bathrooms we frequent. No male point of reference in public bathrooms, and this boy learns by visual model and physical example. Not by talking about it, or by social osmosis. I imagine this when-cute-isn't-cute-anymore behavior of my 10-year-old foreshadowed onto his future 18 or 22 year old male body in a public restroom, horror strikes, and I know we must act on this. Everything must be overtly taught, even pissing at Target.

I enlist the assistance of Teachers Jeff and Horacio at school, and Dad at home for the across all domains quest for appropriate, safe public bathroom etiquette. "Across all domains" means that we must target this behavior in the home environment, the school environment, and any other location my child frequents for continuity, to properly extinguish, educate, and replace this autistic behavior. I must admit that I have never been too involved in his toileting, and I commence the breakdown of yet another skill set for mastery. I write a vocabulary list of appropriate bathroom terms to share between my husband, and the two male teachers for consistency in potty language across domains. I watch my husband stand up and pee with new found intrigue and interest, asking questions such as, How much of it do you pull out? Do you aim? At what? Do you unbutton the top button on your pants? What if you have sweats on? Is there a secret to the final shake? And the biggest safety question on my mind: How do you make sure to not accidentally catch your junk in the zipper?

Shit, shit, shit, I think. Yeh, and by the way, you don't shit on the urinal. Only for pee. Everything must be taught.

The next few months, when Thad would return from school, I would load him up on a few glasses of water, and direct my husband to take him out on the urinal tour of our fine city. Take a leak in as many public restrooms as you can, use the following appropriate toileting vocabulary, and check for mastery and comprehension. He drinks another gallon or so of liquid I send along on ice, and he is instructed to go pee at a few more places. He practices at school and at home, we compare notes, acknowledge challenges, take data, make progress, have setbacks, and eventually declare this particular bathroom adventure a success.

Thad's terminal playground mantra is, "Find a friend," and I decide to take this advice, and I do the same. I get involved with parent groups, I coordinate parent groups, I assemble moments of parent self-care, to get parents talking, to get parents together, to help others know that there are possibilities and there is hope and friendship and lightness in this disorder, that there are avenues and options and we can support one another in many significant ways by banding together as parents. But we are also a slippery, wiley group, us, those crazy special needs parents, familiar to feeling alone in a sea of people, so used to feeling like odd man out, no one gets my crazy life, and I point out the fact that we must get together for support for ourselves and for each other. We may isolate, sequester ourselves because we feel depleted, overwhelmed, or make excuses why we must hide in our misery and confusion because no one else would understand. Except other Autism parents who experience the same.

Find your people, I recommend, as they will become your extended family of sorts, those who mirror your life and can help you make sense of it. These are real people who understand that all the wild things you say are true anecdotes of daily life. They will pull you out of the familiar eye of the storm, that place where we all understand Autism sucking on time and resources in our family, the abrupt reasons for canceling engagements, and provide an ear that doesn't judge to the reasons that make sense to no one else but others who have similar life experiences. I challenge the idea of "Parent Participation" to expand from parents engaging in the IEP to parents engaging with each other.

And Autism parents have certain amazing skills in tenacity, laser-precision, and research. We will talk longer, harder, and with more passion about minute details involving the gut and brain processes of our kids, we will illuminate, inform, and impress with our graduate-level knowledge in so many educational, remedial, legal, sensory, auditory, behavioral, and neurological domains and speak with large, scholarly-sounding medical words regarding the most precise description of our kid's health and illness. We have a big voice and an even bigger heart, put out there on public display.

We, the Autism Parents, also excel in the art and magic of the ability to pull money out of our asses. For example, an AUT mama might find a new therapy that she would like her child to try to ameliorate or hopefully eliminate a symptom, characteristic or by-product of Autism that is messing with the kid's body and soul. And then, that particular mother-warrior might beg, borrow, steal, or just push an invisible button on her body in order to get the twenty-grand that that not-covered-by-insurance protocol costs. Cha-ching, out pops a thick grip of Benjamins from her ass, as my friend Teresa swears that's how she pays for all of the uncovered therapies for her boy.

Get your support pod, I offer as solid *madre-a-madre* advice, and make time to refuel yourself even if it feels uncomfortable, wrong, or selfish. Refill and replenish your coffers so you can be your best. Allow people in, allow people to help, and allow people to listen to you. When I say that I have had a bad day, my friends with kids on the spectrum understand. A tantrum, a meltdown, a crash, or a "stink" happens, and it is important to process the events so they do no long-term damage to your heart and soul. Autism doesn't take a break, Autism does not take summers or weekends off, and neither do we.

And as a support to my parent posse out there in the world, I have provided a reference section for parents at the end of the book entitled, "Thad's Tribe." I give contact information for Thad's providers as scaffolding, as a roadmap for those on the Autism Journey. Here's what worked for us, here are some ideas. I hope that this information might be helpful to you. As always, be informed and make choices that seem true to your soul.

Marisa and I have an agreement that if needed, cuz shit goes down quick in Autism Nation, that within 10 minutes, wherever, whatever, we can talk. Tammy, Gina, and I regularly go out to bitch and booze. "I had a bad day" means lots of different things to different people, and my people participating in Autism Nation understand and support this critical piece of me and my emotional health. Last year, Ana and Eden sat me down, and convinced me that it was all right to send Thad to overnight camp for the summer. Yes, they said, it is okay for you to not be on 24-hour surveillance for 5 days while he is supported at this great special needs camp. Tears in my eyes, I agree, almost needing the green light from another Autism parent to go off-guard for a few days.

Alivia will whisk me away for breakfast when my emotions are heightened to calm and soothe me, and I kvetch with Carolyn while our boys run wildly around the sweaty rock-climbing gym. I recommend the friendship, love, care, and respect of another Autism parent in your world for emotional support because they get it, they understand how hard you work, how hard you cry, because they do too. We celebrate each other's details, those winking glimmers of progress that maybe don't seem as huge to others as it does to us.

I am a parent mentor, and I coordinate parent education and support groups with a sort of primal drive toward no one be subjected to the ignorance and sadness and mistakes I have had related to Autism. I feel a certain level of responsibility to educate others, and my advice to anyone on the Autism journey is to get a mentor, or be a mentor. I know that I help people when we talk, and I wish that I had had a mentor in the early days. I help in various booths at Resource Fairs and Awareness Walks, and I try to say yes as much as I can to as many ways to help the members and causes of our Autism Nation.

I highly recommend talking to Autism parents with kids older than yours to see the possibilities that can and could happen for your child, almost like talking to your big sister about the college experience or how it feels to french-kiss a boy. And then, Leah and Emily tell me about their older boys on the spectrum who take the public bus alone to get around. I had never considered that Thad's movement around the world might be able to be independent from me with the support of public transportation. Granted, each of these boys trained with a professional on how to manage and maneuver the red and green lines successfully. But, the exciting piece for me is that I accidentally and happily got my horizons and expectations stretched by the happy words of other Autism parents. The possibilities for my son were placed before me by hearing about the success of their boys. Good stuff for the soul, I highly recommend hearing as many Autism success stories as you can.

I remind myself through my conversations with other Autism parents that we must be realistic in our expectations of ourselves, our children, and others. I read and support and believe that we must trust our guts, that we must trust our parent instinct when choosing interventions and avenues for our children. Mothers and Fathers, we need to get out there more, and find our new sources of strength and energy. We need more energy, more vigor, more hope. Get in there with your kid because you love them the best, you love them the most. Don't drop them off at 8 and expect them to be better by 3. Be there for the kids in whatever way you can, and as you are there, learn other ways to get in. Be with the kids and be with your peers, other Autism parents, for strength, camaraderie, and the sharing of resources and information. How comforting it is when you have a very precise question about a very broad topic that might have huge implications if implemented appropriately? How comforting to know that you have a friend who is an expert on the topic, or has just recently tried out that new therapy, service, provider, or protocol, and is willing to discuss it with you? Very.

And then, Autism Awareness Day falls like a loud, empty thud on me each April, and it is my most unfavorite day of the year. To celebrate an illness I do not love, the fighting Autism camps, what color to wear, black or blue, what to light up and where to go dark, words filled with venom and machetes on so many sides of our so many deep emotional issues, one liners and vindictive messages, I wish we could all unite and agree to differences and continue to help our kids with a united Autism front, and I wish we could all come together. I find comfort and support in various Autism organizations and events and theories and protocols, and I feel so worried always about being judged as a scab, crossing the line, with us, with them, the big fucking million dollar question, who do you stand with, who are you against, although we all just want justice and health for our kids, we all just want our babies to stop hurting so bad.

I like the idea of Autism Action Day better, as so many Autism parents scream those words on that particular day in April. I am already aware, they yell, they post, they write, they tell, so aware, so consumed. I concur. The A-word that bounces around lightly on talk radio and as the lead story on the evening news that day, celebrate, celebrate Autism for one 24-hour stint per year when everyone is aware, and then they put those ribbons and T-shirts back in the box until next year, as we see a few days of puzzle pieces colored by children for a buck hanging in the grocery check-out lines, and whiz by so many multicolor ribbon-magnets on the back bumpers of so many cars.

I think about my traintrip many years ago to visit California from my then-residence, Colorado, which happened to coincide with the LA riots, and acknowledge that my time in California is always momentous for sure. Why don't we all just get along, Rodney King begged, as I stood by Kelly, my friend I was visiting who worked in a drop-in center on Venice Beach. We stood there with homeless, hungry people listening to and seeing those directly affected by the violence towards others those sad days. I wish all of Autism Nation could all unite and work together in a puppies-and-rainbows-and-lack-of-reality-and-full-acknowledgement-that-there-are-so-many-sides-to-Autism-issues kind of way. I have friends on so many sides of issues and I have many Autism friends with whom we don't discuss certain topics or agree to disagree, validating each other's diametrically opposing views on big heavy subjects in our community, like food, diets, medications, therapies, laws, education, money, vaccines, dripping in so much politica, all for the health and wellness of our beautiful sick children.

But what are we all really doing? What is society doing? What is the government doing? What is science doing? What is education doing? Why are more people not paying attention to this health tragedy that has been named a health epidemic by the National Institutes of Health? Most people know a relative or a friend with Autism. These autistic individuals grow up, and are unable to participate fully as contributing adults that gives back to the community without appropriate training, services, and supports. As state and federal budgets continue to ignore and slice opportunities, these people continue to get older, and their parents eventually die. Their care falls squarely on the state and federal government programs. Paying attention yet, People? If Autism doesn't affect you directly currently, don't worry, it will.

Adults with Autism, the logical outcome of Children with Autism, very often with the few emotional and physical go-to places are engaging in public masturbation, ripping out their own teeth out of boredom, unnecessary violent acts, getting lost, accidentally killed or drowned, and destroying things in homes that are sentimental, irreplaceable, replaced repeatedly or cheap or expensive. I met an Autism mom once told me that she buys televisions at garage sales every Saturday because her adult autistic son throws them at the wall so regularly that they just pick them up weekly at garage sales. Rages and meltdowns in adults with Autism are scary and sad.

Even though I tell my tale here with intrigue and sadness imbued, I feel that we are lucky to have had some resources, circumstances, and supports on our side in this tragedy. We were able to have to the support of an amazing lawyer to get Thad the help he needs (We had some financial resources, and the benevolent generosity of friends and family to pay for the long battle towards Thad's appropriate placements and services), we have a team of providers second to none who truly understand his unique challenges (Good providers are critical), we only have one child with Autism (Many families have multiple children on the spectrum, and must attend to each child with individualized intensity), we are not second-language English speakers trying to navigate a confusing educational, insurance, and legal system (Autism is color-blind, indifferent to race, ethnicity or language), and I am able to stay home and devote my full attention to this situation (Many families need both parents working to support their household). Again, I feel gratitude toward the resources, the kindness, and the people who support us in our Autism life.

And the big fat question was asked one fine day on Facebook by one smart AUT-mama to Autism Nation, "Would you 'cure' your child of Autism if you could?" Here is my response, sitting amongst the many:

I would absolutely level the playing field of life for Thaddeus by "curing" him of Autism, a very heavy weight on our family, a universal burden that screws with his mind and his body, a sickness that makes understanding others' words difficult, a disorder that challenges him physically and emotionally, an imbalance that demands constant vigilant attention, and a health tragedy that makes difficult the very things of life we aspire to celebrate with our children, such as a friend, a party, or a cupcake.

There are so many ways to engage ourselves, the Mothers and Fathers, that are little moments of self-care that can help us keep on keeping on. It is important to show up for a date or a moment with yourself, with punctuality and reliability, just like you do for your child's appointments. Give yourself the same grace, the same courtesy, the same care, you so deserve it, Mothers and Fathers, all of us, as I walk in and out of practicing what I preach, as I try as hard as I can and sometimes hopscotch in and out of my own words of advice depending on the day and the circumstance.

I feel emotional peace, physical release, and mental rejuvenation through regular journal-writing, just for me, no one else reading it, time as I reflect, review and wonder without any judgement but my own. And writing this particular story of my life has dipped me back into a series of powerful emotions, as I go back to my feelings about places, people, and events, and I almost feel hung-over from my own memories. I am grateful that I am dredging up many strong feelings to process, as I move toward peace. I manage my thoughts as much as I can. I allow some to stick around, and demand that some leave immediately as I release the tension in breath to the Universe. We must challenge and manage the monkey mind, the loud bitch-cycle of the Ego that tells us we are never enough and our attempts are worthless. Attempting anything for the good of our children is admirable and should be celebrated.

Last Saturday, I hear "That kid's got potential" from a famous surf legend as he watches my boy charge waves, and stand on the surfboard. These were the first positive words about my son from a stranger that I had ever heard, as I usually receive unwanted, unwarranted parenting advice in the line at Target. I hung those words around my neck like an amulet, a shiny talisman, a fancy good-luck charm, pointing me north in my darkness.

I am always in the car, I am always focused on my breathing, I am breathing and sitting and driving with precision, I am walking and writing and wondering and dreaming and volunteering in his school as a smidgen of giving back to a school I am so indebted to for helping me reach in and pull out my boy. Breathing as I walk, breathing as I see people in spaces around me as I wait for the remediation of my boy, the slow process toward the next process toward a step forward toward more goals and more ideas with so many breaths of hope, breathing into all three lobes of the lung, pressurizing myself for my next happenings. Practicing, repeating, practicing, repeating. Completely exhaling the bad, the frustrating, the old, the misunderstood, and deeply inhaling a new perspective, a new angle, a new day.

Always aspiring that my words might crest an online contest and get me something cool, I plop another poem out onto the internet trying to win a bag of medicated Methyl-B12 lollipops:

THE BIRTHDAY PARTY
Look, there is a cake
the little sweetheart begs
no, I say and remind--
Your allergy to eggs
How about a little piece
it will taste so sweet
no, my little darling--
Your allergy to wheat
The frosting is fluffy
what fun for a young boy
alas, allergy to soy
not so much joy

My emotions continue to bump and grind me from behind. I acknowledge them, process them, and still feel in my heart that I'm not doing enough for my child, although in my head, I know I am. Machinations of my own lolly-gagging and impermanence, the sturdy assemblage of heavy issues, stacked-tall amalgamations of problems and solutions, the swirling anomia of answers in my head and in the world, my karma ran over your dogma, as I pick and chose the various versions of myself that I will celebrate or squash, tenacious and arduous as I force myself to move forward, placating myself to fill my own dance card with appointments and days and hours as I continue to extrude the essence of my boy back into his mind.

We move into "transferring instructional control from the therapists to the parents," a transition towards parent-directed ABA at home with Thaddeus, that is we begin to expect Thad to comply with our directives in the same way that he does with his therapists. We spend every Friday afternoon and all-day Saturday on the ultimate goal of transferring instructional control, us being in charge of our own kid and him complying with our directives, to us, the parents. Parents acquiring and sustaining behavioral control of the child is a critical piece of the ABA process because if parent doesn't ultimately retain this control then his behavior can lapse without a therapist present, which is not a logical or well-thought out long-term plan. His Speech and Occupational Therapy interventions transfer entirely to SLDC for continuity of care, and he continues to go to Vision Therapy once per week, making slow strides in reading comprehension, eye-tracking, and memory.

And sometimes certain things happen that are awesome, funny, and perfect. Right before Thad joined Room 905, we heard so many stories about a particular episode in which Teacher Jeff rode a rollercoaster on a class fieldtrip, experienced nausea, and blew chunks in the girls' restroom at the amusement park because it was the closest toilet in his acute state of vomit. Thad is a black and white, all or nothing thinker, a huge fan of rollercoasters, and the idea that Jeff, one of his main idols of manliness and coolness would do something wimpy like barf after riding a rollercoaster, and in the girls' bathroom at that, never sat right with him, and he was constantly emotionally bugged by this. I ask Jeff, as an end-of-school-year gift to Thad, to release Thad's tormented soul and ride a coaster successfully. Jeff agrees because Thad and him are big buddies. We did acknowledge the queasy stomach possibility regarding rollercoasters, so we frontloaded Jeff with the location of the boys' bathroom nearest to the exit, just in case. And, for Thad, if Jeff re-barfed, it would be unfortunate, but at least he made it to the boys' bathroom to do it. Jeff and Thad took a spin on the Silver Bullet rollercoaster together, Jeff turned green and kept his lunch in the box, and Thad's soul was finally freed.

Thoughts become things, I remind myself over and over, and I begin to consciously focus on monitoring my thoughts as a practice toward gratitude and happiness and life-satisfaction. The masters continue to whisper insight to me in "soundbyte enlightenment," so much concise one-liner inspiration and guidance for myself and my child from deep in my cells, deep in our world history, our earth genetic fingerprint, intrinsic messages from the ancestors, storyboards of the seekers. We are all from same source, caring for all, not just self, as the masters in the movie, "The Secret" tell us, we attract everything that happens to us based on our thoughts. Simply put, good thoughts attract good things, and where we focus our mind, on the good or the bad aspects of our existence, is where we will see the good or the bad energy reverbs manifest in our lives.

I think about Peter Drucker's important words, "The best way to predict the future is to create it," as I consider Thad's unique needs in his current and future programming, the things I will do, create, and advocate for to support his goals, and the significance of active participation in his programming because "To be is to do," says Emmanuelle Kant. I think about Carlos Castaneda's directive to "Be deliberate, be impeccable," as I work through the levels and varieties of challenges we face, reminding me to be forthright with my intentions of his wellness and success with each detail considered to the best of my ability. And Rumi asks me, "If you are irritated by every rub, how will you be polished?" as I move toward breathing through stress and unhappy thoughts because "Nothing is to be feared, only understood," says Marie Curie, and I believe Picasso's musings on "Everything you can imagine is real," as I consider Thad's possibilities as positive outcomes, ever acknowledging the uniqueness of our life, the poster-child for the Grateful Dead's bouncy assertions that "Sometimes we live no particular way but our own."

I experience feelings of blustery grace from these intense kerfuffles that have simmered my soul and sensibility for so long, and I celebrate the flaws of reality and being human as part of my life experience. I wear the memories of this experience of Autism in the small lines that glisten around my lips and sprinkle from my eyes. My skin has a little less luster than before, and I believe that my eyes are still bright and thoughtful, yet retain an intermittent brooding eye-gaze from so much hard memory. Silver tangles try to overtake my hair, and I engage in aggressive hair-dying behavior because I aspire to always get carded for buying beer. I look to myself, to my friends, to my family, my children, my thoughts, my world, and I feel deep gratitude that I am a participant in such an amazing story, a history, a piece of humanity that has transformed me into a lunatic truck-driver transporting precious cargo, a chef to the most discerning of palates, a monitor and recorder of vast unknown universes to be discovered and translated, a voice and a friend to a complicated puzzle that provides great joy in finding the right pieces that fit together, and a seeker of the flashes of sunshine I crave in his mind and in my aspirations for his future. I am a person who reads too much, thinks too much, dreams too much, and probably could have a cleaner shower or a less dusty back porch.

Mark tells me that he has planted the first grape vines at his beautiful farm in Temecula called Spero Vineyards, and that he has dedicated a row of Zinfandel grapes to Thaddeus. How long until we have wine, I ask. It will take five years, he tells me, are you available then for the first harvest? Yes, I calculate, I'll be around, and I smile. Then, later that day, I buy an eighth of a local grass-fed cow, and plunk it into my deep freeze. I feel sexy and liberated.

Chapter 8

I.E.P. = I Eat Pizza

THE LAWSUITS ARE played out in unending arguments about how to appropriately educate Thad and span for years, and then on 11/1/11, with so many ones and whispers of fresh beginnings, on All Souls Day, with ancestors and masters wiggling and stirring in their graves, we finally settle with the School District with the determination of me as his case manager for the next three years which results in Thad at SLDC for school for the next three years. I have a chance to reflect back on his life and his progress. I think about Thad as a three-year old, circa 2003, a silent save screaming boy, short and belligerent, who hated life and everything about it or at least acted like it. We had just been excused from Regional Center services because he was misdiagnosed as non-autistic at age three, and we had no idea what to do with this writhing tornado of boy. The doctors, agencies, and specialists we saw seemed to think there was a normal explanation like a chatty older sister as a reason my three-year old didn't talk or that he's a boy or that he's a late bloomer or perhaps just a really defiant child with uneven development but still totally good, nothing to work on or remediate as an explanation for his blatant Autism. I mean he had Autism 101 going full force at that point, only I hadn't taken the class yet, so I didn't know how fucking obvious it was then. Only in midnight sleepless self-reflection, and guilty hindsight.

I remember the early days before we knew of our family Autism, when we just knew we had a big problem but could not figure out what it was. I remember the days of hiding my emotions because I could not give myself permission to cry, to feel sorrow, remorse, fear, attacking myself for what I did wrong, replaying a thousand moments of pre-Autism history, if only I, if only I, finding the reason, the message, in our life path, and striving to celebrate and embrace the path chosen for us not by us. And now, I understand that I have every right to feel anger, feel sadness, defeat, remorse. But I also have the desire, the right, the responsibility, and the ability to heal myself and others in various ways from this tragedy by my vigilance, my knowledge, my words, my calm, and my comfort.

I recall, I remember, and I think about that long time ago of Thad that seems so far away and so fresh in my mind concurrently. At age two, on Christmas, he took all the "weapons" out of the Clue game and would not give them back without ceaseless hitting and crying so that the pieces were eventually, officially, terminally, his, and then he buried all the cars from the Life game in the backyard sandpit, tantrumming if we tried to unbury or use the pieces to play the game. Game over, our sad minds thought.

Thad was three years old, and he was convinced that the phrase, "Wash your hands" was a put-down as it required him to unhappily comply with an unfair adult directive, and he did not perceive these words as a request for sanitary fingers before snacks. He screams, "Wash hands," at the top of his lungs in a *fuckyou* kinda way when we request he do, participate, eat, walk, work, sleep, start, or stop anything, everything, Thimerasol whispering in his ear to forget, to succumb to the darkness in his mind, aluminum convincing him to get mad, to get stuck, antimony telling him false things, heavy metal poisons cajoling him into not caring, not bothering, him all the time mad or asleep, except when he experiences sand between his toes at the park, as we try to comfort and console the boy who hated and kicked at the nasty grains that poked into his toes like barbed wire.

At four years old, he had a lack of knowledge of nursery rhymes because he refused to look, learn, repeat, or engage, and would whisper under his breath, "The Lord is NOT good to me," at preschool when the kids gave thanks in song for their daily snacks of apples and crackers. Whisper, whisper, if I cannot hear you, it doesn't count that you said it and you have to say it again, I would tell him. The prosody and volume of his voice were too sing-songy and too soft, it was difficult to know if he was talking to me or to himself, and then if he was talking to me, the strange melody and intonation of his words left me puzzled most of the time about the boy's attempts of communication messages to his mom. He began circumlocating words, labeling objects whose name he did not know by referencing things he did. For example, in Thad-speak, "finger-socks," were gloves, and "bad-guy-dogs," were coyotes. He would lie face down on the bench at preschool during freeplay, he would only paint in the color blue, and spent a significant amount of his day in a little white plastic playhouse scripting unkind words out of the tiny window that he had noticed elicited emotional responses from cartoon characters, which ultimately ended as failed attempts at social engagement.

In the early years of Autism, we went hiking and camping a lot, cramming the screaming, writhing 5-year-old Thad into the baby backpack harnessed to Rob. He would screech and kick and we would march through the woods, far far deep in the woods, where we could leave our home without others' hurtful words and awkward stares, and his behavior could not be seen or heard by others, march, march, moving forward, straight line, as we attempt to find things he perceives as scary or dangerous in nature to calm his clattery mind and our jangly nerves. We hike up a volcano in Lassen National Park in August and find snow on the top, we pass through a million migrating butterflies, butterfly wings touching our arms and our faces, surrounding us, touching us, perhaps attacking us I suggest, calming him by invoking Pretend Peril in our environment and happenings, as we pretend-worry about being eaten alive by giant Sequoia trees, or pretend being melted alive in the sulphur springs in Bumpass Hell, so many days deep in the national parks, down long windy paths, as we walk, march, march, march, trying to focus on the faraway sounds of peaceful birds, and not on the sounds of our child's endless screams.

In Yosemite National Park, I taught Thad how to write his name at the picnic table. Letters meant nothing to him, and the only thing that he would do with a pencil was draw a snake, basically a tenuously-drawn vertical line. So we start where he is, me hell-bent and determined that my 6-year-old will learn to write his own name as I tell him to draw a snake. I ask him to give the snake a hat, a squiggly horizontal line is produced, and we have written a capital T. I think about how to imagine a letter H, and I say, snake, snake, bridge, directing him to construct a capital H out of other known entities, and preferred salient features from our hikes. We then discuss how if you slant the snakes, they look like playground slides, and we have created a capital A. And the moon quite often did look like a capital D, so D moon it was. Hence, the way he spelled his name when he entered Kindergarten was, him writing a series of drawn images and saying aloud, "Snake, give it a hat, snake, snake, bridge, slide, slide, bridge, and a D moon."

At age seven, he flips off the Aide during class and gets in trouble. Although I was pretty sure that Thad did not know the nonverbal *fuckyou* communication message of the middle finger, I was very sure that he was overjoyed at the heightened quality of the unfavorable responses by the adults when he accidentally at first, and then continued saluting everyone in his immediate proximity with his middle finger. He is sent to the Principal's office, and I am called. The Principal asks Thad, where did you learn that, and Thad responds, My dad. He also starts an accidental rumor at school that a friend of mine has "good weapons" at her house, meaning to him that he is pleased by the selection of plastic light sabers that my friend has in her children's toy closet. Yes, out of context, a different meaning, and again, punctuated with a not-so-jovial response from school administration. In frustration, again I attempt to explain Thad's global perspective and interest in Pretend Peril as his unique form of communication, and his lack of global perspective to these words. Again, I am unheard.

That spring, our friend, Chris, coins the term, "faux falls for the media" to describe the devious act of Thad stressing out onlookers with pretend danger at the climbing gym or at various rock outcroppings full of dirty cool climber dudes. Thad would engage in so many cartoon moments of "Dad, help!" as he dangled by one arm, harnessed and about halfway up a moderately hard climbing route, with a suspiciously mischievous grin floating on his face. Others would freak and stress about his safety, and Thad would be so psyched that others were worried he might fall. He wasn't making any progress in the school environment at that point, but he certainly was dominating on the rocks, and we were in awe of his superb comedic timing in his endless dangerous physical comedy routines.

At age eight, we took an airplane to go to my sister, Emily's wedding in Ohio, he eats gluten from the buffet, and then pees on every flat surface in our hotel room. I think about windows of time, how, in only a moment, life can change, the push of a needle, the signature of a name, the nod of a head in agreement, turn of the head when you look past injustice, walking on by, venom released from a spider's fangs, or poison passing through the blood and brain barrier. I worry about walking the aisle as a bridesmaid, and that Thad is one minute behind me as the ringbearer. I worry about the open church door to the busy street behind me. I think about the words "marriage" and "elope." I particularly think, in my flashbulb-popping wedding saunter up the aisle, about how the multiple meanings of the word, "elope" can be defined as, running off secretly to be married usually without parental consent, and how it can also mean, an autistic person making a break for it, running off overtly, without parental consent. I ask my brother, Pete, please watch him while I walk and please catch him if he runs, yes, I trust you, my brother, my family. Pete hangs with his nephew in the back of the church, my ringbearer boy does not run, and he walks a straight line up the aisle into the safety of my mommy arms.

Perception of the world includes seeing, looking, and interpreting the vision. Dr. Robyn explains the different neuropathways involved in drawing, writing words, and talking. We talk about interpreting words, images, and text, and inferring and predicting responses to each. How do we know that the person is happy or mad on paper compared to looking at a face. Different parts of our brains enliven, light up, come to life, connect and strengthen with each pass of communication we attempt with him. We train and support the different neuropathways of his brain associated with reading aloud versus silently in a home program called Dynamic Reader. I notice that Thad has to count the series of dots between one and six each time he looks at it, like on a dice, I notice that I automatically can recognize this as a four or a two, and he always begins, 1-2-3, and this act slows him down.

I tell Dr. Robyn my concern, and she eases my worry by saying that they are already working on this skill-set in Vision Therapy, called Subitizing, the ability to automatically recognize numbers through visual counting. My sisters, Ellen and Emily are twins, and my brother, John and I are fourteen months apart, and our mother used to dress us alike in photos sometimes. Sometimes I will look at pictures, and think that I see myself and my brother, although I question, I don't remember being there. My mom will respond, oh that's not you. Incorrectly recognizing yourself, perceptions of our own face, finding ourselves in our own reality, locating ourself in the world, breath.

Thad uses his iPhone to text various people for various reasons. Sometimes we will be sitting somewhere and he will appear to be not happy or checked out, as we continue to remember that perception is everything, and then he will text me from across the table, Mom I'm having a really good time. I am so excited for technology that uses different neuropathways. And the understanding and listening to our child with special needs should be equally as respectful and present as to your typical children. I always listen to Thad's "why," why he wants to do something that might be perceived differently because of an idea that he is having. I do not initially say no because he is my poor little disabled boy because very often he is doing stuff that is actually normal for his age, and I am just not cool enough to realize it yet. For example, he turns twelve and gets a cellphone cuz he wanted to text, and take and send pictures. Sounds a lot like he is wanting to communicate. Sounds a lot like a typical kid actually, and I smile.

My sister, Ellen, survived the Thailand tsunami in 2003, as another family member who was saved by the water. During the crash of the large killer wave that destroyed the town of Phuket, she was snorkeling underwater in a nearby inlet and the wave passed her by. The town was pummeled with so much media about bodies floating around where my sister had just been when we had talked on Christmas. We did not know Ellen's safety situation until over 24 hours after the wave hit when she finally was able to call from a payphone, and ultimately secure safe passage back to her home in Japan as an English Teacher. It was so scary to have a loved one missing from our world for that period of time. I feel inspired that she moved away from the wave and toward safety.

Ellen lives in Japan for 6 years, and she tells me that the word "Autism" in Japanese is 自閉症, pronounced Jiheishou.

The character 自 means Oneself.

The character 閉 means Closed/Shut.

The character 症 means Sickness.

We moved through behavior issues, sensory challenges, auditory processing woes, and find the issue at the bottom of the heap, hiding, tricking us, his low vocabulary levels, and such labored comprehension of words, ideas, concepts, and the big picture. The holy trinity of comprehension, memory focus and attention, the trifecta of difficulty for my son. Almost like the time, one fine day, when a substitute teacher and I think that the problem is his shorts worn special-ed-style, pulled up to his armpits, and as I put my fingers in the waistband of his shorts to pull them down below his bellybutton, I realize that he is in addition underwear-free. You came to school commando? I shriek, and then realize neutral, ground zero, normal, whatever is reality or basic is sometimes blurry. Sometimes there are underlying issues that need to be addressed first such as the lack of undies or attention to the fact that he did not understand the language and that is why he does not respond verbally, to go under the surface, pre-beginning to find the source of the discrepancy, where the actual breakdown occurred in order to remediate appropriately, in order to fix his broken comprehension, to repair the bridge for his thoughtful mind.

I begin to realize that his vocabulary is dangerously low when one day he asks me what the name for those "tall lightbulb sticks" on the side of the freeway, pointing up. Um, telephone poles, I respond. Besides the fact that we see these things every day in our million mile commute, there were street lights everywhere. Confused, he inquires further about the "wood sticks growing out of the ground," and then I point to the street lights and ask him for a label. Poles with lamps, he says. Street lights, I correct. We spend years getting through his behavior, sensory, auditory processing, and social issues, and all of a sudden, I then realize that a desperately low vocabulary level is significantly impeding his academics and social comprehension. I start to wonder which words, concepts, and social phrases he truly knows.

I remind him again to "ask a question," not to "tell a question," as his brain does not recognize the spoken error, and automatically self-correct his words. His splinter skills are unique and quirky. He can tell the main idea of the story, but cannot make up a title. Higher Order Thinking skills and the harder stuff seem to be easier to him than the stuff that appears easy is desperately hard. Gaps in comprehension and inferences and words with multiple meanings confuse such seemingly concrete words as "barbeque" into a multi-day, multi-part discussion of meaning which goes something like me blathering out the following, Barbeque can mean the pulled meat slow-cooked in sauce served up on a bun, and it can also mean the thing that we grill burgers on, not necessarily where we make the barbeque itself, we can also go to a party called a barbeque where we can eat barbeque or not eat barbeque but that party can be a barbeque and we don't necessarily need to eat barbeque for the party to still be called a barbeque.

Thad hurts his "heel," and we know that it needs to "heal" as we discuss the caboose piece of bread in the loaf, the "heel" and how dogs coming to their masters is called, "heel," and how some words sound the same and are spelled differently, and how some words sound the same, are spelled differently and have different meanings, how some words are spelled the same and have different meanings. We think about "corner," and talk about the corner of the room, the corner of the paper, turning a corner, or stopping at the corner, each subtle in its meaning. Sara talks about a "skinny" sad homeless dog that she found near her house, emphasizing the sad emotion of how poor and skinny that little pup looked, "like it's a bad thing," and after the class, Thad asks me about "skinny," remembering on television that some girls wanted to be skinny, "like it's a good thing," he says. Good and bad contexts for the same word, o my little sweet concrete thinker, how do I teach this to him? How do I make this salient, concrete, understandable to him, I wonder, as I continue to mull over these abstract language concepts.

Touching the thumb and forefinger to make a closed circle means "OK" to most, and it also represents the letter, "F" in American Sign Language (ASL). Thad generalizes and conflates these signs inappropriately, and writes OK when shown the letter F last Tuesday on his ASL weekly quiz. I ask him to tell me when he doesn't understand the words, as I am now constantly checking his comprehension. Perhaps he looks like he is not paying attention because he actually doesn't know the words we are using. He asks for clarification between "on time" and "in time" as I express our lateness to an appointment. We talk about how it is preferred to be on time, and to get there in time means you got there on time and maybe even earlier but not necessarily, and we talk about the different time increments that that statement represents.

Words with multiple meanings, and words with multiple contexts continue to confuse him and all must be explicitly taught. A button can be pinned on a shirt, a button can present as a metal disc with a witty saying, and to Thad, this entity is a "pin with a picture." Because a button is on a shirt, and a button can only be one thing, according to Thad. I get depressed and have a minor tanj when I realize words he doesn't know. It's so cheesy but I would take it personally, and feel responsible concurrently, with personal records of up to 10 minutes per meltdown due to my bummedness of how long his vocab continues to bump along. Seriously, how can he not know the word "freckle" or "location," I would wail. It's weird though because I feel sad that his vocabulary level is so low, and at the same time, I feel happy that I have finally realized this.

He learns the sign for "salad" in ASL, and then shows me his interpretation of "tossed salad," with a football-style go-long pass and the sign for salad, he likes "punch and cookies," with includes a playful sock to the arms, and the sign for cookies. Thad is rigid in his interpretation and continues to feel confused about swapping out words, synonyms if you will, as we talk about how "ill" means sick, and I ask him how to spell it. He says, I-comma-L-L, and I say, "apostrophe, please," and he morphs the "I plus will" contraction into a misrepresentation of what I am sure he is trying to answer with correct words. He starts to ask what things mean. "What the word means" versus "the definition" are different ways of understanding the same word, I explain. Is it possible for you to write it this way Thad, I ask as I reexplain the difference between a comma and an apostrophe. What's "possible" mean, Mom? Punctuation continues to elude him in relevance and necessity as he sees adding this particular information to a sentence confusing, and he is challenged in the accuracy of choosing the right squiggly pencil mark to satisfy this particular grammar task.

I ask his Speech Therapist, Trish, to explain Thad's learning style to me. She says that she uses multi-modality instruction, particularly gross motor movement and kinesthetic involvement, using "Pretend Peril" techniques like jumping jacks, push-ups, starting the task over, mock punches to the arm or slashing off of limbs actually engage him, and she tells me, "against all laws of human interaction," this way of engagement keeps him bonded in a twisted, affectionate, and positive relationship with me. Working with Thad is like learning how to rub two sticks together, to create fire, heat, warmth, energy, and connection. If you can light his fire, you will be successful, she continues. To me, her words are the mark of an excellent therapist who does what's necessary to access the child emotionally, and does not give up. Even if the child is complex. Even if standardized assessments do not highlight his strengths. Even if it seems hopeless. Never gonna give up on this guy, she affirms. I know he knows, just have to figure out how to access this knowledge, she says.

Trish continues, "Thad had no prior strategies to repair communication breakdown. He wasn't even aware that he had not received information. If he did receive the information, he didn't demonstrate the ability to rectify his own comprehension difficulties, and he was not inclined to ask questions for the sake of clarification or gaining new information. Through direct, extensive practice with Trish "trying to trick him" as the name for his comprehension challenge, and a loud red game-show buzzer, he learned to ask questions to further his own understanding such as "Can you say that again?" or "What does that mean?" compared to the previous strategy of leaving it at "This is too hard" or emotionally checking out. Trish says Thad can advocate more effectively in getting his communication needs met. He is participating in the present, and he is working toward furthering his understanding of his immediate interactions with others.

Trish talks about his "splinter skills," the uneven development and confusing representation of his actual skill sets in the following way:

"While working with Thad, I noticed a strange gap in his problem solving abilities. Since I've known him, Thad could always decode at a higher level than he could comprehend. I frequently had text available to him when we were working on higher-level comprehension tasks so he wouldn't have to rely on memory. It was then that I noticed that Thad was not referencing the text to find information that was being asked of him. I had read it to him, he had read it aloud. I would ask a question or present a fill-in-the-blank type of prompt and he would respond, dumbfounded, "I don't know" or "Let me think." He eye gaze was anywhere but on the written text where the answers--the information he needed--could be found. He had no strategy to access it. When I asked him, "Thad, where can you find the answer?" he responded in frustration, "I don't know. Can you just tell me, please?" It was then that we started focusing on how to glean information from written language. We started with vocabulary labeling using pictures, internet searches and real objects, labeling their parts. Thad now shifts back and forth from written text to the object or picture, actively searching and usually, successfully finding the information being asked of him.

Vocabulary is a by-product of this activity, with the grand prize of him implementing strategies of accessing, understand and applying information to solve a problem."

How can he have a speech delay when he talks, others say to me in confusion and a little bit smug, as if they had outed my little secret cover-up. Oops, I say, embarrassed for them in their arrogance and ignorance, your stupid-pants are showing. Cover up please. The snufflebumble of this senseless balderdash pendulums to and fro in my mind. It besmirches me relentlessly, as I hobnob incessantly with reality.

I think about engaging with Thad, and practicing parent participation in the IEP process and in his life through rockclimbing, through cooking together, through camping and travel adventures. I think about checking in with our family strengths and working from them. If you like it a lot, maybe they could too. For example, we find that a way to connect with him is through rockclimbing, starting with compliance, then working through sensory challenges to put on shoes and tolerate harness and ropes, and ultimately we move into sequencing, as in "Climb up the pink tape route, and don't step on the blue tape," an exercise that began in compliance and eradicating autistic behavior became strengths and moments of friendship with others. Parent participation in the IEP in a child or young adult's program, in the long and short term, because parents are the ones ultimately left sitting at the IEP table when our children age out of the educational system at 22, that fall off the cliff moment that sneaks up on us just like the cartoon vulture that eats us up in one gulp, burps a satisfied gas balloon, and spits out the bones, the end or the beginning.

Sometimes I feel like I am building on a flimsy foundation, a non-retrofitted house sitting on a fault line in California, one rumble and he tumbles. I keep trying to reinforce, fill in, build, help, and strengthen him. I sit in a pile of mortar and bricks often trying to piece together where to smooth the concrete in the cracks and the crevices, a mother with handfuls of smooth cream that can solidify a structure, but where is the biggest crack, and forever concerned with who will provide that same structural stability to him that one day I am ultimately gone, and he remains? Panic attacks wash up and over me like salty waves, and I shudder and shake like an early morning California earthquake that jacks up traffic and nerves, as I continue to rebuild my offspring, my structure, my masterpiece in worry and wonder, amazement and despair, sadness and delight.

The first time we make gluten free, casein free, egg free pizza, it tastes like shit. The second time it tastes like cardboard. We moved through flavors resembling plastic, and eau-de-none-of-the-above. Trying to cook a pizza with many unknown powders and substitutions is such a challenge, we realize. We substitute gelatin for eggs, flours for other flours, and the first time I cooked gluten free was his sixth birthday party, and the brownies that looked and tasted like the residue on the bottom of the barbeque. Oh yeh, and in addition to IEP meaning "I eat pizza," it can also mean, "Individual Education Plan,"

For his annual IEP that year, I make a series of gluten-free goodies, and I bring local coffee and citrus smiles to share with my friends, who are also Thad's teachers and therapists. As the blueberry crumble and almond shortbread come to life on their tongues, I listen to the expertise and knowledge of the beloved members of his IEP team. So many ideas, so much openness to collaborate, reconsider, try, understand, and to push him in new, unfamiliar yet hopeful ways. It is critical that Thad's providers understand him and his unique ways of learning and engaging.

We realize that his vocabulary level is so low for Fifth Grade, and that he has been working on Third Grade math since Third Grade, every year revisiting the same set of math tasks that he masters as he is working on it. Things like how to carry and borrow in addition and subtraction, and times tables are mastered at the moment when taught, but when checked six months later for review and retention, it is gone. So many vocabulary words taught again and again and we change our IEP game plan. Could we change a series of his academic goals to functional goals? We ask each other, with the reasoning of having his goals be meaningful, manageable, attainable, and functional. Working on something for a purpose compared to working on something just to pass the time or move through standardized grade level expectations. Our team decides to switch his IEP goals from academic goals to primarily functional goals.

IEP goals are annual progress predictors and targets for children in all academic, behavioral, sensorial, social, auditory, and counseling aspects. The IEP goals drive the service a student receives, as in if there is no goal, there is no need. And we have plenty of goals to work on and work from. I feel grateful that we design his goals to support his challenges, and celebrate and use his strengths. In the domain of Pragmatics and Conversation Skills, we write goals like, he will "participate in small talk with a peer during a semi-structured situation over five exchanges three out of five trials given one verbal prompt and one indirect cue over a two week period," with quarterly benchmarks. In Nonverbal Pragmatics, he "will pair a facial expression and a body posture which correlates to his verbal message," and in Problem-solving Pragmatics, "during a structured activity, he will be able to identify a hypothetical/situational problem and provide two possible solutions." We support and dissect his deficits into measurable, meaningful bites of progress.

In the Writing domain, he will "write a basic paragraph based on a concrete experience he has had," and notes describe that he will require prompting with topic sentence, details, transition words and a conclusion. We aspire to master the act of telling time accurately with a goal, and that he will use a calculator on iPhone to produce correct answers in addition, subtractions, multiplication, division, use the 'on,' 'off,' and 'clear' buttons. We write goals regarding using money to make purchases with correct amounts, how to receive correct change, and identify currency (paper and coin) values accurately.

Through tech, we sync our minds and our devices, as we are supported in using the iPad, Wii, and various apps to help him understand the world, using technology for remediation all the way through to pleasure and down-time. Susi says to me, you know that space on the iPad from the drawing app between the picture and the actual written story, I'll take that space on, idea creation. Thad and I will work on coming up with great ideas, how they work together with our words, and ways to represent a storyline. He has goals about Paying Attention, in small group instruction, in large group instruction, and aspects of him providing details from others" information during sharing, and social time is also addressed.

Reading and decoding words, providing concrete details, and answer WH questions from sixth grade text measure all around grade level for Thad. But the comprehension of the word, the meaning, and the bigger picture of the words continue to escape him, although I must say I am deeply pleased with his progress at this point. I feel sad that he is developmentally behind still but I feel so fucking psyched that he is so far away from where he started, and I see different outcomes for his future now that I could not imagine prior to so many amazing people he has had the honor to work with, and so many pivotal therapies he experienced.

We write goals for him in the area of Receptive language, with specific guidance on remediating his deficits in referencing spoken and written information from multi-sentence length texts. He also has goals in Emotional Regulation, which ask him to identify his emotional state, and provide an appropriate response to the situation, such as verbalizing the need, obtaining help, or offering support. He has a Keyboarding goal, as I silent jump for joy, hooray for appropriate goals for going-into-6th graders, and he's good at typing. Of course he is.

We decide to create a place, known as the "red binder," named this due to the red-ness and the binder-ness essence of the item, for all of his speech, reading, spelling and homework. To make definitions salient by drawing each vocabulary word, to re-address novel and previously targeted words, to teach strategies at decoding multiple meaning words through Semantics goal, and the on-going need for intensive interaction with vocabulary words as we sought to work on "marked deficits in both receptive and expressive vocabulary both academically and during spontaneous speech."

The team agrees that a red binder shall serve as his vocabulary, spelling, reading, homework, and language comprehension book as concrete learning, mining his life experiences to check comprehension. A history of binders and page protectors that started with his work with Kelli, his life neatly stacked. A progression of his developmental expectations, milestones, academic, behavioral, and social skills safety kept in page protectors in colored books piled high in Mom's office.

We add the red binder into his program for another important reason, Independence. The language arts homework packets started getting very hard at the end of last year, and we had worked very diligently over the past years getting him to total independence in his homework tasks. Yet, the level of vocabulary was getting abstract, and I found myself assisting him with anagrams of abstract words like "loyalty" and "fluctuate," me wondering if this was the best use of his time. The team felt that it was a better choice to use more concrete words, and to modify the homework expectations and continue his independence in those written tasks.

The team decides that the calculator on his iPhone will support his functional math goals. I want him to feel smart and not frustrated at school, and I'm not a math whiz why should I expect my son to be? He doesn't not recall math functions and facts and operations without a lull in instruction, but he can demonstrate spacial concepts, and notions of geometry in his drawings. It is so important to remember his strengths as we remediate his deficits.

He has Social Skills goals that support his challenges on the playground, with specific breakdowns of skill sets on how to initiate play with others, how to sustain emotional and physical engagement with friends, and lots of strategies for him to use if things get rough or confusing. To help with organizing behavior, the teacher will give the child an array of choices for recess, the teacher frontload expectations for unstructured time by asking the child to pick a friend to play with, to choose group in process or join an organized sport. Sometimes the teacher will To support children with social challenges at recess, very often the teacher will review the rules of the game, practice outcomes of winning or losing, practice the ingredients of the game, like getting a basket or a goal, being tagged or being "it." The teacher will also help the students know how to process the emotions associated with the happiness of getting a point, or how it feels when you get hit in dodgeball. How to be a good winner and a good loser, kinda like life skills.

I am aware of the monkey mind, the ego, and their unhelpful tricks. They yammer, they whisper, hateful hearts and evil mindgames, not enough, never good enough, you can be a better mother. I hear and listen and release these thoughts to the universe to be reabsorbed as energy for a more constructive purpose, and I look to another master, Morticia Adams, to help me define "normal," as I thank her silently for inspiring my son to want to snap his fingers like they do in the Adams Family song, all the while understanding that we can find inspiration, resources, and possibilities everywhere if our minds are open to it. My son likes the Adams Family hand in the box because it is so scary and so very dangerous, and Morticia reminds me, "Normal is an illusion. What is normal for the spider is chaos to the fly."

As I tell this story, I remind myself to feel gratitude each day for my amazing, funny quirky son who brings me joy like no other, and teaches me so much. I embrace an "attitude of gratitude" as a way of striving to be for my health and happiness and I was so happy that he was engaging in a certain way with his friends at school. Unique ways such as Butt-guts, a show-and-tell Powerpoint we made that documented the removal and biopsy of a mole on Thad's butt. The cool doctor let me take pictures, him posing with a scalpel full of Thad's ass shrapnel. Thad told and showed his class all about his graphic bloody butt incision. I feel so much gratitude and loving grace toward the amount of blessings I experience in the world.

I think about Saint Anthony, patron saint of lost things, and Saint Jude Thaddeus, patron saint of lost souls, and I wonder if they participating in any active way toward saving autistic children. I also wonder if there is a connection between these saints, my child, and his loneliness, and I hope forever there is not. Sara texts me a picture of Thad not paying attention in group, a little image on my phone of everyone sitting on the floor and Thad still oblivious to the directions, still perched high on the chair. I feel gratitude that he is able to sustain the requirements of a group that lasts one hour, and that he no longer requires an Aide to stay seated. Thad asks me about summer time with his cousins in water-based activities in Maine, Rhode Island, Cincinnati, Cleveland, and Chicago. I go to the chiropractor regularly to get my hips adjusted. Smooth like water, the chiro says to me. T has a moderate level tantrum in the office, his spine is adjusted by the chiropractor and promptly, swiftly, he stops talking all that autistic smack.

And then I bust down the men's bathroom door at the Denny's in San Dimas on our way to school on a Tuesday morning because Thad needs to barf right now. He runs into the stall, and I refuse to leave because my autistic child is actively barfing in the first toilet to the left, as various other patrons enter and exit, some pee discretely as I avert my eyes, and some offer to keep watch for me. We generate quite a ruckus as people rush in and out for coffee and sausage biscuits, I wait until my boy is done heaving, we drive to school, and

I write, "Traffic" as the reason we are late on the check-in clipboard in the office. "Yakking at Denny's" for the reason he is tardy might be misconstrued as an excessive amount of unnecessary information, and could be considered as socially unexpected behavior by me. As I attempt to honor social norms and respect social nuances, I try to downplay the series of events that had just happened, and then, Thad loudly announces to his class, Guess where I just barfed, as I deposit him that morning in Room 905.

Thad is fascinated by Spanish speakers, and he is so interested in how people speak Spanish to communicate. My mom talks to Horacio and others in Spanish, he notices outloud. A foreign language that seems sometimes like it might be more attainable than English, as sometimes I see him watch Youtube videos of known movies dubbed in foreign language, fascinated with the idea of communicating with language, how those people communicate with a language that might sound similar to the garbled English he must experience on a regular basis. Spanish is a language like English, except I understand words like "hola" and "adios," he must ponder. Sometimes I think he must think fuck this English bullshit, and let's start over in a different language. He would draw pictures of ice cream, and write, "helado," underneath, and so many pictures of particular interests like keys, "llaves," drawn to many specifications, and gentle language sprinkles of, "hola," "adios," and "como estas" throughout like verbal whipped cream.

Because I stay down near SLDC during the day while he is at school, I begin to volunteer in his ASL (American Sign Language) class and in his social skills group, and I do yoga and movement with the kids in 905. I think about my time in these environments at his school as little morsels of me giving back to those who are so awesome in Thad's tribe, and as real-time parent training for me with some very smart therapists and teachers. As I volunteer in his environment, I learn.

Working on language comprehension continues to be frustrating for both of us when even the definitions in the homework include unknown words and nuances to explain meaning. For example, one night as we work on vocabulary words, I describe the word "tolerate" to Thad as "being okay with something you don't really like." He questions, Like eating salad? Me, well sorta.

Then, we set out to decode the following sentence with the targeted vocabulary on his worksheet:

When your little brother tags along, you *tolerate* it.

First of all, he doesn't understand the concept, "to tag along," because it is not exactly come along, it's more of a come-along with a sense of enduring what we intrinsically understand as irritating sibling behavior. He is a little brother, and he adores his big sis. To him, the idea that it would be anything but glorious and awesome to have him come along on his big sister's adventure is inconceivable. Why would she not want him to come? Would that mean that she doesn't like him? Again, nuances of truths, feelings, and so many emotional shades of grey. The idea that little brothers could be annoying is beyond his mind, and again we quietly close the packet. I realize that these words in the homework are too abstract for my concrete thinker. And that the homework pack on bullying is challenging because the only way I know to explain the concept of a "bully" is to ask him to recall prior uncomfortable events that make him sad where he was targeted by mean kids because he looked or acted different. He still talks about specific significant events of bullying early on.

His next IEP is a triennial year which means we assess his performance levels in all relevant domains. It is also the year that our settlement with the school district ends, and we must return to a conversation with them about Thaddeus and his future. I continue to feel nervous and hopeful.

Yesterday, Thad had two teeth pulled by the dentist to make space in his mouth for the adult choppers, he doesn't understand the visceral sensation of his teeth moving, he starts trying to wiggle his adult teeth out of his head, and I issue some pretty big consequences to quickly extinguish that behavior. Many autistic people have pulled out their adult teeth for various reasons, as we talk about his forever teeth, and about being a grown-up person in the world. Inside my clattery brain, I worry about what's next for him, about Middle School placement, the confusing puberty waves he is riding, and the associated challenges of growing up as a boy in our world. I worry about how to pay for his future therapies, and I wish on every star I can see that night for an educational and biomedical sugar daddy.

A poignant moment of emotional viscosity becomes an ethereal rainbow of hope one day as we commute. Pouring rain is causing troublesome traffic, and then, the sky is drenched in sunshine. We smile together, look upward, and see both sides of a rainbow for the first time ever. Thad and I discuss leprechauns and pots of gold like friends, and I feel so much gratitude in my life.

CHAPTER 9

Passion Flowers Smell Like Mom's Shampoo

THE PASSION FLOWERS smell like Mom's shampoo, and they look like dinosaur flowers, Thad says. I enjoy his social referencing, as I automatically start thinking about which academic domains this statement belongs in within his IEP goals, considering the points of reference when he says this to me as we admire the showy blossoms, cutting samples for friends, teachers, and therapists as gifts. Always on my mind, more ways to get the message through his mind with so many repeated attempts of comprehension and communication. Again, I am sure that he must experience it viscerally to truly comprehend the meaning of a word. What do they smell like? My hair as a tangible reference point for my son's understanding of the olfactory experience of the crazy pungent blooms out on the autumn fence is a lesson in perspective taking for him and me. Why yes, my hair does smell like those delicious flowers, sweet boy.

Gorgeous purple and white passion flowers grow on the long, rough, deeply stained brown fence in my backyard once per year, somewhere between Halloween and my mid-November birthday, these prolific, sweet-smelling, delicious magenta flowers overtake the spiky trellises. Vision of prehistoric times in flower form as literally hundreds of invasive blossoms overtake the fence each year. Born from the single plant I put in the ground ten years ago, I now have this vine full of fat green leaves thriving over all over 50 feet of full-sun fence. This setup is great because the plant grows well without my assistance and it flowers once per year with attractive colors and a showy display. Yet, I have created an accidental expansive experiment in one entity taking over an entire pathway happening right in my backyard. Passion flower is invasive to the point of killing other plants around it, taking up all the space and the resources. One way to consider the fence full of a single plant might be hooray for invasive plants, as a gardener with limited time and an affinity toward beautiful surroundings. From this perspective, yes this is a good thing.

Perspective taking, the ability to see multiple points of view fluidly and automatically in social situations, to know the appropriate social response, and to be able to anticipate with relative usual accuracy the other person's mood, feeling, and response toward you, your actions and your words is an important life skill, and a very challenging skill for people on the Autism spectrum. To see the various aspects of differing viewpoints is an exhaustive list, and a challenging series of many social skill-sets that must be taught, retaught, and reviewed and does not come naturally for those with Autism. Accordingly, we must consider all of the positive and negative angles of the lush greenery on my backyard fence.

Like what about the other plants that tried to thrive in that part of our garden, those plants that I lovingly laid in the moist dirtbeds before I understood the level of intensity the passion flowers pushed against those equally beautiful, viable and diverse plants and flowers? Many of the other plants and vines all eventually died, even with me aggressively hacking back the fast passion flower foliage as it choked and invaded lovely stalks and stamens, sweet cactus blooms, vibrant desert colors, all placed by me with love and intention. The passion flowers took the space of any other plant that got in its way.

I think about passion flowers and "Candida," a yeast overgrowth in the gut commonly experienced by autistic people, both as arrestingly beautiful and very dangerous snowflakes in our swirls of nature and reality. I remember seeing candida on a cellular level under a microscope for the first time in massage school, and there was a particularly eery gorgeous scary aura around it. So visually appealing, quietly floating through our digestive track, attaching so easily to the innocent pink lining of the intestinal walls with barbs impossible to dislodge, the candida reproduces like fucked-up rabbits intent on taking over the power and function of the host, my child. I try to make the intruder leave with supplements diets and drugs, and the collateral damage sloughs off at farthest points as the embedded points of the snowflake dig deeper into the delicate lining of our children's emotional centers, their second brain, their gut walls, their gut-brain connection.

Our kids feel physical, emotional, social, and communication misery from the candida overgrowth presence and destruction, as this fungal form of candida with barbed appendages called rhizoids literally cuts through the intestinal walls, and allows undigested proteins and toxins into the bloodstream, and eventually into the brain. In this unending quest to heal his leaky gut and seal up his digestive track into wellness again, we battle yeast overgrowth every time he takes antibiotics, eats too much processed food or sugar, and sometimes for no apparent reason at all. I will suspect the yeasties are up to no good when we see his foggy eyes, forgetfulness, and spacey lethargic behavior.

I imagine a bubbling mire, the excruciating pain of a yeast infection on the inside of his body, corrupting his brain, his organs, his sensibility, and it makes me so sad. I wonder about children with no words, and how they scream with no voice. I imagine their explosive behavior as a form of communication, telling us of their pain, confusion, and isolation. I imagine the innumerable connections among gut health, proper nutrition, and autistic behavior that should be paid attention to, made a priority in funding decisions for medical protocols and research, and I shout foul play, liar, money, money, money towards those who staunchly won't consider, won't dialogue, won't learn, and believe and espouse unfound garbage otherwise.

I hope that so many more people continue to consider the significance, educate themselves and the public at large, highlighting the myriad of connections and concerns among healthy digestive tracks, brain and body function, proper nutrition, Autistic people and their life-satisfaction and well-being, financial emotional and spiritual support to Autism families, and solutions to very serious questions about the long-term care of our kids. And I hope that there are new and better ways very soon, like immediately, like now, that can support families because it is devastating how far the horror of Autism stretches, a whole body disorder that affects the whole family daily. I hope that the seriousness and the urgency of an epidemic of Children with Autism (who eventually become Adults with Autism) finally makes it to the daily news, as an epidemic, as a tragedy, as a call to action, and onto the desks of those with the money and power as ultimate importance. Our beautiful, unique, damaged children currently sitting motionless, stacking up, like endless piles of blank papers waiting to be signed.

Passion flowers grow well in the swelter-fest concrete corridor between our house and the neighbor's, a fluid digestive system for smooth passage of green garbage cans, dirty mountain bikes, and salty surfboards that can get upwards in temperature of some serious triple digits. If I do nothing, the flowers will inch to the left and kill my red pink and white roses too, one of the few other plants hearty enough to survive and enjoy the heat in this swath of Hell's Kitchen. I could do nothing, as the passion flowers aggressively growing in that spot in the yard do not directly bother me. But without my help by keeping them at bay, the roses will ultimately be overtaken and die. The plumeria only holds on nearby with my constant attention toward removing the curly choky passion-filled wandering flower-tendrils. Jasmine planted with my big plans of delicious aromas wafting into my kitchen on warm summer nights, bouncy agrapantha with purple and white balls dance in the strong sunshine, and French and English lavender, all survive because I help, and if I did nothing, the passion flowers would also overtake the concrete walkway and eventually swallow up the garden tools propped gently to the side.

I think about the day I purchased the passion flowers from the local flowermongers. They say, it's invasive, and I say, great, I'll take two. I think about Darwin and the "survival of the fittest," and the way that this theory of evolution could be where we are with our kids, the priorities, and acceptable human collateral damages we see in modern society. I think about the Canary Party political party, my preferred political soupbowl, and again recall their motto, we are sick and tired of being sick and tired. Our sweet canaries in the dark coal mine, our sweet children with injured minds.

And once again, Gentle Readers, in a celebration-for-the-peculiar kinda way, I invite you to consider the intent and interest and weird perseverations in my strange and wonderful life as I visualize my garden path as a digestive track, as I imagine Candida as a feature in my yard, as we all take a moment in appreciating and celebrating the blathering musings of a focused Autism parent. Normal, what's that? Yak, yak, yak, a terminal freaky diatribe about my thoughts on how too much yeast jacks his system, and then after these intense intestinal considerations I realize that I am a little jacked up myself, lost in dreamy thoughts swirling outside my kitchen window, seeing all of these connections in my immediate circumstances that just might board me on the crazy train itself.

As I strive to find passion in various activities and people and moments attached to Autism, it is important to consider the secret ingredient in the soup of success for our kids. I consider the foundations of his therapies, the notions that we must start where they are, we must help them to manage behavior and teach skills, strategies, and support them socially academically and sensorially, yes. I believe that the secret is to identify and to start with their passion, an intense interest, an entryway into the so many ideas and opportunities that these kids have locked in their brains. I recall that so long ago there was a very small singular porthole into Thad's mind. Seven years ago, human interaction and engagement with my child was only successful if based solely on his ideas and directives regarding Buzz Lightyear, Pretend Peril, and chicken eggs. Fast forward, and I extrapolate so many ideas about him, his future, and appropriate care for him from so many extraneous places. Now, I see this young man who is growing up and developing into a handsome, sweet, thoughtful friend with some cool talents and unique interests to enhance his next life-steps. We will highlight his creative talents and unique perspectives as a way of furthering comprehension and social communication for him, as a foundation for future job skills training, as thoughtful attention to his future of best outcomes in adult life, and a basis for meaningful social interactions and life relationships.

And then, one morning, Thad is finally taller than me. He is so excited because according to his internal playbook, those who are taller are in charge. We commence a multi-month discussion that begins every morning, as he shoots up like a tall sunflower in the middle of the night, towering further and further over me, eyeing me sweetly and menacingly, demanding that I relinquish my power to him, that he is now in charge because he is taller. In the past few months as he moves toward cresting the I'm-taller-than-my-mom wave, he would constantly rise to his tippy-toes when he stood next to me, making sure to look down on his shrimpy mom with a pretend-evil gaze to support his plans to renegotiate with me who is taller, and therefore in charge. Sorry dude, so onto your shenanigans and so not believing the hype, I say. I'm still the boss, I remind my tall son.

Children and adults on the Autism Spectrum very often have a particular interest that is highly motivating, a way into the mind. I believe we should find that passion, that intrinsic motivation, their price-point, the porthole into the soul, be amazed at the beauty, and build his future life and learning around it. Thad's passion? That's easy, a simple recipe: Drawing, Farming, Cooking, and being in movement and outdoors, with a dash of Pretend Peril infused into it all.

I think about Thad, and his future as a capable human being who meaningfully participates in the world, in life, a person who gives back to society as an employable adult. What does he want to do in the future? As we move into his teenage years, I consider his interests, and I start to plan his plans for an adult life now. Honestly, I don't really care if he can fill in a worksheet of facts about North Dakota, or if he knows the symbols for various heavy and soft metals, but I do care about his future and plan to now start now. I plant seeds of jobs, interests, and possibilities in him, starting now with his interests to nurture and grow into employable skills sets. 90% of adults with Autism are unemployed or underemployed, and I think about this statistic constantly as a consider fostering skill sets in him that could eventually become a job.

Thaddeus creates visual representations of his feelings, and depictions of real-life experiences by drawing pictures, and animating cartoons. This strategy helps him overcome his communication challenges in verbal language, and supports his strength as a visual learner. Drawing is an organizing cognitive process for Thad that captures his unique humor and attention to detail, and help him communicate his important, thoughtful ideas. Attending to the process of idea creation, aspects of attention focus and memory, his interests, Pretend Peril, organizing, storyboard sequencing, vocabulary and comprehension, social skills, communication of his ideas, nonverbal gestures, eye contact, eye gaze, and abstract written ideas, such as "meanwhile" are so important to the advancement of his mental places, and his happiness in life.

Drawing pictures started as an exercise in ABA compliance and a drill in Speech Therapy to draw and name the parts of the picture. Then, it became a way to visually describe feelings, perception, emotion, and a way to communicate with a friend that is not oral-language intensive. And then, it became a pasttime for him, a unique interest, and the process of drawing helps me tease out different domains to focus on in remediation. While drawing, he superseded his IEP goals, by appropriately demonstrating emotion, facial expression, layering story-lines, turn-taking, conversational turn-taking, and empathy in his drawing. He and I hang out and draw, that's our social time together. We do vocabulary, story creation, ideation, sequencing, and planning because the words he says, what he writes, and what he draws in each panel all must match. Sometimes, that's hard.

We use his particular interests as a focus, as a hook to engage his mind, and to help him to be present with the tasks of drawing and story creation. If he is thinking about dripping faucets, light switches, and sink handles, for example, we build the stories forward and backward using these interests as a starting point. Once, he felt quite mentally stuck on the visual of the cool vintage bathroom sink handles at my parents' home. He talked about the hot and cold faucet fixtures to me incessantly, and we began to draw. I asked him to tell me about the "before" and the "after" of his story, his ideas, and his intense focus on the faucets. An elaborate story emerged about the aquarium, a particular penguin stuffy he had just acquired, and the way Grandma's dog had beheaded the stuffed animal just as Thad came to the stuffed penguin's rescue, and sewed his black and white body back together. Usually, in Thad's story, there is someone or something being very wronged, Thad swoops in, and saves the day in an opulent fashion.

We use a "storyboard," a series of pages that he draws on, writes on, and numbers as a way to organize his thoughts, his ideas, and the flow of his prose. This way of capturing the visual, verbal and emotional parts of him started many years ago in a summer camp about cartoon animation. The first time we tried to make a storyboard, what he drew, what he wrote, and what he said did not match. I thought about how it was so confusing how he was trying to organize his thoughts, and then it became a lesson that we worked on. I told him that what he says, draws, and writes must match. For others to be with you emotionally and hear your story, you must make all of the pieces match, I tell him constantly and we work on his words, his pictures, and his ideas falling into a uniform march of consistency and appropriate communication. Sometimes the ideas start on the iPad as a little written story he pens during our long commutes, sometimes in a conversation little flickers of funny flow and ebb in his words as I see him picturing so many funny scenes in his mind that I will then ask him to draw, and sometimes his time at his animation class has me doubled over in laughter as I see his creativity accessed by a very special, talented teacher named Ian.

And then we have a very significant moment one day, a tears-of-joy kinda significance, the day that he first vocalized that he was having perseverative thoughts, that he couldn't make them go away, that the thoughts were scary, and that he didn't like it. He tells me, Mom it's back, the flying car is back and I cannot get it out of my brain. His perseveration of the flying car from the Harry Potter movies plagues him intermittently like a virus that lives deep in his cells. It's back Mom, I am scared of it, make it go away. I am floored that he verbalizes to me that he is looping a movie scene in his mind as usually, I have to guess and surmise why he is emotionally absent or not paying attention. I am also happily freaked out that he tells me that he doesn't like it, that maybe perhaps he prefers reality to the Autism-loop that churns him so often. And, I always had thought that those monkey reels in his brain were comforting to him, again so happy to be wrong.

He draws the flying car on the first blank paper and uses his written words to explain it, then he draws his brain and a bouncing ball on the second page describing the feeling, and then he grabs a third paper, and writes words about how it scares him, how he doesn't like it and how he wants it to go away. I call this a "brain dump," as we do this regularly to release his thoughts, and to get the images out of his head and on paper. For example, I will pick him up from school, and he will be yammering on about hot-dog people without a context or reference point for me. I ask him to draw what he is thinking, and with this action, context is provided to me in the form of a series of step-by-step instruction panels on how to make little hot-dog people with cut up weenies and tooth-picks. Yep, I tell him, I like it and we can definitely do it. I get the context, I embrace the idea, and I am in. We make a family of frankfurters that night for dinner.

Some recurring images in his brain are more damaging than others to my son. Buzz Lightyear, Harry Potter flying cars, and certain cartoon snippets are heroin to my kid, and again we separate fantasy from reality, an uncomfortable loop that pulls him away from us so regularly, a loud script in his head that demands his attention to a mind-numbing loop of words characters sounds and sensations that his brain incorrectly interprets as soothing and familiar, yet damages him in so many ways. This experience with the flying cars was the first time that he actively asked for it to stop and asked for help, as we are always asking him if he is in his head, and if so, to get out of your head and be with us. He asks me all the time why he cannot watch certain movies or see certain images he craves, I tell him that anything that gets him "stuck" he cannot be exposed to. If something gets him stuck, he goes away from me and it makes me, his mom, his friend, deeply sad, and it is my job to take it away to save him from the Autism spin back to a lonely pretend world of nothing and nobody real.

He learns how to use "talk bubbles" and "think bubbles" to identify thoughts and words, and he demonstrates that he understands the difference. We talk so much about how you can be thinking one thing, and saying another, and that it's okay and it is expected behavior. I am reminded of a particular drawing in which Thad drew a particular tantrum involving a tall tree in our yard, him yelling at the therapist, and him refusing to get down out of the tree. He draws thought bubbles with words and feelings like, leave me alone, I need time alone, I have too many "thinks" in my mind, and his therapist issuing consequences for his defiant behavior with sharp lines and mad eyes. I see on paper his perspective on how wronged he felt when she wanted to work on alphabet flashcards and he just wanted a moment of peace, high up in the tree.

Perspective taking is so difficult for people on the Autism spectrum, and I try so hard to make each moment of confusion a teachable moment for him, to help him understand how to act and react if he perceives or misperceives a situation because I believe that if he incorrectly perceives that something happened or it actually did, it is the same and he needs to have appropriate responses either way. I remember the days of public school when a boy would brush by him, Thad would incorrectly perceive the unfamiliar touch as the boy hitting him, he would strike back, get in trouble for hitting, be mad, and he would not understand why he was in trouble for getting hit and defending himself. I would then teach him that if a boy hits, if he did or did not in reality is immaterial, to tell his teacher, and to not strike back.

Drawing and computer animation are also ways of introspection, self-reflection, and communication for Thad. He will take picture of his face with his iPhone, and then study the image of his expression he plans to draw. I am also known to be his live model, as I strike poses in the kitchen of the precise arm formation when using a bow and arrow, or with Ursula, as a demonstration of how two people's bodies look when they hug, as he captures the angles of arms, elbows, and hips in his mind and on the paper. The confidence he derives from drawing is also a place of creative problem solving for Thad. As he drew one day, I directed him to divide the page into three panels. He did not know how to equally represent three parts on the page, but he did know four equal parts. So, he made a large cross on the paper, and then wrote in the unwanted fourth square, loser, bad, no, wrong. Compensatory strategies and problem solving skills currently at work, I say fuck yeah.

He draws his protests in the margins as one-inch wide ban signs, the circle with the diagonal line of protest, all the things he will not do, such as capitalize the letter B, erase a mistake, or feed the dogs. He draw his freaks, his stinks, and his tantrums, all different qualifiers for various levels of meltdowns and explosive behavior, and then we talk about it afterwards. He also draws his places of happiness, interest, and focus engaging skill-sets of language and word comprehension, vocabulary usage, and perspective-taking. We push forward in strings of cheese, vegetable chips of communication, and melodies of his laughter, as he puts his ideas on the page and we share joined moments of communication.

And then something cool and amazing happened in my cross-talk with Thad's providers. I say to Jacque, we are still trying to figure out the attention, memory, and focus pieces of his puzzle during his most recent assessments and I feel somewhat dejected and frustrated. How can I think about this differently, where can I go next, I ponder to her aloud. What if we change his EEG hook-ups toward points associated with memory, attention, and focus. We found Thad's brain's sweet spot, and his storyboards girth up from four pages to 55 pages, almost seemingly overnight. We had found some particular neuronal connection that was stimulated, a connection was made, and his first cartoon animation series was created. Like a cerebral vomit of ideas, the kind of barf I like.

His cartoon dreams come to life, and "Saving Nick" is born. Thad begins creating his first animation webisode series through Exceptional Minds Studio in Sherman Oaks, a non-profit vocational center and computer animation studio for young adults on the Autism Spectrum. Thad works with the amazing Ian, his 1:1 instructor in Adobe Flash, and his ideas take shape in the assets and scenes he draws. We drive on the Hollywood Freeway one afternoon per week to get to this mecca of calm, acceptance, and motivation for my son. He feels so confident and excited at the cool vibe of the community of students and instructors at the school. He loves to hang out with Ian, and he works so hard. The vibrant red walls and blue room welcome him into a sweet space, and he feels proud that he hangs with a bunch of guys who do animation, and shave. Yep, he's getting older and shaving is what grown-ups do. Social awareness, his knowledge that he is getting older and how he must act appropriately in grown-up environments, as he steps up his game when he walks into the studio, with the big guys, the cool guys, the grown-up men, hell yeah.

Check out his awesome cartoons:
PART 1
http://m.youtube.com/watch?v=YtMrZZR-t3o

PART 2
http://m.youtube.com/watch?v=FyB7JvrsUOY

PART 3
http://m.youtube.com/watch?v=pWPU2PD10OA

Thad begins to draw his ideas for his first cartoon in an elaborate story-board. We smile at the "dangerous" series of events Thad describes on paper. A bad man named Jack wants to steal Thad's dog, Nick, and take Nick to his house in the mountains to keep him as his pet. Thad grabs a few weapons from his virtual "weapons closet" and begins to explore a series of interactions and emotions from his anger as a response to someone swiping his dog, his parents' worry that he has left for the mountains on his rescue mission alone, his sister's concern about his whereabouts, and the deep battle fury that Jack and Thad experience together as Thad sneaks around Jack's hideout, to Nick whimpering in joy at the sight of Thad,

Thad rejoicing in finding his dog-buddy, Thad's family so relieved at his safety, so proud of his bravery for saving the family pooch, and Jack ultimately realizing how Thad has tricked him. Thad learns a new vocab word, revenge, as he explains the final fight-scene-turn-close-up-to-Jack's-mad-face concept as Thad tells me that Jack "wants to do a mean thing back at Thad for stealing Nick."

And then, we have the next series, in "Jack's Revenge," the sequel to "Saving Nick," and we discuss the word "sequel," and Thad describes to me the five things that will happen, and very often he wants to go back to "Saving Nick," and re-describe or re-draw what he has already drawn in the first story. It is important that we talk through his ideas before he draws to be clear on his intentions, and he is allowed to change his idea for the story as long as it is a new idea, not a recycled or perseverative thought. As we progress in his stories, we make a plan of what will happen in the story, and how it will go. He tells me, and I write it down. For example, we have a written plan for the next storyboard called "Jack's Revenge" with five new significant things that will happen in the story:

1. Jack will superglue the floor shut after he steals the dogs from Thad.
2. Thad will feed Jack a spicy food-bomb to trick him while he rescues the dogs from Jack.
3. He will shop for "fresh" weapons at a "weapons club."
4. There will be an epic battle between Thad and Jack with the theme of "He was my dog first."
5. In the final scene, Jack will attempt to punch Thad, miss and round-house-punch himself, causing him to fall off into the waterfall at the end of the story.

Sometimes, we discuss and discuss minutia of points to be sure all of his story aspects match and make sense, and sometimes we argue if he gets stuck on wanting to redo a scene, recreate a scene from a popular movie lightly veiled as his own, or if what he wants to draw next is not logical or very off-topic.

"In the story, the following things will occur," is what we think about out-loud, and talk about for weeks as part of his idea creation. We discuss ideas, the why, the compare and contrast, but why would he do that? The "And then?"

Could that be possible? What does the other guy see? I see the wheels of his mind churn the images into words that I understand, images he will draw, and a storyline that is silly, unique, and PG-13 level scary. The agreement that Thad and I make is that he has to tell me the story idea, the main idea, five or six things that he plans will happen in the story, the details, and then he has to draw a storyboard representation with pictures and words that match the list. We talk and battle through the storyline and slowly his ideas emerge. He finishes "Jack's Revenge" on paper, and sets it in the queue for production. His series of funnies that he is sharing with others is so thoughtful and creatively silly, like my boy. I feel so proud.

The "dangerous" tale that he is currently working on is in process as the "prequel," the reason why Jack initially turned evil, and "prequel" as yet another vocabulary word and concept for Thad to master:

The Mental Process and the Backstory of each part of the
HOW JACK GOT EVIL:

1. Jack's parents made him brush his teeth with spicy Sriracha sauce. (I am trying to get him to eat new stuff, to dip with sauces, not for a particular sauce, just to keep the channels of introducing him to new stuff and him happily accepting new foods open, and as he complies with my request of trying ranch dressing, dunking his food in ketchup or spicy honey mustard, and he is particularly taken by the bottle of Sriracha and happily submerges his forked hunk of chicken in for a "sample," another vocab word I am actively trying to push into his brain.)

2. Jack's zombie friends are bugging him for "just a taste" of his brain. (Thad is reading comic books about zombies and he is very interested in the zombie lifestyles and zombie culinary choices, and how zombies are killed by stabbing them in the brain, compared to a vampire demise of being stabbed in the heart.)

3. Jack's zombie friends also bug him by eating his nose like sushi with chopsticks. (Recently, Thad had his first sushi experience as part of his on-going training for being a teenager. I brought Ursula and her friend along to demonstrate as cool real-time teen aficionados in sushi,

to model appropriate teen behavior, to teach him to go out with friends, how to hang out, and how to mix the wasabi and soysauce with the chopsticks.)

4. Scary monsters are riding their unicycles around Jack's house all night long, keeping him up, and he cannot get any sleep. (This idea is based on his unicycle riding, and on his first animated cartoon about you guessed it, scary monsters riding unicycles around his house. He particularly likes the residue of the frustration that his parents used to feel when he would keep them up all night prowling the house in search of mischief, and demonstrates this outward frustration with his facial expressions and exasperated sighs.)

5. Scary monsters trick him by gluing the channel changer to cheesy little-kid shows, not cool teenager shows. (He has always had a particular interest in glueing things. He uses a lot of glue when making the dudes house, and he is always asking, What other stuff can we glue Mom? He demonstrates a knowledge of what is appropriate for kids and teens to watch on television, although he maybe does not always follow these rules when left alone with the channel changer, and also he insinuates that the worst thing to do as a teen is to be subjected to little kid cartoons and humor.)

6. The culminating moment at the end of the story is when Thad has a swarm of bees in his nose, and then he sneezes on Jack. (We found ourselves in my car one day, waiting for a red light to turn in the middle of a mobile swarm of bees, a crazy hive in-transit experience that took a multi-minute rest on top of our car, and we were enveloped in the swarm for what seemed like a dangerous eternity to me. Thad loved it, particularly loves the danger of it, and always remembers and recalls it whenever we see or discuss bees.)

7. Jack's friendly body changes and morphs into EVIL JACK. (He likes characters that morph from one entity to another, popping, bubbling and physically changing from one thing to another, like the cartoon Danny Phantom, Harry Potter and the Poly-Juice potion, or anyone who physically manifests in a visual change from good to evil.) I cannot wait for him to animate this idea particularly because his pantomime of the issue was so hilarious.

Mom I wanna go to Exceptional Minds twice a week. Mom I wanna go to school there when I am a man someday, he says to me regularly. He normally never asks to increase the frequency of any type of organized instruction, and I wildly dream and bliss out over his request, seeing so much goodness in this environment of creativity, respect, opportunity, and possibility for my child and for so many creative cool young adults on the spectrum. My child being motivated by respectful instruction, fun, thoughtful words and responses, in an environment imbued with real employable skills and instruction that embraces unique strengths and supports unique challenges. The people are so important in every equation of his process that we experience.

Thad derives intrinsic motivation from the animation masters as he tells me, Mom we are in Hollywood, every time he sees the freeway sign because he had learned the significance of then awesomeness of Hollywood early on with his movie watching, and now with the newness of movie industry, cartoon animation and post-production. We talk about it, he listens, and works so hard to understand. I love to watch him think about his future, to consider that he could go to school all day when he is older to just draw, to go to school and do stuff that he likes and he is good at, what a concept, what a way to imagine learning, deriving motivation from a child's special interest or skill.

Exceptional Minds Studio (EM) is set to graduate its first class of students completing the three-year computer animation, and post-production certification vocation program in the spring of 2014, with so many movie credit accolades already under the studio's belt, EM students with legit paying jobs and IMBD credits to place proudly on their resumes, concrete representations of their creativity and employability. I feel proud for all of the students, and their parents with this huge accomplishment that highlights their unique talents, celebrating each student as a viable, employable adult, and I feel honored that my son is part of such an amazing organization.

After many months of weekly instruction, Ian tells me that Thad is finally relaxing into the experience of animating, and is allowing Ian to teach him stuff about nonverbal body movements, face expressions, hand gestures, and eye gaze as ways of nonverbal drawn communication. Thad's cartoons get richer and more layered with every loving spoonful, as Thad loosens up to be taught, as

Thad loosen up to learn. Thad and Ian draw together, conjure cool ideas, sample various musical scores to accompany the exciting adventures of Thad and Jack and Nick, as cool hip-hop vibes ooze out of Thad's bedroom when Thad realizes Nick has been stolen, superhero cool jams as he flies through the air with his jet-pack to save his beloved dog, and ominous tunes backdrop the anticipation and uncertainty that blanket the screen as we all collectively wonder, What's going to happen to Nick? I smile.

At home, animation happens on the computer and the iPad with a particular spin on the current series, "Thad and Dad" where unfortunate things befall Dad at Thad's hand, such as Thad shrinking or increasing the size of Dad's head with particularly elaborate cartoon space guns, or Dad making one false move and Thad dumping a bucket of spit on his head, vaporizing Dad into a pile of goo in the living room, or swallowing Dad up with Thad's cartoon mouth that grows exponentially as needed for Thad's cartoon wrath. Loving his dad more than any other, this series of drawings is the greatest display of love from Thad for his dad.

The belly laughs that Thad experiences when he tells me the stories he makes up in his head charm me into a puddle of adoring mom-putty. He tells me so many silly Thad-stories in the car during our long commutes, and I continuously remind him that his verbal words, his written words, and his drawings must match. If you let people hear your story, I tell him, if you explain it and don't just keep it in your mind, you can share a humorous thought or experience with a friend, always trying to help him understand the idea of using his cartoon as the jumping off point for joint-attention, a shared moment with a friend. Thaddeus wants friends for sure, and we are still working diligently on those skills.

Pizza making forever continues with baking, creating, considering, and dreaming continues in the kitchen as we assess, we bake, we try, we muse, we pucker in yuck and reconsider, we bake again, eyebrows raise in agreement with murmurs of delicious bites of gooey and warm and soft and pleasing to the eyes, nose, and mouth, as we experiment with different flours, nut meals, meats and cheesy additions to concoct the ultimate perfection pizza-style. We try different toppings, and make up crazy names for the pies, we try special pans and stones to make it taste like we think pizza should taste without all of the neurotoxins and fucked-up autistic behavior that gluten and eggs unapologetically offer our boy.

Thad wants to be a farmer when he grows up, and has his "Who's your farmer?" t-shirt from the Farm to Consumer Legal Defense Fund as a favorite piece of his daily attire. Farmer t-shirt and blue shorts, let's roll, he's invincible. He likes to carry watermelons and pumpkins around the markets and our house when they are in season, I realize the sensory calm he experiences when carrying around heavy fruits, and we endlessly buy watermelon and pumpkins seeds that he plants all over the yard with wild abandon. He is so excited and motivated by rides on the green tractor on "Mark's Farm," also known as Spero Vineyards in Temecula, a unique public-private collaboration of resources toward meaningful job training and employment for adults with disabilities with the focus of wine production. Training at Spero Vineyards awards these Global Citizens a certificate in Viticulture and Hospitality, preparing our children to be essential workers in the community.

I think about Thad's attention, memory, and focus as he asks regularly to go down to the farm and work, as Thad grows like a weed and I buy "Who's your farmer?" t-shirts in increasingly bigger sizes every few months. I am always thinking about his future, teaching employment skills, and ways to give him meaningful lifestyle choices. After he rode on the green tractor with Mark for the first time, he said to me, Mom, I could maybe do that when I'm a man someday. Yes, my boy, absolutely, I say and smile in happiness.

Ursula, Thad and I visited my friend, Heidi's urban farm in San Francisco to relax my nerves while I waited for the results of the Due Process. Itty Bitty Farm in the City is a mishmash of sweetness, great food, love, and creativity in the form of chickens, goats, vegetables, rabbits, bees, and a dog. Thad is in heaven perseverating on the chicken coop and the eggs but getting a ton of functional work done motivated by hanging out with the chicken. He moved dirt from a dumptruck, fed the animals, and Skyped with his class. He was so proud of himself, showing his 905 friends around the farm via high-speed internet.

Me nutty like the almond tree planted by my son, sweet like guava and soft like figs as I consider his possibilities, tart like Meyer lemons if anyone says it is not possible, inspired by all the goodness in the soil, the goodness in the world, if I look I see opportunities, if I seek, if I believe in him, in myself, as we move ourselves forwards. As I see other parents, like Mark and Eva, founders of Spero Vineyards, and Yudi Cathy and Ernie, founders of Exceptional Minds Studio, bringing to fruition real employment pathways and meaningful methods of happy, sustainable futures for our kids, I feel deep gratitude toward them, standing in awe at parents who see our kids' needs and take steps towards their beauty, growth, and realization in the world.

It is never to early to think about his future as an adult who will need support in work and living, and I graciously and gratefully join the FRED (Farms and Ranches Enabling Adults with Disabilities) Conference, a group of parents and professionals with a focus on disabled adults' meaningful work leisure and housing options, each year to brainstorm, create, and learn from each other. To take the very large, very looming problem of lack of services and options for adults with disabilities, and actively come together in the spirit of collaboration and creation of new ideas, new models for living a full life is the creative, passionate cause of this intuitive band of fore-thinkers.

This past summer, I tour Bittersweet Farm in Ohio while visiting my parents, and I learn of their respectful living options, and meaningful work opportunities for adults on the Autism Spectrum. The Director, Jan, tells us about an adult with Autism who had a particular interest in ripping cloth and how they turned this potentially disruptive behavior into an artistic skills that yields some seriously beautiful Christmas wreaths made of wire and cloth to be sold in the farm art galley gift shop, and I hear another happy tale of an adult with a particularly focused interest in tire treads and how this individual now creates art as beautifully-painted clay flying fish wall art with intricate scales made from the impressions of tire tracks in the clay. At Bittersweet Farms, the staff understand residents' particular interests, and create meaningful work around these interests. And the love and respect that hangs heavily in the air is palpable, like the comfortable aroma of summer sunsets lingering in the trees.

Mark tells me about his recent visit to Coco Winery in Japan, a working vineyard for adults on the spectrum. He learns that the vines are purposely grown on a hill so a tractor can never replace a human, so our special population keeps these jobs. He tells me about jobs of precision that adults with Autism excel at, such as champagne riddling, the process in making high-quality champagne of slowly turning the sediment in dormant bottle a small fraction of an inch with precision and regular attention every certain amount of hours, a repetitive task and they excel. We muse about artisan creations of a thousand different treats for the palate.

An angle on Thad's success includes using his particular interests as rewards, and making everything functional so there is a purpose even within the reward. We find motivation in drawing, farming, cooking, and physical or movement-based activities. I tell him, if you do the following reading task, we get to go out this afternoon and "shop" for RVs. Double-quick, those academic tasks are completed, and he soon is in ecstasy taking pictures of particular mobile estates he fancies, as he happily darts in and out of RVs all afternoon. A fun social experience with my sweet boy. And now I also want an RV for our future adventures, as we took this special interest and spun it into a reward and so many opportunities for social engagement, as he asks the salesman to see that one over there, and so much new vocabulary, and all kinds of cool adjectives to describe particular qualities of an RV. He took pix and darted in and out of RVs all afternoon. Me smiling inside.

He has babysitters and tutors and we fashion these supported experiences into moments of hanging out socially with his friends, and being creative as a hobby, something he does with his friends. Thad likes to construct elaborate dollhouse miniatures houses from kits into "dude houses," which become farm houses and beach houses, which eventually may become sets for stop-motion animations that he creates, placing himself in the story of how he aspires to be a farmer, a surfer, and an animator who owns a lot of dogs when he grows up. I love that he thinks about his future, I love that he plots and plans how he will be when he grows up. Good thing that is on both of our minds.

We also incorporate physical movement and infuse functional skills into everything we do. For example, cooking is a functional task, and he is my prep chef many evening because he particularly likes knives. With my support, he cuts the vegetables for the stir-fry using an appropriately sharp knife for the task, he grates cheese with a hand-held grater, and uses Mom's Vitamix, with the plunger that looks like a weapony bat, to make aggressive smoothies, beating cream and fruit into frothy submission. We climb our friend's persimmon trees to get fruit to carry home, let ripen and make into persimmon fruit leather in the dehydrator. The recipe, the chopping, the cutting, the waiting, estimated time is a few months, a few years, a few minutes, a lifetime, to slow it down and make it all functional, rewarding in its process, equally amazed by the product and the positive emotions we feel as we do.

Julia Child, a beautiful lively cookbook full of matronly love with a fabulous voice comforted me by saying, If you are afraid of butter, use cream. I am pretty sure that I believe that this motto should be applicable to all things as a method of how to jump into life, to be present, to be here, to be now. I say live a full-fat, saturated life, be truly present in your life situation, do not be afraid or embarrassed to feel the way you feel, and talk about it with another soul who listens. Beat your butter, whip your cream, be alive, and be proud of the whorls on top of your cake of life, moments, and memories.

Julia's words recall childhood in me, as my parents stood in awe, fascinated with her on our little black and white television in the kitchen, providing direction in our meal-making with her words full of the love and pleasure of food. Thad and I plan a chocolate pecan pie, and a pumpkin pie for our Thanksgiving feast. We relish all food holidays as ways to expand culinary and gustatory horizons, and Thad names himself "the boss of the whipped cream." We practiced working with the beater so many times to desensitize the whir, to teach a cooking skill, and now happily he is an expert. He remembers how the sensations of the beater used to scare him and eventually make him angry. Now, he knows how to safely get the beaters out of the cabinets, plug it in, and hold the bowl even if it seems unnecessary. We continue to think about everything as a life-skill, a meaningful activity in his bright future. He like farming, he enjoys landscaping tasks like pruning with sharp shears, he can water the plants, and sweep the walk. We are so happy that he is interested in these thoughtful, worthy, and respectable jobs, and consider all things that he engages in as a piece of his puzzle, an answer toward his future, and a training towards his unique life and hopeful independence in the world.

Success and failure bounce in and out of our family life like green and red rubber balls from the gumball machines at the pizza parlor we no longer frequent, and I freshly vow to myself once again to never give up. Rob plants chewing gum in our garden to organically get rid of the gophers who are feasting on our nectarines, tomatoes and peppers, they will chew themselves to death on the packs of Trident Rob has buried into the furrows, he hypothesizes. As we try lots of things to make something happen or something stop happening, as some things work, some things don't, we embrace these life experiences with grace, and we feel gratitude for the successes and the failures that happen in the human experience of living.

The importance of motivation is critical in everyone's life. Disabled or not. We all want passion to motivate, to propel us forward. I plan to help my child have a rich and delicious life by fore-thinking this experience now. I recall one smart mama at the FRED Conference saying, Children with disabilities will have great adult lives if the parents make sure that they have that great life. It is up to us, it has always been up to us. Parents who love their children, all parents, caring, as we build Thad's life and learning around his passions, flowing and ebbing, my life like moontide, like a midnight swell, gracefully riding the waves, and brushing off my ass and getting back on the surfboard, the storyboard after the wipe-outs that do and will happen. I polish my rough spots with the grace of uncertainty, and slough off the dead cells of fear as I push my feet deeper into life's sandy beachwalk.

Somewhere between love and loss, between beauty and madness, misery and peace, the ether of his progress allows me to peacefully unite with myself and dream of positive outcomes in his future. Somewhere, I find myself on a map at the crossroads, a street corner, an entrance to a large farmers market, or a party of friends. As I feel hope that maybe one or two or more of my millions of dreams, prayers, requests, heavenly appeals of healing and recovery for my son might be answered, heard, considered, or rapidly moving up the almighty celestial list of divine consideration.

My life as a pomegranate, the life of Persephone, six months up and six down, as I contemplate my existence in a piece of red fruit, and Gayle challenges readers and writers to mindfully eating berries in her luscious book, Fruitflesh, (Brandeis, Fruitflesh: Seeds of Inspiration for Women Who Write, permission from author) where she brings forth the importance of human perception in the form of a strawberry. Give yourself a full five minutes to look at and consider a single berry, and another full five minutes to eat the succulent fruit, she invites, daring us to examine our ways of seeing, and asking us to slow down in life to appreciate the process as much as the process, the details, and find joy in the moment. I consider my little piece of fruit, my boy, the details of my sweet son, his juicy bounty, his seeds and flesh encoded with joys and wonders, his perceptions of life, my perceptions of him and our world, the power of slowing down to savor what we eat and what we do and what we see and how we see, and the importance of slowing down in life.

I bite the red flesh, lick my lips, and feel gratitude to my child, to his therapy team, to our family, and to my life. I realize that I can choose to perceive my life as I like, as I want. I imagine the good, the love, and the magic in my life stretching around me like a warm encompassing hug, and I am empowered and healed by the strength and conviction of my own thoughts about my own life in my own mind. Thoughts become things, and my life is so rich, so good, so delicious.

CHAPTER 10

His Future is Ripe with Possibility

THADDEUS STARTS FIFTH Grade, and I think it would be the appropriate moment for him to practice learning some new skills, and such a good idea that he learn to ride the unicycle.

What I did not realize during that flash of midnight OMG brilliance was that him joining the Beginning Unicycle class at the local YMCA was the perfect thing for him to do. You are doing what, everyone asked. I did not give particular concern to everyone's response because "You are doing what?" was a common reaction to my acute, seemingly all-of-a-sudden gut-level need to change move or modify Thad's time usage. What I did not realize until later was the why of my deep maternal urge to force the boy to ride around on one wheel in a sweaty, loud gymnasium. We had inadvertently, effectively leveled the playing field for him in this particular activity, when usually in most activities he attempted, the field that seemed to slope uncomfortably steeply against him as he tried to learn and keep up with his peers.

Most of the time, when he starts something new, Thad is at a disadvantage due to language demands and expectations. Usually, I am trying to catch him up to everyone else's starting point along with keeping up with the demands of him progressing adequately with the group. Usually, he does not catch up or is not able to stay with the typical peers. Unicycle class was unique because we started with boys and girls of all ages. Everyone is a beginner, no one can do it, it is not a language intensive environment, and the class will learn all the new skills together.

Of course there were small challenges, such as teenagers teaching the class. Very often, saying one thing and doing another, typical teen behavior. The unitard-clad teacher says go left, and she walks right. This type of instruction delivery is confusing to Thad, who relies on peer modeling, when a child watches others for cues on appropriate behavior, as a compensatory strategy for when he misses verbal directions. As a strategy to support his challenges with verbal language and to help him understand the anticipated next steps when tasks are delivered orally, he tries to be acutely aware of the kids around him during the routines which helps him work on his focus and attention in the company of neurotypical (a word used in Autism Nation to define "those with normally developing brains," usually as a direct contrast with those affected by Autism) peers. I am sure that I have found a new answer, a fresh way to unlock my boy, and we begin unicycle class twice per week.

To help support his comprehension of the oral directions given that are not necessarily what the teacher physically demonstrates at the moment, or are muffled words because of the way sound bounces in the gym, I ask Lindsey, an amazing Speech Therapist at school, for some help with some hand gestures, some visual language and commands to support him, and I add a little American Sign Language into the unicycle recipe. I sit on the benches on the sidelines of the gymnasium, and discreetly gesture directives such as 'change direction,' 'follow him,' or 'go left.' Thad hears the message of the instructor, looks over at me for clarification, I sign the message, and away he goes. Brilliant execution on his part, and I smile inside. The instructors know about his Autism, but the other kids and parents don't because he is doing so well. In unicycle class, he doesn't look any different from the other kids. He's shy, the other parents say about my boy. Yes, I say, as I sit with my secret. When he passes for "normal," whatever that is, I feel proud of him, and his progress out of Autism.

Thad is still always trying to get out of whatever I ask him to do, even if he does truly want to do it. I probably look like the meanest mom in the world as he continuously, constantly tests life's boundaries, and his mother's rules. I cannot do it, he whines. No one can mount the unicycle independently yet, so we all must practice, I remind. I'm thirsty, his face contorts into childish whispers of defiance. You don't need any more water and you don't need a break, I snap. I imagine others thinking of me cracking the metaphoric whip with my poor little innocent thirsty child cowering in the corner. Behavior, behavior, always follow through on your requests, Bob's voice terminally in my head. All he wants is a drink of water, they prod. He's had enough water, I retort. I follow through with the directives I give him, as Thad fires many clay pigeons to distract me out into the universe, and I don't believe his behavioral hype. And honestly, at this point in my life, steeped in Autism nation, I no longer give a shit about bitchy glares, and disapproving stares. Whisper, whisper, point, knowing glances. Unfortunately, I am used to it.

Thad lives a life of behavior modification, meaning that I believe that if I keep him on a higher standard of behavior, as much as I can, as often as I can, and with as much consistency as I can, in as many real-life circumstances as I can, he will ultimately ingrain how to act as appropriately, as independently as he is able, to be the best he can be, and he will ultimately have a better, more fulfilling life. So, fuck 'em and let 'em stare is my motto. Those who are staring should probably check themselves, and the behavior of their kids too. My excuse for his behavior is Autism. What's yours? And the little girl that tried to bully him at the park because he could climb higher than she could, um, Mom, get off the cell phone and pay attention. Looking in that mirror and seeing the reality of life is sometimes such the bitter pill. Teach your children to be kind to other kids who might look and act different. Everyone ultimately just wants to be liked and accepted.

That spring, Thad is all ready to participate in the nine circus performances at the YMCA in the Beginning Unicycle troupe, and he heads out to the trampoline park one evening for a little fun with his superbuddy, Bernycia. He is trying to make a friend that he has sought out on that particular Friday night, so very appropriately and so very happily. Bernycia is hanging back, watching a who-can-jump-higher contest in the corner of the blue trampoline, and thwack, Thad breaks his ankle in one dramatic crunch. While trying to make a friend is the part that still makes me cry inside.

A sad, tear-stained boy is carried into the house from the car by his dad. Mom, I have a splinter, he tells me as he gestures to the watermelon attached to his shin. I realize that he has inappropriately generalized the experience of a having a splinter, a small sliver of wood that sometimes happens after climbing a tree, into language to describe every physical injury that might befall him. Much of his comprehension and ideas and understandings are experience-based, and that if he has not experienced it or done it, it is possible he will not understand the meaning of it. Because he has had splinters in the past and because never had a broken bone before, he has no point of reference, he has no visceral sensation, no muscle memory of an event to tie it together, no words to describe, therefore he has no meaning or understanding of the idea.

Sometimes he understands a unique concept without experiencing it first-hand and sometimes he believes outright if someone tells him about the idea, but usually he must experience it to fully comprehend it. This challenge makes reading comprehension extremely difficult for Thaddeus because one could consider how reading expands our mind through words on a page, and for him, he must do to understand. For example, Mark is a farmer, but also a surfer. Thad has no context of him surfing because he has never seen Mark surf with his own eyes. So when Mark makes killer wave references, Thad looks at him suspiciously. Why is the farmer talking to me about surfing? Or perhaps, the California state standards-approved reading chapter on Chinese New Year. Words like ginseng, apothecary, and the fact that the little girl lives in an apartment above the family restaurant perplex him and me. He doesn't get it and I have no idea how to meaningfully teach it. Thad has no point of reference for any of these ideas, from Chinese herbs to people living above restaurants, and therefore misses the meaning of the story.

We go to Urgent Care the next day as his ankle continues to pulse and swell, and we meet a doctor who demonstrates overt ignorance about Autism, and poor listening skills in the first few minutes of the appointment. I explain that Thad has Autism, and a significant expressive and receptive language delay. I explain that he is sometimes challenged by localizing the source of pain, especially in moments of distress. I say that I will help the doctor discern Thad's words, and that sometimes what he says is possibly not true for various cognitive reasons. The doctor dismisses my diatribe, names himself an expert in the spectrum disorder, and begins the assessment.

Dr. Smartdoctor, looks up from his clipboard, and inquires smugly, hyper or hypo? Um, what? Does he have hyper or hypo-Autism? I telepathically let him know that I am clear that he must have skipped that entire three-page chapter on Autism in medical school because these prefixes are not terms that currently exist in modern medicine to describe Autism as the whole enchilada. Hyper and hypo, as in "too much" and "not enough," are used more accurately to describe a child's presentation of the Autism in specific physical, emotional, communication, and cognitive domains. For example, I might say that he displays hypo-arousal when attending to classroom desktop tasks, and he has associated IEP goals to sit up straight in the desk for a series of minutes at a time, or I could discuss a hyper-sensitivity to loud sounds in a crowded movie theatre or the incessant buzz of fluorescent lights in public school classrooms.

I am further under-impressed at this medical professional's claimed plethora of knowledge about Autism when he questions Thad directly about his ankle pain. The doctor pushes on certain parts of Thad's black and blue appendage. Which one hurts more, 1 or 2? 2, responds Thad. Which one hurts more, he asks, 1 or 2, pushing on a new purple and yellow stretch of his calf. 2, says Thad. I tell the doctor that he is not getting an accurate read because Thad will parrot back the second thing that the doctor says, no matter what it is. I am ignored. This characteristic of Autism, echolalia, is the phenomenon of repeating back what is just said to you. Very often, it is misinterpreted as actual communication. Nope, just a refrain.

1 or 2? 2.

1 or 2? 2.

1 or 2? 2.

1 or 2? 2.

After this absurdity continues for a stupid while, I interject and tell the doctor where specifically on his leg Thad has told me previously that it actually hurts him. A different place than all the 2s that are noted on the important clipboard.

The doctor then begins to question my language-delayed child about the quality of the pain--Is it more stabbing, or throbbing? Sharp or dull? Does it subside when elevated? The doctor is lobbing questions at Thad full-force like a popcorn popper with the lid off, and I begin to answer these questions on T's behalf, also. By this point in the medical assessment, Thad is now way more interested in the weird saw-like machines in the room, and highly concerned if his foot is going to fall off or not. He asks this question about 100 times during the next ten minutes. This characteristic of Autism is called perseveration, the unfortunate state of getting stuck on an idea, phrase or desire, and the inability to cognitively move past it. Thad is interpreted as being rude because each time the doctor tells him that his foot will not fall off, there is a quick inhale, pensive 3-second lull, and Thad fires out the same question again with fresh interest in the doctor's anticipated response.

Back at home and headed to school the next day with his leg safely encased in a bright blue cast, I decide that this new accessory will be used as a teaching tool to work on his social and communication skills. Every moment is a teachable moment and every moment, I continue to access this place of teaching it, learning it, checking comprehension, demonstrating it, seeing if he is understanding it, filling in the blanks, and overtly showing him the places in the cryptic communication he missed. Rinse. Repeat.

Thad is sure that maybe no one will notice that he is laid up currently. I tell him, darling, people will notice a bright blue cast, but I try to spin the positive for him. I see this as unique, as I explain the word "unique" and check his comprehension of what I am trying to impart to him. Honey, you are the only kid on campus with a cast. That's different. That's cool. Everyone in Room 905 will want to sign it. I wonder what they will all write on your cast, I consider outloud. He acts like a teenager, and doesn't let Rob, me or Ursula sign his cast until his friends in 905 do. It's developmentally appropriate to be cool and to want the acknowledgement and feedback from your peers and friends over your family at this age, and I smile inside.

I thought he would like to use the wheelchair that I requested he borrow at school for the next few weeks until the ankle swelling went down. The campus is quite expansive, and with a freshly busted appendage, hobbling on crutches could be exhausting and time consuming. Yet, he recognizes that using a wheelchair for mobility is different from the other kids in his class, and did not want it or like it. He was aware that the wheelchair was different, and again, I smile inside at this social awareness. When he forgot his crutches in driveway one day because he was distracted by a movie on his iPad, the consequence was that he had to use a wheelchair to get around for the day.

Pay attention, I remind him. I don't want to look like I'm broken, he tells me, remorseful of his lack of crutches. This follow-through of 'be in charge of yourself and your stuff,' my terminal mantra, helps him realize the seriousness of my statement. His perception of cruising in the chair at school and the awareness of other's eyes on him motivates him to hobble around each morning making sure all of his stuff is in order for school. Sometimes behavior modification is counterintuitive, and definitely looks odd from afar.

We also review, plan, discuss, and frontload concepts about the small talk and conversations that would probably happen regarding his injury. First, we talk about how it is socially acceptable, and that it should be expected that people at school will ask him about his cast. We also discuss how people at the grocery store or the bank might inquire too. We also have a rule that Thad follows to not talk to strangers. Because the breaking of rules is not tolerated, a social nuance of the sometimes its okay to talk to strangers and sometimes it's not is broken down into a new rule we agree upon, it's okay to talk to strangers if they ask you about your broken ankle. We discuss how people that he doesn't know might ask him in the line at Target, and that they ask to be kind, and to acknowledge his injury.

We also practice the script of how the conversation might go. The person will ask you, what happened? I broke my foot, he says. No, I tell him, you broke your ankle. The next questions to anticipate would be, how long will you have the cast? An hour, his go-to response when questioned about time. No, I tell him, two and a half months. We settle on "ten weeks" because it is easier to remember. The little bits of chit-chat that surround the novelty of a leg cast, the stuff of life, must be practiced the night before, in the car on the way to school, and I write it on a small cheat sheet in case he forgets. Again, we break down and practice the human experience so he can successfully participate in the world, so he won't miss his own life because he doesn't understand social nuances, and so he can have the appropriate words to tell others about his life when they question him because people are genuinely interested in others. We practice and practice this little script, a small part of this big skill, communication.

Oral communication continues to be so difficult for him, and Thad has always been interested in boys who talk with their hands. He is so fascinated with deaf people, and how they communicate without words. I think he likes the idea of losing the words which continue to be so challenging for him, and just communicating visually or physically. Usually shy with strangers, he notices that Lindsey's husband, Charlie, who is deaf, talking with his hands, and Thad marches right up to him and says, hey, how do you say, "zombie" with your hands? After a bit of deliberation, Charlie came up with "walking dead person." He signs this phrase, and Thad is thrilled. He is also interested in friendship with a deaf boy at school named Michael. Michael is my friend who doesn't talk with his voice, Mom. He talks with his hands, he tells me. Michael and Thad are both smart, kind boys who really like Star Wars. They met on Halloween, with Thad dressed as Jengo Fett, and Michael in a Star Wars t-shirt. Michael signs to Thad, I like your costume, and Thad signs to Michael, we are friends.

We move forward, and I reflect back. Response to Intervention (RTI) is a method of academic intervention that looks at how particular supports, therapies, and teaching models have worked for the child to gauge the effectiveness of the treatment over a particular period of time. In this spirit, I have asked many of his current providers to give their insights on the changes in Thad that they see comparing the first day they met him to currently. I feel deep gratitude to those who champion my child, I experience my forever gratefulness, I am indebted to their kindness, expertise, perseverance, and to each one's desire and unique ability to be Thad's friend in addition to his teacher or therapist. "Every day is a journey, and the journey itself is home" says Basho, as I honor the process, human relationships, and as so many of his important people tell me how he has changed, from their perspective then to now, how has he changed, grown, matured, and progressed.

Teacher Jeff tells me that his first impression of my son way back in 2009 was sweet, quiet, and shy boy, who was academically challenged but not an outward behavior problem in the classroom. His behavior was self-absorption, turning inwards, so lost in the movies playing in his mind. Socially, he was developmentally only engaged in peer parallel play, and by last year, he was hanging out with adults at recess or willingly interacting with peers with adult support. His preferred conversations went from incessantly asking about Jeff's cat to learning to using many appropriate conversation starters, as Thad started to learn to retain social information, and to participate with support in class.

He began in my class with an FM trainer for small and large group instruction, with aide support in large group instruction and he was academically at first not tuned in. And now he participates without the FM trainer and without an aide during instruction, says Jeff. He could not get the big picture, the gestalt, the magnitude of the words and concepts, such as the "President of the United States," and now he is using functional skills, and drawings to provide context and meaning to his thoughts, and his considerations of the thoughts of others.

Initially, Jeff adds, he couldn't comprehend by simply putting the pieces together, and it was necessary first, to get him to care about the actual learning of information, and then move into actually teaching him concepts. Higher order thinking questions, inference, predicting, and social information continue to challenge him, represented in the functional IEP goals we now have that emphasis process, and the product being a way he could contribute meaningfully to society as a capable adult someday. Fast forward to 2013, and today, he continues to be more comfortable with concrete ideas and well-defined tasks and expectations, and he is now happily manipulative, non-listening, and eye-rolling in an appropriate teenager way.

Dr. Jerry says that Thad is more connected, more personable, and more engaged with peers than before. He is more Autism-compliant now but less teenager-compliant, which is so very normal, as he blows me off in the gym with his "teenager face" when I request he do something he doesn't really feel like doing, Jerry tells me. He is now beginning to understand and care about competitive games and winning which he was indifferent to before, he tries to win, he aware of who is winning, he has favorite games and preferred tasks in the sensory gym, and when before the answer was no to all questions posed, he will sometimes ask for clarification of the questions. But, usually he is engaged and he has an appropriate response to share or consider. He's good at scooter-board hockey, he keeps score, makes small talk as they play seated card games, and cheers his friends on, Dr. Jerry recounts.

Susan says that she sees differences in Thad that include connection and love for his family as evidenced by a willingness to share in the social skills group, and how his eyes lighten up when talking about his family. Activities, vacations, and even family dynamics are shared and discussed by Thad, and he loves to co-lead yoga class with his mom, and when I need to set firm and clear boundaries for his behavior in group, she says, he accepts the corrections, and he emotionally handles himself. His new normal has nearly erased my hippocampus recall of his past, she tells me in our collective smile.

Dr. Susi tells me that Thad deserves credit for his ability to share more things that are happening in his life by tell me what's going on in his mind, and what he did today and plans to do tomorrow. He is more cooperative, flexible, and tolerant, he has an increase in gross motor skills and posture, and he has an increase in control of his body. And we introduced drawing, he took it, ran with it, and made it his own, she continues. He owns it, uses it as a way to connect with others, and show his sense of humor and funny personality. He took drawing where it went on his own, as a form of self-therapy and communication of his ideas. We thought him drawing seemed like a great idea, and then he manifested it into an amazing reality, she tells me.

Dr. Gwen commends his positive changes in affect regulation because before, she tells me, his limbic system was taking him for a ride, and he was constantly challenged with the ability to control his emotions. And now as he works to perfect his calm and alert states, he is able to emotionally engage with others which was impossible in the past. For example, when I present him with something new, he now wants to know how to get, fix, and engage with it, she says. When I started treating him seven years ago, he immediately became angry, oppositional, and emotionally stuck in the need for same, or if the plans did not conform exactly to his wishes he would shut down, she tells me.

His parasympathetic and sympathetic nervous systems have moved out of the primal "Fight or Flight" mode, and his "Executive Functioning," the cognitive control of attention planning action reasoning flexibility and problem-solving, is coming online, as he is able to move more fluidly and effectively through a perceived problem. He is not as impulsive as before, he thinks before he does, and he is starting to hold "self" and "other" separately, "Theory of Mind" glimmering in the distance, and a smile broadens on his mom's face. And, she concludes, drawing is not, "A way in for Thad," it is "THE way in for Thad," as I hope to see drawing continue to support him in communication, comprehension, social engagement, humor, and future life and job goals. I smile at these words from such a beautiful person who has actively treated him through his entire Autism journey.

Sara says that when she met Thad for the first time, she saw a beautiful, quiet child with long dark eyelashes who was completely disconnected from the world. She tried to connect with him using what she knew, all the *status quo*, the standard ways, and it didn't work. Then, she tells me, she got "permission" from Thad to get into his mind, starting from his place of emotional comfort, as she admits that maybe "finger-eating" isn't appropriate, but I know that we are in that place together, recalling so many moments with Thad, she tells me.

She continues, Thad has taught me about how his "mad face" is his way in, the way to engage him, to be with him emotionally, and understanding how to get into Thad's world has helped me with my work with other kids also. I appreciate my friendship with Thad, as she tells me about their moments, as we sit together in counseling groups, and although we both want to sprinkle salt on my finger for him to eat, and then trash-talk battle it out, I say not appropriate right now, he understands, and growls under his breath to me in a humorously menacing tone, Losing the finger later Sara, meaning we will continue our fun moment together when it is socially appropriate. He gets it, and I am elated.

I ask Trish about her memories of Thad and she recalls Thad, so handsome, so wrapped up in his own head, and so difficult for her to "reach." I was so worried about how to bring him out of his mind, and into the moment we now share together, she says. I saw glimpses of opportunities, she continues, when he would wow me with his charm, the compliments, his sweet smiles, eye contact, and personal questions about my family as an avoidance tactic, but I found that it was also as a way to establish introductory chit-chat. And I swear his eyes actually twinkled when he spoke, she remembers. Early on, he used to speak so softly that it was difficult to understand him and even more difficult to discern if he was talking to me or just scripting a movie in his mind. She continues, he had to sustain engagement with me, and if he broke the connection by going into his head, we had to start over, and Thad hated that.

Thumbs up, thumbs down, he spent so much therapy time successfully improving on vocalizations that are meaningful, directed at a person, and audible. She tells me, I know that I will never meet another "Thad" in my lifetime. I have learned that he will never fit nicely into any single diagnosis, character quality, or cognitive aptitude. I know that any attempt to fully describe his unique essence is futile besides actually knowing him. He has been one of my greatest clinical challenges, and one of my greatest joys, she affirms.

Jacque commends his unique sense of humor that is now authentic and real. She tells me that his funny banter is not scripted or canned anymore, and that she enjoys watching Thad connect to others using "words with feelings attached." She talks about watching my handsome boy grow and mature through the years, and recalls when, for Thad, words were just words, sounds and growls devoid of feeling, and now how he accesses life and himself with emotion, "loving those he loves" through his physical humor, drawing, and animation. He communicates in so many ways now, she tells me, as we talk about his ocean of emotion that is now so much more regulated, so much more inviting, calm, and approachable.

Thad visits Kelli for the first time since he started school and left her clinic almost five years ago, and I ask her the same question, what differences do you see in my boy. I am again taught a valuable lesson by Thad's tribe, as she responds, I guess I thought more about the similarities instead of the differences. I remind myself again to first consider his similarities, his connections, and his strengths, and then parse out the differences. Kelli says, I could see the wheels turning as he was trying to process a flood of memories looking at the rooms, and the slideshow I made of his years in the clinic. It made me really wonder what he was thinking and feeling, as I watch the two of them fall in line, old friends, re-bonding over the crazy times of years ago, as I see him thinking about his friendships and the past experiences he shared with Kelli and his buddies at the clinic.

Thad requests that I wait in the lobby as Kelli and him chill because he is a teenager, he is hanging with his friend, and his mom doesn't really need to be all up in his business. Kelli remarks that the once pancake short-stack of a child is really tall and smells like a teenage boy, and oh so developmentally appropriate to forget to wear his deodorant on that day. She tells me that she is impressed that he initiated asking about people who meant something to him five years ago, and that he wished a particular boy would come back because he missed him. She says, his body seems more calm and organized while he was engaged, and his artwork has really blossomed from the days of simple stick figures, and copied letters. I watch his eyes light up, recall, and engage Kelli in memories as he walks through the rooms of the important clinic where so many paths of his journey away from Autism and toward his recovery and healing began.

And Bob continues to show up unexpectedly now and again in Thad's world, like a behavioral booster, a safe vaccine against the symptoms of Autism we target in our therapies every day. Thad's teachers and therapists are his safe vax against regression into Autism, a type of inoculation I can get on board with. Thad pipes up, straightens his spine, and gets right to work when he spots Bob in his midst. Thad's demonstration of appropriate behavior in this way is an indirect loving hug, a high-five show of respect to his therapists and teachers because I see a boy who choses to not engage in autistic behaviors when he sees someone who knows him and his true abilities. Thad understands that they expect better from him, and his care toward what his tribe thinks about him is a critical ingredient in the large pot of love and gratitude I feel toward all of them.

I continue to have endless epiphanies as I traipse through my life, craving, acknowledging, recognizing my lust for normalcy, and a primal need to feel sane on a consistent basis. I fall *verklempt* at the demonstrations of engagement, love, and devotion of Thad's people, his village, his loving farm of friends and support, and I continue to shun monkeyshine disguised as empty promises, trust me I've got it, and bitchy indifference toward my expertise in my boy. As I move forward to the next pieces of his history we shall write together, I think about Nelson Mandela's words, "I am the master of my fate, I am the captain of my soul," as I retain my personal power to determine how I feel, act, react, compose myself, my words, and my journey, remembering that, "You only fail if you stop trying," says Einstein. Both masters speak in thoughtful brilliance, as their words and ideas and focus and fortitude have changed so many life paths in history, me brightly inspired by their strength and perseverance.

Life continues its distinct pulse, and successfully separating reality from fantasy is still a problem for Thad. I remember him playing the game, Minecraft, on the iPad during our school commute a few weeks back. I request a hot lava swimming pool in the beautiful house made of purple wool and with a front yard full of chickens and cows that he has built for me in his game. Your farm, Mom, he smiles. We get home, I pull out an organic chicken to roast, and a bag of veg-gies from the CSA. As I begin to dress the chicken, and cut the carrots, parsnips, and onions, I request that Thad take a shower. He goes upstairs for a while, and suddenly, comes flying back down the stairs in a pile of tears.

Mom, Mom, he wails, I am sooo sorry, I burned down Dad's house by acci-dent. I am sorry, I am sorry. I hold my sobbing boy close, and ask what had hap-pened upstairs that has made him so sad. Mom, Mom, I was painting the walls with hot lava in Dad's house on Minecraft, and I accidentally burned his house down. He shows me the iPad, and there is indeed a green wool house ablaze on the screen. I don't want Dad to be mad, it was an accident, he cries over and over. Unable to separate reality and fantasy in this sense, my sweetheart boy is a magnificent mess of unceasing apologies to Rob. I am so sorry I burned down your house, Dad, so sorry, so sorry. I will never do it again.

In addition, he telescopes the sadness and remorse he feels for his perceived bad deed to the benign, yet necessary task of showering, which is what he was supposed to be doing when he instead chose to sneak his iPad into his room and play. I will never take a shower again because of this, he declares, crying more than just a little. He overgeneralizes his sad emotions into every action that is, or is supposed to be happening at that moment. Showering what he was supposed to be doing instead of playing Minecraft, and sometimes when his emotions are heightened with feelings of fear or remorse, it is confusing to him and difficult to practice emotional regulation, a big challenge for most people with Autism. These sensations of big emotions, strong emotions, and especially uncomfort-able emotions can cause a jumbled response as he tries to process the feelings, and verbalize his tangled thoughts.

Another reason why I feel so much concern about him understanding the thin veil that separates virtual and "for realz" in our world is that one can never be sure which detail the autistic mind will grab onto as a perseverative moment. In my child's mind currently, he is experiencing a deep bother regarding the destruction of a two-dimensional house made of virtual animal hair. Yet, it is always probable that the physical motion stabbing the other person in the chest, the intense excitement of lighting a match with intent to burn something tan-gible, or the cool visual of a gun shooting someone dead might be the moment that endlessly plays in his mind, as I recall my intense concerns for the potential hazards of first-person shooter games on the autistic mind.

As parents, educators, therapists, doctors, family, and concerned friends, we can never be sure what will stick, loop in their minds, and then want to be reenacted endlessly. So, if my very visual child watches television that repeatedly delivers gory moments of inflicting pain as exciting and adrenaline-producing, or if he plays video games that glorify violence, then we are doing every disservice possible to him by allowing his vaccine-damaged mind to determine the course of his actions, whatever they might be. Sadly, children with Autism have accidentally killed their parents, and spend the rest of their lives, waiting forever, incarcerated without understanding, forever wondering where she is, when she will be back, and when Mama will tuck them in again.

The mind is a tricky playground. It is a wonderful servant, and a terrible master, I think as I watch my child intermittently gripped in the clenches of this invisible disorder that envelopes him, and takes him far from me without notice. In the jaws of the beast, the emotional carnage, I track the animal who attacks my baby, and vow to slay the monster. We settle in that night with an evening of shark attacks on Animal Planet, and wish outloud to each other for snow to fall on the cactuses in our southern California backyard.

Thad tells me later that he jumped off the tower at school today, that he re-hurt his leg, and did not tell the teacher. I worry that his impaired sense of safety will negatively effect the complete healing process of his freshly un-casted ankle. I make a mental plan to talk to Teacher Jeff tomorrow about not letting him aggressively play chase at school for another month or so. I tell Jeff that Thad has told me he hurt his leg, and did not disclose it to the staff. Yes, Jeff tells me, he did, and he went to the nurse. He didn't tell you? We told him not to jump off the taller tower. I then realize that Thad has told me a skewed version of the truth because he did not want to get in trouble from Jeff or from me for doing something he knows is wrong. I realize that this concern is not a safety issue at all, and it's about Thad lying. He lied, I internally rejoice because it is more developmentally appropriate for an almost-13-year old to lie to adults than to have an impaired sense of danger.

On Saturday, I attempt to meet Gayle and her writing class by the lake in the park. I had been looking forward to her workshop, yet I am confused by the location she gives along with my prior significant directional challenges, my wonky spacial awareness in a north-is-always-in-front-of-me kind of way. As I walk, I think about looking for more answers, protocols, persons, and methods to further heal my boy. I text her to request further clarification on her whereabouts, as I continue looking for the round pier under the pepper tree, to the left of the gaggle of old men feeding the white geese. I keep walking. Eventually Gayle texts me, stay where you are, I will find you. I'm sorry I missed your class, I tell her, I was looking for you, I was trying to find you. She gathers me up in hugs and smiles. It is not a problem, I am just so happy to see you, she tells me with a kiss on the cheek. We go to the farmer's market for breakfast, and she introduces me to a new fruit, jujube. We drink rich black coffee, celebrate friendship, and discuss the importance of never giving up on the ones we love.

I continue to rely on the soundbyte enlightenment told to us by ancient masters, soothsayers, and mystics from earlier times to comfort and soothe me in times of strong emotions and gushing feelings. I hold on to Rumi's important words that remind me to "Let the beauty we love be what we do, there are thousands of ways to kneel and kiss the ground," when I ponder the course my life has taken and the way I will rise up to the challenges presented to me with love grace and acceptance, and Tom Robbins's observation that, "I believe in everything. Nothing is sacred. I believe in nothing. Everything is sacred," regarding the difficulties associated with creating and managing an appropriate intervention for my child, and the way that I will cherish and celebrate every moment he is with me, every advance he makes, and find the divine nature of the small footsteps that are endlessly moving forwards toward a more giant goal.

As the parent of disabled child, I ponder Nietzsche saying, "You must have chaos in you to give birth to a dancing star," defining the "chaos" in myself as a positive spin of creativity uniqueness and possibility, harkening to the Greek goddess Eurynome, born from Oceanus and Tethys, who separated the earth and sky, and gave birth to the universe. I think of the Marine quote, "Pain is weakness leaving the body" when times are hard, and the old adage reminding us to "Leave no stone unturned," as I consider new ways of thinking about remediating his Autism.

I find calm and hope in the Buddhist consideration of "Samsara is nirvana," personally interpreted from a loosely defined translation of "Suffering is bliss," and upgraded to "Strive to be happy every day no matter what," as a way of focusing to keep happiness and emotional calm as my baseline, not a lofty or future goal, no matter what shitstorm befalls us. I crave insight into his bottled mind that is begging to be released, and once it happens, the beauty that is inside. I want to be in his world, in his space, in whatever way I can, and to commune with him because, as Pierre Teilhard de Chardin says, "We are not human beings having a spiritual experience. We are spiritual beings having a human experience."

And we continue to perfect the homemade pizza pie that supports goals of deep nourishment, improved health, focused interaction and appropriate behavior. Currently, we mix up almond meal, extra virgin olive oil, pink Himalayan salt, and raw organic full-fat yogurt for a crust. We bake it on a pizza stone, and add delicious grated organic mozzarella cheese, grass-fed ground beef, and yummy green olive toppings after first browning the crust. The crust doesn't contain eggs or any gluten (wheat protein) as these two substances continue to cause physical and behavioral spikes if he eats it. Six years of no casein (milk protein), and we slowly are introducing it back into his diet with good success, and anything gummy or chewy still produces an allergic response we call "hot ear."

The "hot ear" phenomenon is a boy with a recent diet infraction, a.k.a. sneaking known food allergens, who gets bright red ears, burning hot like an angry sun, usually accompanied by a significant stomachache and an unhealthy dose of lethargy and brain fog. Hot ear is uncomfortable to Thad, and he knows that if he eats forbidden foods, from an open buffet at a party, for example, he will end up with hot ear and the associated symptoms. In true boy form, without adult monitoring, very often he will take on the physical challenges of feeling like shit for the rest of the night based on a poor food choices. At least, he is aware of the outcome, and I am grateful for this. A step in the right direction, and we just aren't finished walking that path quite yet.

And sometimes the masters are in right front of us, acting in real time to change the world, to positively influence the trajectory of this tragic Autism epidemic. I am a giddy schoolgirl as I anticipate Dr. Andrew Wakefield as the keynote speaker at the Weston A. Price Foundation international conference in Atlanta. I come to this conference each year to educate myself further on nourishing food prepared in traditional ways, to learn more about gut health and remediation, and as a personal respite from the pressures of my daily life. I hold his book as we wait to file in, and I realize I have willed him literally within arms reach from me.

I excuse myself from the food tribe, and approach Dr. Wakefield. Thank you, thank you, I gush. You are my hero, thank you for fighting for our kids, you were my hope in the early days, thank you for telling the truth and standing by your findings in the most challenging of circumstances. I tell him about Thaddeus, his story, and his progress. Keep fighting, he says. Promise me you will keep fighting. I will, I say.

He spoke in front of our group to doctors, therapists, scientists, so many members of the whole food revolution, and to so many parents. He showed a disturbing graphic about the relationship between the 1 in 55 epidemic proportions of Autism in 2013, and the prediction that if the current trends continue, that by 2025, 1 in 2 children will have an Autism Spectrum Disorder. How can society allow the sacrifice of entire generations of kids, I think, as tears well in my eyes and I see small innocent, lovely, round-faced babies suckling mama breasts at nearby tables. We must keep our children safe. Dr. Wakefield recounts the witch-hunt, the misinformation and damage of the Lancet paper, and how all fingers pointed to the mother as the guilty one.

Dismiss the mother, investigate the mother, blame the mother. As so many other mothers and myself have detailed the undeniable physical changes, the horrible physiological upset, the heart-wrenching emotional vacuity of our children after being damaged by vaccines, as our children's gut-brain axis is destroyed, we are told to remain silent, to continue to trust Big Pharma and misinformed doctors, and to be complacent about these reprehensible, toxic, money-making choices that will affect my boy forever.

They ask us to trust, to be quiet, like sheep in a large herd, unnecessarily and extremely immunized, lifeless, brain-dead zombies. Wakefield then quotes one of the masters regarding the vaccine injuries happening to our children, our future. The death of one man is a tragedy and the death of a million men is a statistic, he says to a silent crowd. Some of the children are dying, but many just remain as the walking wounded. A cloudy wind blowing between life and them, without the luxury of human communication or physical touch because they have been twisted and spun into an existence of painful brain-body chaos.

Boys are being damaged, and women will inherit the earth if they like it or not, he says, referring to the fact that Autism affects significantly more boys than girls. It is time for us to rise together, to trust our maternal instinct to protect and heal our babies, and to stop this rampant, unnecessary vaccine jabbing for the almighty dollar. The Foundation presents Dr. Wakefield with an Integrity in Science award. Sally Fallon Morrell presents him this award, and reminds us that there is "grit," in the word "integrity." I believe we must propel forward with tenacity and momentum relying on what we believe in our hearts to be true. If there are children who have lost their voice because of the circumstances that we, as mothers and fathers, accidentally allowed to befall them, then, as mothers and fathers, we must rescue our babies from the hell, the isolation, and the pain of Autism.

Dr. Wakefield discusses the media outcry of no connection between vaccines and Autism early this century, and I recall so many walks over the years through the shopping line, the drop-off line, the buffet line, and I how I try, try, try to explain, and eventually say fuck you to anyone who tries to tell me with absolute venom there is no connection between the two. Happily, at this point in my Autism tale, I am moderately in control of my emotions and I know that the ammo of facts and emotion I possess on this topic can strain or end relationships. With shotgun precision, I can deliver facts related to the population of ASD kids being under 21 and the universal consequences associated with the epidemic, and unfortunately, many people take it personally that I dare insinuate that vaccinating might be unsafe. I only say it because I live it, and I only repeat my life experiences to you because I don't want you, whoever you are, to repeat my ignorance, my oblivion my blind trust, my mistakes, my waiting, and my worry. Read, learn, get educated, ask questions, and make informed decisions

A shout-out to Thad's awesomeness because he teaches me so much about him, about myself, and about the richness of life in this Autism journey. So much gratitude to the maternal instinct that I feel so strongly which directs my choices in his recovery, my second brain, the gut emotion that constantly reminds me to trust those intuitive feelings, and to continue to clean up, support, and heal my child's intestinal health.

Props and endless fist-bumps to the people on the front lines of research, advocacy, therapy, teaching, legal strides, and Autism Awareness, who put themselves, their names, and their livelihoods on the line for the precious canaries in our coal mine, and who remind me to never stop fighting, to never stop learning, and to never give up.

And to the wonderful Mothers and Fathers, I offer heaping platefuls of love, respect, and encouragement for the days and days of cleaning up poop (the physical kind, the financial kind, and the emotional kind), for driving far distances to therapies and doctors, for taking copious notes and researching new ways for your precious babes, for paying for endless therapies, tests, and services for the kids not covered by insurance, for believing in their children, and for never giving up hope.

We have come so far with Thad already in his life and his remediation and healing from Autism, and we still have so much to do. I believe in him, and he believes in him. I like these thoughtful words I associate with the human experience of living in a family affected by Autism, "Sometimes something strange can be beautiful too." To live fully, to learn deeply, to change in positive peaceful and thoughtful ways, and to become a better human being in the process. I strive to find that space between act and react, that space between what I thought it would be and what it actually is. And there, in that space, I find peace.

Hey Mom, he says as we walk out of the YMCA one evening. We had just taken five months off from unicycle riding to heal his broken bones, and he's back at it, happy and on fire to learn more tricks. I had just complimented him on his effort toward his goal of mastering the skill of riding the unicycle backwards, a few seconds to begin. And a few more. And a few more. He's working on it, he's sticking with it, he's practicing a skill, hooray! He falls off and gets back on. I am so pleased at how far he has come in unicycle, and in his life. His progress delights me, makes him proud of himself, and propels me forward like food.

Hey Mom, he says again as I see this taller-than-me young man looking up to a dark sky. The moon is empty, he tells me referring to a crescent smile in the heavens. He had just learned that a "circle moon" is called full. And he was probably concretely thinking about "opposites" as he said this. We stopped, shared a hug, and looked up into the sky, ripe with possibilities, together.

Disclaimer

I ONLY CLAIM to be the parent of a child with Autism describing an experience, and I espouse only my opinions on my life and my circumstances. Nothing else. I am not a doctor or an expert in any way, and if you take what I say as ultimate truth or advice, your bad. If you have questions about your child's well-being, please ask the appropriate professionals, learn about health and education choices and protocols, and don't believe the hype. This story is uniquely mine, and it is born from happenings in my own personal human experience. I speak from my perspective as a mother, a teacher, a seeker of truths, and an advocate for her young spawn. I appreciate and welcome thoughtful dialogue regarding the opinions I express in my book, but I am not too keen on absolutist bullshit flung in my general direction. In other words, if you don't like what I have to say on particular issues, I invite you to write your own book.

The names of the Autism parents and children have been changed to protect their privacy, and their unique journeys.

Thad's Tribe

I WOULD LIKE to honor and acknowledge the following providers who have graciously agreed to provide their contact information as my Thad-roadmap-of-services-that-might-inform-others. The following information might work for you and it might not, so please accept all responsibilities and liabilities for your choices.

IN ORDER OF APPEARANCE IN THE BOOK

KELLI

Early Intervention in Speech Therapy, Occupational Therapy and Development
Kelli Wilms, MS, CCC-SLP
Playworks Center for Development and Learning
www.playworks.cc

GWEN

Cognitive Therapy/ Clinical Psychologist
Dr. Gwennyth Palafox, PhD
Meaningful Growth
www.meaningfulgrowth.com

JACQUE

Realtime EEG Neurofeedback/ Thoughtfield Therapy/ NAET (Energy Medicine)
Jacque Smillie, TFT-ADV
www.banishingfear.com

BOB
Applied Behavioral Analysis (ABA)
Bob Chen, MFT, BCBA
ABA BEARS
www.ababears.com

MARK
Special Education Law
Mark Woodsmall, JD
Woodsmall Law Group, LLC
www.woodsmalllawgroup.com

DR. SUSI
Occupational Therapy
Dr. Susan Spitzer, PhD, OTR/L
www.drspitzerot.com

DR. ROBYN
Behavioral Optometry
Dr. Robyn Rakov, OD, FCOVD
Vision Development Center
www.visiondevelopmentcenter.com

CAROL
Behavioral Audiology with a speciality in Central Auditory Processing Disorders.
Carol Atkins, MA, CCC-A
Available for consult: carol@carolatkins.com

SLDC
Non-Public School
Speech and Language Development Center
www.sldc.net

DR. DIANE
Developmental Pediatrician
Dr. Diane Danis, MD, MPH
www.danismd.com

SPERO VINEYARDS
Vocational Program for Young Adults with Autism
www.sperovineyards.com

EXCEPTIONAL MINDS STUDIO
Vocational Program for Young Adults with Autism
www.exceptionalmindsstudio.org

BITTERSWEET FARMS
Residential Farm for Adults with Autism
www.bittersweetfarms.org

Cover Concept

THADDEUS STAUDER DREW the cover of this book during his lessons with Ian Anderson at Exceptional Minds Studio. I gave them the loose directive of, "Draw Thad on a surfboard, riding through waves full of monsters and sight-words. Both are equally as scary and dangerous."

Ian told me that Thad had drawn his nipples red, and that he adamantly refused to change them. Acknowledging Ian's concern that this might be seen as socially inappropriate to draw nipples in color, I responded, Look down, he's correct in his interpretations. All hail the concrete thinker!

Cover layout by Ian Anderson.